by EDWARD SANDERS

EDWARD SANDERS

AMERICA
A HISTORY IN VERSE

VOLUME 3 1962–1970

For cindy
w/ best wishes
for your art
Ed
4-29-04

A Black Sparrow Book

David R. Godine · Publisher · Boston · 2004

This is
A Black Sparrow Book
Published in 2004 by
David R. Godine · *Publisher*
Post Office Box 450
Jaffrey, New Hampshire 03452
www.blacksparrowbooks.com

The Black Sparrow Books pressmark is by Julian Waters
www.waterslettering.com

Acknowledgments
Thanks to Erik Dailey for excellent research help, to Miriam Sanders for examining and correcting the manuscript, to John and Barbara Martin, to Austin Metze for help with the scans, to Mike Liebler for the loan of crucial books, to Pat Jackson for locating important articles and books, to Mike Golden for sharing his work on Martin Luther King, to Tuli Kupferberg for the loan of the protest buttons from his vast collection, to Jeff Cohen for research help, to Karl Helicher for loaning some key material on 1968, to Brooke Horvath for inviting me to the 25th anniversary of the Kent State tragedy, and to Jeanne Somers for the photo of the Guardsman.

Front-cover photographs
Top: Berkeley, California, 1969 — National Guardsmen, called out by Governor Reagan to quell demonstrations, surround a Vietnam War protester in People's Park. Copyright © Ted Streshinsky / Corbis. *Bottom:* Selma, Alabama, 1965 — Martin Luther King Jr. speaks to a rally of civil rights demonstrators before leading them on a march to Montgomery. Copyright © Flip Schulke / Corbis.

Library of Congress Cataloging-In-Publication Data is available.

ISBN 1-57423-189-8 (pbk. : alk. paper)

FIRST EDITION
Printed in Canada

Contents

The poem of America has reached the time of my
                                    youthful rebellion
the years of Civil Rights marches
& what they used to call the
                            "mimeograph revolution"
with its stenciled magazines & manifestoes
& the recognition of rock & roll & folk-rock
                                    as an art form
years when we searched for meaning
in the sawdust floors of rebel cafés
or the stardust soars of psychedelic haze
or mind-stretching hours in front of
            4- and 8-track tape recorders
                        getting our brains onto friendly oxide
while we outlined our livers
                like a Dan Flavin sculpture

                & tried to keep our dreams afloat on
                drunken barges packed with
                            notebooks & albums & jotted schemes

The cloth of these nine years is
woven of longing & joy, evil & dread, fun & threnody
& patched with the thread
                of silver guitar strings
                        & the shredded steel of armor

It is a thousand-throated song both beauteous & hideous
whose vowels are of napalm and Fender amps
prepared pianos, screams in jungles
the sweet silver ooo's of Byrds, Beach Boys & Beatles
& 5-part harmony in burnt churches & dog-growl streets

Its consonants are the clicks
of kisses in tipis & rapes in huts
of fists in gloves & skin in rainbows
of death more common than hamburger
and life more plentiful than wheat
of women more certain & men more willing
to wake up thinking each day could be paradise
                & weeping or shrugging when it wasn't

It was the time of a randy young President
                                with a bad back
who attracted the squint-eyed scorn
& even the hatred of the
National Security Grouch Apparatus

It was a time when nuclear war
                        nearly swept the world
a time of fierce debates over nuclear tests, a time of
dog-bites in Birmingham & "I Have a Dream"
                        at the Lincoln Memorial

It was a time when millions figured out
there was a glut of freedom
guaranteed by the Constitution
                        not yet being used

and two roads seemed to split
                the American vista

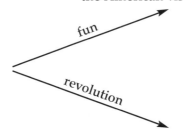

and off we sprinted
        as if to run down each
                with oars for Orpheus.

It was the time when a generation
                of mostly nonviolent activists
expected a great change in America
at least a Social Democracy
"from California to the New York island"
though by 1970
        when this volume of *America* closes
                their hearts were broken
                        at least for now.

It was also the time of an empty-saddled horse
                        on Pennsylvania Avenue

when the president who vowed to
                    break the CIA
                            into a thousand pieces
was himself broken into a thousand days

It was the time of a strange man named Johnson
& his Great Society where violent passion commingled w/
                            passionate violence

It was the time of a shrieking war
                    that would not stop
                    no matter what was done

& then the reappearance of an even stranger man named Nixon
                            & his assault on free elections

It was a time when Kent State could come
                    just 300 hours after the first Earth Day
and when the Phoenix of death
                    would try to supplant the Phoenix of life.

It was a time of too much governmental secrecy
& strange, secret police programs such as
Chaos, Cointelpro, Garden Plot &
                    the plot to tear away power from Martin King

It is a secrecy which lasts to this day
so that the tracing of these 9 years
has a shape like one of Sappho's
                            shredded papyri

and history tends as gappy as our FBI files
blanked out stupidly for reasons of
national dolority

yet things kept hidden keep dribbling forth
so that even as I wrote this volume
sections had to be rewritten
in the flow of the new.

I realize that history is like a trillion-stranded phone line
& often there's a huge impactment of no's

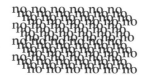

before a single yes
in the search for sequence

but still I apologize for not including things
so many hold vital
such as the details of sports & contest—

Golf has been sorely neglected, for instance, and what about
the high hurdles, curling, speedboat racing, college wrestling,
ice hockey, bowling, tennis, darts, rugby, archery,
fencing, lacrosse, ice dancing, skiing, high school football,
soccer, volleyball, badminton, bridge, chess, rings,
the marathon, the javelin & discus, barrel jumping,
Ping-Pong, demolition derbies, NASCAR,

& the forward one-and-a-half somersault
with a half twist!

It busies my every day
to figure out what gets put in!
and I know that in my reaching out to Muses ancient & modern
I must not forget the Muse of Fun

for the weave of America can't just be the Blake-gloom graspings
of would-be Metternichs
& 4-year kings

as I wander the time-track looking for Grace
　　to place in a thrilling flow
　　of events, ideas, currents, strands & vistas

　　while always seeking the footprints of the
　　　　　　　　　　　　　　Muse of Fun!

And then comes the question of evil.
It was hard for a person like myself
　　　　one of whose first poems at 15 began
　　　　　　"America the fair and beautiful land
　　　　　　you stand like a rock secure
　　　　　　beneath the sea of trouble & strife
　　　　　　like an angel fair & pure"

　　to realize my Nation veers in & out of evil

　　but evil
　　　　is the only word
　　　　　　　for some of it

—the ancient word Apopis comes to mind
(from the entity that tried to devour the morning sun)

　　yet the ability to do good
　　finally takes the Nation forward
　　A compassionate helicopter pilot
　　　　　　　stopped, at last,
　　　　　　　　　the murder at My Lai
　　Someone finally wept
　　　　　　& halted the slashing

　　Finally the napalm ended & the defoliants too
　　Finally
　　　　the warriors stopped
　　　　　　had a drink at the officers club
　　　　　　　or a hit of Jimi Hendrix
　　　　　　　　　& some weed out back of the air base
　　　　　　　　　in the dusk of peace

　　& flew home to the quality of time
　　for it's never too late for Reconciliation.

Between my country right or wrong
& my country sometimes right sometimes wrong
or my country terribly wrong

lies the
Feather of Justice

Ancient Maat

from a very imperfect ancient nation

yet Maat shines forever

and may all the muses ancient and modern—
Sequentia, Retentia, Euterpe, Condensare
and ancient Clio most especially—

plus also the Muse of Fun!
stand by my pen
in the Boat of Information

for the singing of America

Long may it dwell in peace & sharing
out on its shining arm

AMERICA *a history in verse*

VOLUME 3
1962–1970

1962 1962 1962

1962 1962

Out of the year of
the Bay of Pigs, the Freedom Rides
& the Russian resumption of nuclear tests
                                        came '62

in a kind of frenzied glory

when many things seemed possible
before denied
such as the end of racist rule
                        in the South
the spreading of wealth
with paid vacations & leisure
                    to every person

in a nation where 1%
still owned half of the

There was a quick-witted President
who'd won a Pulitzer
            for his writing
& now demanded a clear, clean civilian control
as Roosevelt had, upon a fierce & pushy
                    military-industrial-intelligence complex.

There were elements of i-yi-yi
                    in the time-track
such as the fact that nuclear bombs
were down to
            three feet in length

& the fact that much of the conservative officer corps
seemed to view the President as
                    a gutless appeaser
                            in Cuba and elsewhere.

He was a man more amorous
                than Thomas Jefferson any day
and if you believe the sources in
Seymour Hersh's book
The Dark Side of Camelot
he liked quick trysts
            by the side of the

            White House swimming pool
                    in the midst of swirly duties

    But there was something of substance
    to the man of Camelot
    at the edge of the 1960s—
    the age of desire & acid guitars
    Strategic Hamlets & napalm
    Love beads & body bags
    & many fierce bumpings & knockings on th'

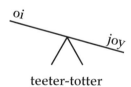

            teeter-totter

In France January 4
    a ghastly cabal of right wingers
        called the Secret Army Organization
            called for a revolution in Algeria against the Motherland

    From January 18th through the 23rd
    The S A O set off 35 bombs in Paris

January 18
  US planes sprayed trees & foliage w/ herbicides
      in a successful field test in Vietnam
      which led John Kennedy to approve Operation Hades
      (later called Ranch Hand) which saw various mixtures of
      2,4-D, 2,4,5-T and other chemicals—
      with names such as Agent Blue, White, Purple,
      Green, or Pink, depending on the colored stripes on their
      metal drums—death-dripped
      from C-123 aircraft dipping low above
              the Vietnamese jungles

January 29
  The 3 power conference on ending atomic tests fell apart
        —it had met 353 times in Geneva since 10-31-'58

January 30
  The Flying Wallendas were arrayed on a high-stretched wire
                  in Detroit

    when one lost footing
      and 4 of the 7
        plunged to th' floor
          where 2 lay dead

    in a further expounding of Juvenal's lines on
    the people's fixation on
    panem et circenses
        —bread, circuses & of course now thrill-fall—

February 3
  JFK ordered a trade ban on Cuba
       —no more of those good maduro cigars
  and not such a great idea since
  it may have helped spur Castro
      that spring to okay
        the imposition of Russian missiles

February 16
  there was a Peace protest in front of the White House
    The President sent out an urn of coffee
    and invited some into the WH to "meet with top aides"

    The students called for the end of atmospheric testing

a halt to the useless civil defense program
and disarmament

two good ideas the Fates would accept
but the third wd wind up
on the cutting-room floor

―――――――――――――――――― **Mongoose** ――――――――――――――――――

Back in November of '61 the Kennedys set up a CIA program
to overthrow Castro called "Mongoose"

Early in the year Robert Kennedy was
using his storied wound-spring vim
to urge the Mongoose team to hurry up &
get rid of Castro

He supposedly announced to the Mongoose squad
that the operation had "top priority" & that
"No time, money, effort—or manpower—
is to be spared."

But then, not long after RFK's exhortation
General Edward Lansdale, "operating head"
of the Mongoose team

complained that there had been no President-level
decision for actual military intervention
in Cuba

The Joint Chiefs of Staff
―――― **Sign Off on the Ghastly Operation Northwoods** ――――

"We could develop a Communist Cuban terror campaign
in the Miami area
. . . and even in Washington"

wrote the US Joint Chiefs of Staff
(chaired by the right-wing general named Lyman Lemnitzer)

in a proposal to JFK to set up something called
Operation Northwoods

designed to rouse the U.S. populace
like crackers to a lynching—

"We could blow up a U.S. ship in Guantanamo Bay
and blame Cuba"
wrote the Chiefs

"Casualty lists in U.S. newspapers
would cause a helpful wave of indignation."

The Chiefs also recommended "exploding a few plastic bombs
in carefully chosen spots, the arrest of Cuban agents
and the release of prepared documents
substantiating Cuban involvement. . . . "

Another brilliant concept of the Chiefs
was to explode an empty drone plane
disguised as a commercial flight
& blame the Cubans:

"An aircraft at Elgin AFB would be painted and numbered as
an exact duplicate for a civil registered aircraft belonging to a CIA
proprietary organization in the Miami area. At a designated time
the duplicate would be substituted for the actual civil aircraft and
would be loaded with the selected passengers, all boarded under
carefully prepared aliases. The actual registered aircraft would be
converted to a drone (a remotely controlled unmanned aircraft).
Take off times of the drone aircraft and the actual aircraft will be
scheduled to allow a rendezvous south of Florida"
The drone would be exploded over Cuba
and then Castro accused of killing an innocent group
of Americans

Thanks, Chiefs

& who were these guys who were chiefing it
in early '62?

General Lyman Lemnitzer, Army, Chair
General Curtis LeMay, Air Force
Admiral George Anderson, Navy
General Earle Wheeler, Army
Commandant David Shoup, Marine Corps

Kennedy rejected the plan
in March of '62.

Is it not proper to think that military leaders
who would propose
domestic terror
could also kill a president
or fashion a patsy?

—————— Perth Turns On the Lights for Glenn ——————
February 20

John Glenn was the first American
to orbit Gaia
and 3 times at that
in the Mercury spaceship *Friendship 7*

When he passed overhead
Perth, Australia, acquired the name The City of Lights
as it switched on all its luminescence
in the middle of the night

to salute the captain of *Friendship 7*

& then on Feb 26
a ticker-tape parade for the likeable Glenn
down Pennsylvania Avenue
for a speech to a joint gathering of Congress

Then it was Scott Carpenter's turn
to go up in a *Friendship* in May

Another Joint Chiefs
—————— Proposal for *Friendship 7* ——————

The Joint Chiefs had proposed as part of the
seamy Operation Northwoods
that if John Glenn's launch had failed
& Glenn had perished

to say that Castro had used electronic interference
to kill the flight

March 2
    Wilt Chamberlain scored 100 points for
        the Philadelphia Warriors vs. the NY Knickerbockers
        in a 169–147 win

That same day JFK announced
        the US would resume atmospheric testing
        in April if the Russians
            did not sign a test ban agreement

        uh-oh, here comes
            the death air of leukemia

    That was a Friday
    On Monday a bunch of us from the
    Committee for Nonviolent Action *& The Catholic Worker*
    blocked the entrance at the Atomic Energy Commission
            on Hudson Street, against the tests

    Some of us were sent to the Hart Island Workhouse
            located off the north part of Manhattan

    where on March 24
    in our dormitory-like cell room
    they showed the Emile Griffith–Benny "Kid" Paret
    welterweight world-championship fight

    Griffith in the 12th
            backed Paret into a corner then
    did 20 quick bashes to the face and head
    baf, baf, baf, baf, baf, baf, baf, baf, baf, baf
    & baf, baf, baf, baf, baf, baf, baf, baf, baf, baf

    The referee stood as in a trance
            and did nothing

    Paret's wife, watching it on TV in Miami,
    screamed, "Stop! Stop it!"

        Paret was already in a coma
        & died at Roosevelt Hospital

& I vowed to turn my back forever on boxing
that awful night in the dark, silent workhouse

────────────────── **Ghastly & Evil Hamlets** ──────────────────
March 1962

It was a thing first urged by the chief of the
British Advisory Mission in Saigon
a human named Robert K. G. Thompson

The shovy Americans took it as their own
& called it the Strategic Hamlet Plan

The Viet Cong, it was supposed
were focused on getting control
                of the 116,000 hamlets of South Vietnam

Guerrillas, the thinking was,
could stay alive as long as they had the
voluntary or forced support of the hamlets

Therefore encampments of hell were built
enclosed in barbed wire and medieval moats

Villagers were forced within the barbed wire/moatage
& sometimes whole hamlets were moved

Residents were given i.d. cards
curfews were in place
                & freedom-fractioning checkpoints

Not a good moment for America

────────────────── **White Roses for Gandhi** ──────────────────
March 12

Jackie Kennedy and her sister Lee Radziwill
        went on tour to New Delhi
        and Pakistan
                for 2 weeks

        and before that to Rome
        for an audience with Pope John XXIII

They were met by Nehru and his daughter Indira Gandhi
                        at the airport

                Jackie was driven
                to where Gandhi had been cremated in '48
                                        and placed white roses there

———— **A Loss for the Upcoming Struggle of the '60s** ————
                        March 20

        C. Wright Mills
                Professor of Sociology at Columbia U

        whose *White Collar* of '51
        & *The Power Elite* of '56 helped shape the
                        thinking of the US left on the
                        actual structure of the nation's ruling elites

                        passed away at 46

———— **A Lunch for Hoover at the White House** ————
                        March 22

Late in February J. Edgar Hoover had sent a memo to Robert Kennedy
noting that mob-moll Judith Exner had made several phone calls
in a week to Evelyn Lincoln
                        the President's secretary.

And then in a rare private lunch at the White House
Edgar filled the President in on what he knew—
that Sinatra had introduced Judith Exner
                        to both Kennedy & Mafia killer Sam Giancana
                with the clear indication that
                he knew of Kennedy's occasional dalliance with Exner

so that, in a decision that would ultimately push the great
and then liberal singer Mr. Sinatra
into the camp of the conservatives, the President
decided not to stay with Sinatra in an upcoming visit to Palm Springs
        but rather to stay with Bing Crosby
                        and to cease all social contacts with Sinatra.

Sinatra was so angry he broke up the concrete helicopter pad

he'd built for the President's visit
                    with a sledgehammer

———————— **Unhappy with Sports-Car Style** ————————

For her part, Judith Exner was not that happy
            by early '62
            when the President only wanted to ball
                    (perhaps because of his ouchy back)

            in the position we used to call in the Midwest the
                                    sports-car style

———————— **Hoover's Self-Decided Bugs** ————————

            J. Edgar Hoover felt he had the right to bug at will
            —that's bug, sneaking a microphone, say,
            as close to a black leader's bed as possible,
                            as opposed to a wire-tap.

            He didn't need authorization, it was felt
            even though a unanimous Supreme Court
                            had ruled such bugs
                            not allowed

            (Back in '54 then-Attorney General Herbert Brownell
            had sent Hoover a memorandum which
            in effect told him to ignore the Supreme Court

            Hence, on his own, Hoovie boy
            began bugging MLK advisor Stanley Levison
                    at least as early as 1962)

March 18
        Premier George Pompidou and Ahmed Ben Bella
        agreed to an immediate ceasefire
        and a French withdrawal by year's end

        There was a plebiscite on July 1
                with over 90 percent of Algerians voting for
                                        independence

        The Algerian war had killed 17,000 French troops and
                                up to a million Muslims

while the Secret Army Org (OAS) of right-wing generals
kept trying to kill deGaulle
                         by planting bombs in France and Algeria

and then in September '62 Ben Bella, now president, proclaimed
                              a neutral socialist republic

———————————————— **Baker v. Carr** ————————————————
March 26

        The rural parts of Tennessee controlled the
                              Legislature

        Memphis, for instance,
                was under-represented in the Legislature
                by a ratio of almost 4 to 1.

        So a man named Charles Baker & others sued
        Sec of State Joe Carr
                hence the case name *Baker v. Carr*

        over the unequal voting districts.
        It was a big case
        & the Supreme Court decided that Tennessee's
        failure to reapportion
                was a violation of Mr. Baker's
                Constitutional Rights

     and thus the principle of one person/one vote
     broke into the hickish-cliquish delineations of voting districts
                  around the nation.

Early April
     CIA officer William Harvey met with
     Mafia killer John Roselli in New York
     and gave him poison pills from the CIA
                         with which to kill Castro

     Harvey had become head of the CIA's Cuban task force
     in February '62, renaming it Task Force W

April 8
     a Revolutionary Tribunal in Cuba found
     1,179 CIA-paid Bay of Pigs invaders guilty

and sentenced them to 30 years in prison
but at the same time offered to free them all
for a payment of $62 million from the US

(in '61 the Cubans had offered to fork over the invaders
in exchange for 500 tractors
but the US had no'd it)

Serious negotiations were underway and then
about a week later 60 sick and wounded were freed by Castro
as a gesture of good will
pending payment of the full amount

─────────── **Like a Horrified Chorus in Euripides** ───────────
April 15

a 400-person US helicopter unit
was sent to war against the Viet Cong in 'Nam

If Euripides were writing it as a play
he would have had a chorus of the snipping Fates
swoon forth with a keening ee ee ee ee
like the eery ee-ing in *Trojan Women*

to grieve in sad harmony
the need-to-kill bloodsongs
of the Power Elite

─────────── **US Nuke Tests** ───────────
April 24

JFK ordered resumption of cancer-spreading
nuke tests in the victimized Pacific
after a 3-year pause

The military started detonating the next day
& by May 4 they'd
death-dusted the world's lungs with 4 bombs

─────────── **Anger in the Kremlin** ───────────

To the Soviets the US purpose was as clear
as the ice melted in a Siberian rocket test:

14

it was to upgrade America's nuclear weaponry—
which would serve to widen even further
the big gap between US & Russian kill-tech
            rather than allowing the Soviets to catch up.

All this was in Khrushchev's mind
            as he pondered putting missiles
                        in Cuba

──────────── *Silent Spring* **Is Completed** ────────────
April 20

The great Rachel Carson
had been a celebrity since 1951
when *The Sea Around Us* became a bestseller

But during the past 2 years she'd lived through the irony
of writing about the health harms from pesticides
            while undergoing the cruel routines
                        of radiation, mastectomy, weakness

Nevertheless she purchased some time to write
& make what the bard Charles Olson termed the "typos"—
that is, her mark or stamp
            upon the world—

pushing herself, sometimes almost blind with iritis
                        to finish her greatness.

That March she began another round of radiation
            working on her manuscript in bed in the mornings
            then heading for the hospital for treatments

so that on April 20, 1962
            Silent Spring
                        in the agony of its creator
                                    was finished!

with installments in *The New Yorker* starting in June
for a culture-shaking stir

            It was a moment for America

April 26
    in a move the public strongly praised
    Kennedy pressured the steel industry to rescind a price increase

    after US Steel announced increases of $6 a ton on April 10
                Bethlehem Steel followed
                and very soon thereafter 5 other steel-co's

            Kennedy was pissed
            & ordered the Defense Dept to send contracts just
                    to those companies
                            which had not raised prices.

    Then on April 26 Bethlehem, US Steel and two other steel-co's
    were indicted for anti-trust price-fixing charges

                    It worked:
                    prices rescinded
                    public huzzah
                    & cap-eyes rolling

May 1
    JFK signed a bill giving $32 million to
                help educational television facilities grow
    with a limitation of $1 million per state.

    In the recent decade the FCC had reserved 273 channels for
                            "educational channels"

            It was the spirit of Social Democracy
            trying to find its home at last
                        on a huge & disparate continent

May 19
    The President celebrated his 45th birthday
    at a party in Madison Square Garden
                with 15,000 on hand

    It was televised to a fascinated nation
    & Marilyn Monroe sang a bedroom-breathy version of
            "Happy Birthday, Mr. President"

in a clingy silver gown covered with sequins
　　　　that seemed to have been grafted to her curves
　　　　　　　　like thousands of tiny sizzle-head cymbals

(Jackie wasn't there
　　　　but took part in a horse show that afternoon
　　　　　　　& spent the Night of Sequins in Virginia)

──────────── **The Wall-Off of Marilyn Monroe** ────────────

It's a murky cloud of Clio
but shortly after the famous singing
　　　　　　　of "Happy Birthday"

Kennedy cut off access from the actress.

May 22
　　According to one book (Donald Wolfe's
　　　　　　　The Last Days of Marilyn Monroe, p. 416)

on May 22 the White House got a call from J. Edgar Hoover
who "wanted to see the president on a matter of national security."
The meeting was allegedly held on May 24
after which, even on the same day,
the Oval Office switchboard operators were told
not to accept calls from Marilyn Monroe
　　　　and a private number JFK had provided her
　　　　　　　　　　was shut down.

(On the other hand, according to Seymour Hersh's
gloomy history of Kennedy's womanizing
The Dark Side of Camelot [p. 404]
　　　　Kennedy and Hoov' did not lunch
　　　　between the March '62 lunch-warning about
　　　　　　Judith Exner *&* a lunch in November '63)

According to another book, *Official and Confidential:*
The Secret Life of J. Edgar Hoover, by Anthony Summers (p. 298)
"Monroe would not accept that the affair was over." In an
interview Summers cited, Peter Lawford later said "Marilyn began
writing these rather pathetic letters to Jack and continued calling.
She threatened to go to the press."

As for Ms. Monroe
> she had been in the midst of a film for
> 20th Century Fox called
>> *Something's Got to Give*

with Cyd Charisse, Dean Martin and others

when she interrupted the film to
> fly to NYC for "Happy Birthday"

A few days later she came down with a severe sinusitis
> filming was delayed
>> & then she was fired on
> June 8 for delaying the project

> In the 11 weeks left to her
> she worked to revive her picture
>> so that, by the day she passed away,
>> she had won! It was to be
>>> rebegun!

> aided apparently by a phone call from RFK
> to the head of Fox pictures

> You can sleuth the evidence of that
> in several books on Marilyn & the Kennedys

> *Come alive, o Clio!*

May 23
> at Massachusetts General Hospital in Boston
>> the first reimplantation of a human limb

> *Good news!*

May 30, 1962
> The first performance of Benjamin Britten's
>> *War Requiem* in the rebuilt Coventry Cathedral
>>> once bombed to a spire & lonely walls
>>>> by the Nazis

Snap
May 31

They tied his ankles and knees
then Adolf Eichmann said
"Long live Germany. Long live Argentina"
The door sprang open
Then "snap"

Pitching for Missiles in Cuba

Just about the same day that the Nazi felt the snap
a delegation from the USSR
pitched a plan to Fidel
for the placing of nuclear missiles in Cuba

and Castro reportedly "reluctantly" assented.

Khrushchev intended a thunder of missiles for the island
among them some 40 land-based missile launchers
with 60 nuclear missiles ready to decimate
the American South
& most of the North
plus 45,000 Soviet troops
and around 80 nuke-tipped cruise missiles
for defense of the Cuban coasts

The Russians also planned to build a submarine base in Cuba
for 7 subs with nuclear missiles

June 4
Supreme Court nullified 6 Freedom Rider convictions from '61

June 8
JFK established the Office of Science and Technology

The Port Huron Statement
June 11–15

The Students for a Democratic Society
had formed in 1960
as an arm of the long-time semi-socialist
but strongly anti-communist

League for Industrial Democracy
& its credo of "Cold War Liberalism."

Now was their moment
　　　　to speak for a generation
as 59 or 60 SDSers
met for 4 days and nights
at a United Auto Workers convention
　　　　at Port Huron, Michigan, north of Detroit

　　　stitching their dreams of
　　　civil rights, the economy,
　　　war & "quality of American life"
　　　　　　upon a cogent cloth

　　　with the result that at 5 am on June 16
　　　they finished a manifesto
　　　　　　known as *The Port Huron Statement*

　　　Among its writers was an activist named Tom Hayden.

Port Huron called for Participatory Democracy
criticized the lack of civil liberties in the USSR
　　　but said that "the American military response
　　　　　has been more effective in deterring the
　　　　　　　growth of democracy than communism"

The SDS had an impact way beyond its numbers
　　　　　　in the war-crazy decade to come
as it spelled out fresh vision of a "new left"
　　　cut free of Cold War commie-noia
　　　& free of the do-nothing components of the labor movement

────────────── **The School Prayer Decision** ──────────────
June 25

The ACLU had sued the school board president
in New Hyde Park, Long Island
　　　　　　a man named William Vitale

on behalf of Richard Engel & 9 other parents
after the New York State Board of Regents
which controlled NY's educational system

had promulgated a morning prayer in the 1950s:
"Almighty God, we acknowledge our dependence upon Thee,
and we beg Thy blessings upon us, our parents, and our teachers"

The case was known as *Engel v. Vitale*
& on this day the Supreme Court
peeled prayer from the edge of the blackboard

in the words of Justice Hugo Black
who wrote the decision
"In this country, it is no part of the business
of government to compose official prayers for any group of
the American people to recite"

> The case caused a swoon of indignation
> especially against the great Earl Warren

———————————— Birch Smirch ————————————

> The looney-tune buffoons of the John Birch Society
> had preached that Eisenhower
> > had been an out-&-out Communist agent
>
> & in the early '60s sponsored an essay writing contest
> with a $1,000 prize
> > on "Why Chief Justice Warren
> > > Should Be Impeached."
>
> Earl Warren joked at the contest
> suggesting his wife Nina enter—
> "She knows more of my faults
> > than anyone else"—
>
> and then came birch-smirch billboards, such as

In the summer of '62
JFK ordered a secret White House tape system
which recorded 260 hours of his phone calls & meetings
till late November '63

Today there exists from this system
some 127 audio tapes with 248 hours
of the talk from 300 meetings. In addition there are
12 hrs of telephone dictabelt tapes.

Of course, who knows how many more hours
the Military-Industrial-Surrealists, hostile to JFK,
might have taped?

July 3
Algeria was made independent
after a huge portion of the Algerian electorate had voted for freedom
from the French control
of the last 132 years

Bye

July 7
The nuke-bats conducted the first nuclear detonation
in Nevada since 1958

& then, 2 days later,
another evil h-bomb test in the Pacific

I wonder if Dr. Teller received royalties
for any of these blasts
from the trigger-tube he helped invent?

And then on July 11 the final atmospheric test
at the Nevada Test Site
in a location called "Area 18"
where Robert Kennedy & General Maxwell Taylor were on hand
as a low-yield Davy Crockett nuclear shell was fired
from a recoilless rifle mounted on an armored personnel carrier

part of an exercise called Operation Ivy Flats
which also included troop maneuvers

July 20
    JFK chose General Maxwell Taylor
           to head the Joint Chiefs of Staff

    The sort of military officer who would never propose
    domestic terror
           in order to drum up support
                    to bomb Cuba

    (Taylor had previously turned down a Kennedy offer
    to head the CIA after Allen Dulles' retirement—
    Would JFK have been assassinated
           if Maxwell Taylor had accepted?)

———————————— **The Mystery of Marilyn** ————————————
Saturday–Sunday August 4–5

She'd won her struggle to restart her picture
& was looking ahead to new projects
one of which was a musical version of *A Tree Grows in Brooklyn*
She spoke with composer Jule Styne
           about the score that week

    But then on a street called Fifth Helena in Brentwood, LA
    her housekeeper saw the light on in her room
    at midnight and then at 3
           but was hesitant to wake her
           because she had been having trouble sleeping

        She called M's psychiatrist, Dr. Greenson
        who came at 3:30 am

        to find Marilyn lying face down in death

        and a phone "clutched fiercely in her right hand"
                as he later wrote

    A swirl of rumors & variously fact-founded allegations
           have dust-deviled the time-track since

    There were her "powerful paramours"
           for which read John Kennedy & others
    who fucked but "withheld their hearts"

& there was her legendary diary
        & its jotted-down disclosures of Camelot

Was it done by accident
when they drugged her then searched
        for the diary?

Was it a mob hit   a hit to grab her sizzling diary
a Hoffa hit   a Sinatra hit
even a Kennedy hit   (very very unlikely)
or an intelligence hit to blackmail the President?

What the hell was it?
or was it a self-hit from
        someone desperately unhappy
          & hungry for the long
            sleep of eternity the *perpetua dormienda*
              that Catullus sang?

The issue whether

   visited

    the day she died
    has not been resolved

That weekend, according to Arthur Schlesinger's
RFK and His Times (pp. 636–637)
Robert Kennedy was in San Francisco
        for a meeting of the American Bar Association
& he stayed with Ethel
          & 4 of their kids
            at a ranch in Gilroy
              southeast of SF

so that a 'copter south that Saturday
was theoretically possible
& so too the chance he may have helicoptered
        out of Los Angeles
          late that night or early Sunday

    It's a murky torrent of Clio

August 17
   The President praised Dr. Frances Oldham Kelsey of the FDA
   and she was given a medal for distinguished public service
   for her work in '60 & '61
                  in preventing American drug duds
                  from forcing thalidomide
                                  onto the market as an "ideal sedative"
                                  for pregnant moms

         after it had been discovered that thalidomide
         caused phocomelia
               —where infants are born with deformed or missing
               limbs

                  Good work, Dr. Kelsey

———————————— **The Communications Satellite Act** ————————————
                           August 31

         JFK inked a bill setting up the
         Communications Satellite Corporation or Comsat

         a privately owned system to own and operate a satellite
                                  communications system

         a kind of Socialism-for-the-rich give-away
                                  to the cap-eyes

         (In '64, however, a global consortium of 11 nations
         formed Intelsat under UN auspices, which
         grew within a decade to over 125 nations)

August was the month
      the CIA reported that Soviet ships were headed for Cuba
      with what appeared to be military cargo

      When they landed, the cargo was being moved to the
                                  interior of Cuba under Soviet protection

      The CIA judged that the shipments were
      likely surface-to-air defense missiles (SAMs) plus radar &
                                                    electronic gear

September 7
    probably to counter US broadcasts
    Cuba began "Radio Free Dixie"
                praising black protests in the South
                        & urging them to keep it up

That same day
    Premier Khrushchev okayed
                the sending of 6 Luna rocket–launchers
                & 12 nuke–tipped Luna rockets

                plus 6 atomic bombs for
                the IL–28 planes already
                        ready to bomb from Cuba

September 8
    Khrushchev met with the bard Robert Frost in Moscow—
    the Shoe Man told the Fence Man
                that the USA & Western Europe
                        were weak and worn out.

    The Shoe Man had no idea
                how lusty Camelot was
    when he quoted the well-known
    words of Tolstoy to Maxim Gorky
                        that on matters of eros
    "The desire is the same, it's the performance that's weak"

    Frost later tonedownedly described the colloquy to reporters:
    "He said we were too liberal to fight."

September 12
    Nixon began a campaign to be Governor of Cal
    & true to his sleazy history, accused Gov. Edmund Brown of being
                        squishy on the com-threat

                If elected governor, Nixon said, in
                an opening rally in Pomona
                he would foist his strength against "the Communist threat"

September 1962

He was an Air Force veteran named James Meredith
who'd first applied to the University of Mississippi
in 1961 and was denied.
The NAACP took up his case in federal court
then RFK's Justice Department joined the case & on
January 12, '62, the US Ct of Appeals for the 5th Circuit
        found that Ole Miss's requirement requiring
        alumni letters of recommendation
                        was unconstitutional

Then, on Sept 10, the great Supreme Ct Justice Hugo Black
ordered Mississippi to admit Meredith

Thereupon Meredith twice sought to enter
        but Governor Ross Barnett
                stood in person to bar him

Robert Kennedy pressured the Gov
after which there was a
        secret agreement 'tween RFK & Mr. Barnett
        to allow Meredith to enroll

Meredith made his third attempt on 9–26
but Barnett broke his word

Kennedy was steamed
Barnett was facing a $10,000-a-day fine, plus arrest
        at which Barnett caved
and Mississippi admitted Meredith
                        the following day

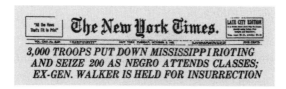

When James Meredith, protected by federal marshals
arrived to take up residence at Ole Miss on September 30

a mob began tossing bottles and rocks
& at least 3 died

The next day JFK sent in 3,000 federal troops
400 marshals & the National Guard

to make a clear point on the
clear changes in America

Bothered and harassed continually
Meredith existed through the 2 terms
& graduated
from Ole Miss
the next spring

September 25
Mr. Castro announced that the Russkies intended
to build a base for its fishing fleet
in Cuba

This was around the time that American papers
printed articles that
Soviet weapons were being shipped to Cuba

JFK replied that
to the best of his knowledge
the weapons were defensive
or so Mr. Khrushchev had assured him.

——————————————— *Silent Spring* ———————————————
September 27

It was one of the best moments of the early '60s
when Houghton Mifflin published
marine biologist Rachel Carson's
Silent Spring

pointing out the ghastly dangers of pesticides
DDT most specifically

She'd been one of the first women to hold an upper position
with the US Fish and Wildlife Service.

The eyes of polluters, chem-poisoners & the chem-bucks crowd
rolled furiously in the months & years ahead
          but after *Silent Spring*
                    nothing could stop the attention
                              given to environmental poisons

                    however much the chem-bucks crowd railed
                    & bribed & demanded to keep on spreading cancer

September
          the Beatles' first single, "Love Me Do"
                              came out in England

          The core of the group—Lennon, McCartney and Harrison—
          had been working little clubs
                              in Hamburg and Liverpool
                              since around 1955

          (In a severe marketing blunder
                    Decca Records had recently
                              turned them down for a contract)

————————— **The Cuban Missile Crisis Begins** —————————
                    October 14–16

          On the 14th, a wide-winged U-2
                    took photographs of Soviet missile bases in Cuba

          and then about 8:50 am on October 16
          an assistant named McGeorge Bundy entered
                    Kennedy's bedroom with U-2 photos
                    showing Soviets
                              setting up nuclear missiles

October 16
          Brazil nationalized the US-owned phone system

                    Roll, CIA eyes, roll!

October 18
          In an evening meeting with his advisors

Kennedy announced he had turned down the
military's concept of a first strike
in favor of a blockade proposed
by Secretary of Defense McNamara

& then on Friday morning October 19
there was a 9:45 meeting with the Joint Chiefs of Staff
in the Cabinet Room
of the White House

They filed into the place of history—
Air Force Chief of Staff Curtis LeMay
Chief of Naval Operations George Anderson
Army Chief of Staff Earle Wheeler
& Marine Corps Commandant David Shoup

The Chiefs knew that Kennedy was leaning toward a blockade
and some of them, especially the bomb-batty Curtis LeMay
were upset.

Beforehand the Chiefs had agreed to recommend
a "massive air strike"
without any warning

on various military targets in Cuba
but they were not unanimous on an invasion of Cuba
with Maxwell Taylor, the chairman,
standing against it

——————————— **Almost as Bad as Munich** ———————————

LeMay plainly hated the blockade.
"This blockade and political action," he said disdainfully
"I see leading into war. I don't see any other solution.
It will lead right into war. This is almost as bad as
the appeasement at Munich."

Grrr   Grrr   Grrr

The braids were always thereafter resentful
at being left out of the decisions
—a little too upset—

but Kennedy thought a surprise attack
was a bit too Pearl Harbory
        & as RFK put it, "Not in our traditions."

(A good chronology of the Cuban Crisis is in the book
*The Kennedy Tapes— Inside the White House During the Cuban
Missile Crisis*, published by Harvard U Press)

October 20
    After the meeting with the Joint Chiefs the morning of 10-19
    Kennedy had gone out that day to the Midwest
        to campaign for candidates in the November elections

but his brother Robert called him
        on the 20th to urge him back to DC

He returned, feigning a cold
& immediately went into a secret session
        with his advisors

    The medium-range & intermediate-range missiles
    being set up to the south
    CIA officer Ray Cline told him
        could deal death on "Dallas through Cincinnati
        and Washington, DC (by MRBMs)
        and practically all the continental United States
        (by IRBMs)."

    During the meeting CIA director McCone
        outlined his opposition to the large air strike
            urged by the Joint Chiefs

——————————— **Grrrs for Adlai Stevenson** ———————————

UN Ambassador Adlai Stevenson
angered the braids during the Cuban Crisis
        for his nonaggressive stances

such as during this Saturday-afternoon meeting
        after JFK had rushed back from Chicago

    Grrr.   He was strongly opposed to a surprise air strike
        feeling it would lead to a US invasion

(though he supported the blockade)
Grrr.   He urged the US to proffer a settlement
                to include the withdrawal of US missiles from Turkey
            and, grrr of grrrs,
                        to pull US forces out of the
                        Guantanamo base

JFK "sharply rejected" surrendering Guantanamo
        but, in the end, the policy he directed the military to follow
        was basically the same as the Ambassador's

                        ⁀⁀⁀⁀⁀ ⁀⁀⁀⁀⁀
            & Grrr   Grrr   Grrr
            from the Military-Industrial-Surrs

            (i.e., the Mil-Ind-Surrealists)

On Monday, October 22
        the President held a meeting in the Cabinet Room at 5 pm
            with congressional leaders,
                    most of them brought back by military couriers
                        on military planes

    CIA chief McCone briefed the senators & congressmen
                that there were now 36 missile launching facilities
                                    at 9 bases in Cuba

12 of which had a strike distance of 2,200 miles
                    able to melt eyes almost anywhere in the USA
                    except the Pacific Northwest

                Right that moment, McCone said,
                there were 4 medium-range nuke sites
                ready to go
                    with mobile launchers
                    that looked like trailer beds

Late that afternoon
            Marines from Camp Pendleton, Calif
                    and other troops were assembling
                                        for a possible invasion

32

The Berlin Factor

In the course of the meeting JFK hinted at a duple battle:
"I don't know where Khrushchev wants to take us.
We've got this obligation on Berlin,
          which is a very difficult place for us to defend.
He may put in a blockade in Berlin and may grab it,
in which case we will be taking action there
                   and also in Cuba."

A Spine-Chilling Speech
October 22

That evening Kennedy spoke to the nation
      one of the most fear-producing
         talks
           in hearthside history

comparable to Roosevelt after Pearl Harbor
         or Orson Welles in his Mercury Theatre
         mock attack of space-killers in Jersey
               back in '38.

He sketched out the missile sites in Cuba
         for a quiet, nervous nation of living rooms & bars
         and announced an air-and-sea blockade
               of the island

    with shot-of-liquor-inducing sentences such as
    "It shall be the policy of this nation
    to regard any nuclear missile launched from Cuba
    against any nation in the Western Hemisphere as an
    attack by the Soviet Union on the United States,
    requiring a full retaliatory response
              upon the Soviet Union."

    Gin and tonic, please. A triple.

No Room for Nina Warren

During the crisis
certain important government people
were given "laminated passes"
which would allow them entrance
to a very secret
          "alternate seat of gov't"
                    in a mountain in "Appalachia"

Chief Justice Earl Warren was given his pass by a courier
"Where's the pass for Mrs. Warren?" he asked

The courier replied there was no room for wives
& so the great Justice handed it back

Planning for Total War

During these days
the military planned for the biggest drop of paratroopers
                              since the battle of Normandy

The Strategic Air Command of B-52s, B-47s &
          172 intercontinental missiles were
          operating at DEFCON 2
                    just a tad beneath DEFCON 1
                                        or Total War

          100,000 soldiers & 40,000 marines
                    & a big navy fleet were ready

          Polaris submarines
          left their bases in Scotland
                    to patrol the Atlantic
                    with missiles
                              computered for specific parts of the USSR

Sweating It at Stanley's
October 24

It was a Wednesday night in the Rebel Café
known as Stanley's Bar on Avenue B
          in the Lower East Side

where a bunch of us sat mugging our livers
as Russkie ships approached the blockade
                with the good chance of a New York Nihil

We were poets, Catholic Workers, anarchists,
civil rights workers & various others

I shouted to my tablemates
that the '60s were going to be a rough rough ride.
We blamed the aggressive Kennedys then
                plus the military and the fangy right
                yet in our minds too the possibility
                                that Khrushchev was unstable
                                & beating his shoe
                                        on the shores of a nearby isle

October 27 in the evening
        RFK met with Soviet Ambassador Dobrynin
        at the Justice Department

The Attorney General was under careful instructions
He said that that the US had to have clear
                indication by tomorrow that
                the missile bases would be removed

If Russia didn't remove them, the US would

Dobryin brought up Khrushchev's idea of
                taking US missiles from Turkey

RFK said there would be no quid pro quo
but that, after 4 or 5 months had elapsed
        he was sure "these matters
        could be resolved satisfactorily."

————————— **An Altercation with the Admiral** —————————

Robert McNamara insisted on tight control of the military
                                                during the blockade

& the Chief of Naval Operations Admiral Anderson
surged angry when McNamara issued specific instructions
on how to manage
                the blockade

The altercation occurred in the "Flag Plot," which was
the naval operations room

where the admiral suggested that McNamara split back to his office
& let the Navy run the operation.
McNamara too waxed miffed and told Admiral Anderson
that the action was "not a blockade but a means of communication
between Kennedy and Khrushchev"
He then commanded the admiral
not to use force without his express permission and insisted
that Anderson acknowledge McNamara's authority.

A few months later Kennedy got rid of Anderson
offering him the ambassadorship to Portugal.

October 28
The Shoe Man agreed to
remove all nuclear missiles from Cuba

& then days later in the November 6 off-year elections
the Democrats gained
thanks to Cuba

& Edward Kennedy was now a senator from Massachusetts

───────────────── **LeMay Grrring** ─────────────────

Air Force Chief Curtis LeMay
thought the Turkish/Cuban missile trade
& the fact that Soviet troops & weapons remained in Cuba
(not to mention the US promise not to invade)
made it "the greatest defeat in our history."

───────────────── **See Dick Lose** ─────────────────
November 7

Out in California in the early morn
came the fine news that Tricky had been beaten
by Gov. Edmund Brown

& Nixon at last made a concession speech
that spanked with the sparks of malice

To be sure he thanked his 100,000 volunteers,
wished "they had gotten out a few more votes in the key precincts
   but because they didn't Mr. Brown has won and I have lost."

    Then he went into his famous mewl of farewell
    which many at the time
            thought ended his politics:

"And as I leave the press, all I can say is this:
for sixteen years, ever since the Hiss case, you've had a lot of fun—
a lot of fun. . . Before I leave you I want you to know
just how much you're going to be missing. You won't have
Nixon to kick around anymore, because, gentlemen, this is
my last press conference."

      See Dick lose.   Lose, Dick, lose.
      See Dick fib.   Fib, Dick, fib.

November 10
    Eleanor Roosevelt
    one of the great Americans of the century
               passed away at 78

      She who had worked so fiercely
      to better the conditions of workers, to ease racial hatred,
      to set up gov't sponsored daycare centers
      to set up a world system, the UN, to stop wars
               & end the evils of penury

On November 20
    JFK lifted the naval blockade of Cuba
    Khrushchev said all missiles
        were to be taken away within 30 days.

    America, in exchange for a UN-monitored missile removal,
        agreed not to invade Cuba
        miffing the right-wing officer corps
           who hungered to bash and bomb

(The US later removed, w/out too many trumpets trilling the media,
its missile bases from Turkey, which both
Defense Secretary McNamara and CIA director McCone
had admitted were useless
        months before the crisis began)

In December
    the great organizers A. Philip Randolph & Bayard Rustin
            met at the Brotherhood of Sleeping Car Porters in Harlem
            and Rustin brought up again Randolph's idea of
            a huge march for civil rights and jobs
                    which he'd first proposed in 1942.

                It was the seed
                that was to lead to the great
                        March on Washington
                            in August o' '63

December 10
    The Nobel Prize to John Steinbeck

    and the Peace Prize to Dr. Linus Pauling
            for his work to help halt outdoor nuclear tests
            —he'd gotten over 11,000 scientists to sign a
            petition to the UN
                    calling for a halt to the cancer-spreading
                    genetic-mutating evil

        (The ceremony awarding it to the great Pauling
        was put off till December of 1963
                awaiting the outcome of the test ban treaty)

    & Dr. James Watson of Harvard shared the Nobel Prize in
    Medicine & Physiology
            with Francis Crick & Maurice Wilkins
                    for discovery of the double-helix structure of DNA

December 11
    the first Minuteman missiles went into op
                    at Malmstrom Air Force Base
                            near Great Falls, Montana

——————— **Release of the Bay of Pigs Prisoners** ———————
                    December 21–24

    For over 6 months an attorney named James Donovan
    w/ the approval of Attorney General Kennedy
    had been negotiating with Fidel Castro
                for the release of the Bay of Pigs prisoners

Early in December RFK asked the pharmaceutical & baby food
companies for contributions

and then on December 21, Donovan and Castro signed a deal
for food and medical supplies
              worth $53 million in '62 cash
              to be handed over
in deliveries that would conclude in July of '63

By Christmas Eve '62 Castro set loose the prisoners
and also allowed 1,000 of their relatives
              to leave the island
                        "as a Christmas bonus."

December 28
      Because of the Ike-era
              Dulles/CIA murder of Lumumba in early '61
              the UN, in the Kennedy era,
              had to take part in severe fighting
                        in Katanga province

in the Republic o' th' Congo.
The next day the UN occupied Elisabethville (now called
                                        Lubumbashi)

Novum Sub Sole '62:
      More subatomic particles!
      as American physicists found 2 varieties of neutrinos,
              one associated with the muon,
              one with the electron.

Later scientists would iso another variety of neutrino,
                        associated with the tauon

in further searches for the meaning of
              Wm Blake's "Auguries of Innocence."

Pop Art pops forth in '62!
      Roy Lichtenstein
              & Claes Oldenberg, among others

A dealer named Leo Castelli gave the young man from Pennsylvania
his first show
and O and W had a show together at the Sidney Janis Gallery

W's commodity painting, *Campbell Soup Can, 19¢*
        was one of the last pieces Andy hand-painted, after which
he switched to a combination of painting & silk-screening
in a series that
        led to some of the best of the Pop Art movement

After the death of Marilyn Monroe
    he cut a still from her 1953 film *Niagara*
    and started a sequence of 23 silkscreen paintings of her face
        —stunning works with thrilling colors & shapes

Also that year the
    Wrapped Portrait of Brigitte Bardot by Christo
    & Ad Reinhardt, Jasper Johns, Robert Rauschenberg, David Smith
        —art for a new time

Michael Tippett's opera *King Priam*
    & Edward Albee's *Who's Afraid of Virginia Woolf?*

Peter Schumann founded the Bread & Puppet Theater

The first communications satellite, Telstar, went into orbit

& the meadow-ruining encroachments of Wal-Mart stores began
        in Rogers, Arkansas

The USA now had 200 reactors in operation
    spewing out mists of cancer-scythe

It was the year of Elvis Presley's "Return to Sender"
the ice-pick vocals of the Beach Boys' "Surfin' Safari"
and Joan Baez gave us her beautiful *In Concert* album

        That April Bob Dylan wrote an anthem for the era in
        "Blowin' in the Wind"
        & then in Sept "A Hard Rain's A-Gonna Fall"

The husband-wife song team of Noel Regney & Gloria Shayne
that fall had written a peace song during the Cuban crisis called
                                    "Do You Hear What I Hear?"
which was famous thereafter as a Christmas tune
recorded by many
                        including Bing Crosby
                        whose '63 version sold a million plus

Peter, Paul and Mary had a
big hit with the Pete Seeger/Lee Hays '49 labor tune
                                    "If I Had a Hammer"

Seeger wrote the Kingston Trio's
                        "Where Have All the Flowers Gone?"

Right-wing repressionists had blacklisted Seeger from major labels
                                                        for years

& speaking of the right wing, the
            economist Milton Friedman
                        proposed in *Capitalism and Freedom*

            a "negative income tax"

            a variation on the "reverse income tax" schemes
            proposed in Great Britain in the 1930s

            With the neg-tax a person or family
            with income beneath a certain level
            would not have to pay taxes
                        and in addition would get a payment

            It had various booby traps in it, such as his
            right-wing hunger
            for the government to be removed from the sacred US
                                    Rooseveltian Safety Net

                        The erasure of Roosevelt
                        has always lurked
                                    in their not-so-secret agendas

During the '60s the physicist John Wheeler
coined "black hole" for a collapsed star whose gravity at its surface
is so enormous than nothing, no light, can escape.

Libri '62:
>*A Clockwork Orange*   Anthony Burgess
>John Barth's *The Sot-Weed Factor* and Faulkner's *The Reivers*
>>Marshall McLuhan's
>>>*The Gutenberg Galaxy*
>*Ship of Fools*   Katherine Anne Porter
>Ken Kesey   *One Flew Over the Cuckoo's Nest*
>*Seven Days in May* by Fletcher Knebel & Charles Bailey II
>*Labyrinths*   Jorge Luis Borges
>Robert Bly   *Silence in the Snowy Fields*
>*Another Country*   James Baldwin
>Doris Lessing   *The Golden Notebook*
>& don't forget *Sex and the Single Girl* by Helen Gurley Brown

'62's final harmony:
>January 13, Ernie Kovacs, fine TV comic, in a car wreck, at 42
>May 13, Franz Kline at 51
>June 4, William Beebe, oceanographer, at 85
>July 6, William Faulkner at 64
>Herman Hesse at 85 on August 9,
>September 3, e.e. cummings at 67
>>>while chopping wood
>November 18, Niels Bohr, at 77
>Charles Laughton on Dec 15 at 63

Films '62:
>John Ford's *The Man Who Shot Liberty Valance*
>Hitchcock's *The Birds*
>Luis Buñuel's *Exterminating Angel*
>Stanley Kubrick   *Lolita*
>*Divorce, Italian Style*
>*The Manchurian Candidate*
>*To Kill a Mockingbird* with Gregory Peck
>John Huston's *Freud*

>and on the tube the cross-class crassness of "Beverly Hillbillies"

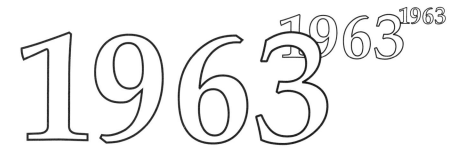

There was news that year from radiotelescopes
of the huge burning vastnesses known as quasars

more bright than a billion stars
        and receding from the earth at
                24,000 miles per second!

What the hell are they?
—a gathering of matter awhirl around a Black Hole?

It was a scary tidbit of *Carpe Diem*
in the year the word "psychedelic"
                first was used

——————— **A One-Line Poem for January** ———————

"Mayflies think they can shake the tree"
        —Mao Tse-Tung
                in reply to Comrade Kuo Mo-Jo

January 14
        Charles de Gaulle said no to the US's offer
                                of Polaris missiles

(the US wanted NATO surface ships to carry them)
& listed his objections to England's coming into the European
                                Economic Community

so that late the same month England was denied entry

Also January 14
        JFK proposed a tax cut
                worth 10 billion in early '60s cash
                o'er 3 years

The Rope

Early in the year the Roper polling org
found that for the first time
more Americans got their news from television
                                       than from ink

January 22
    The USSR said that a US attack on Cuba
                would lead to war

            & then on Feb 28
            Robert McNamara
                        was upset when, even though Russia had
                        pulled its missiles out of Cuba
                        10,000 soldiers remained

January 23
    Britain's secret service liaison with the CIA
    a human named Kim Philby
                vanished, then wound up in Moscow

    He was an MI6 officer, and was working in Beirut, Lebanon
    Philby's defection badly rattled the
                        Military-Industrial-Surrealists

George Corley Wallace
January

When the demagogic George Wallace
was inaugurated as Governor of Alabama

            he said "I draw the line in the dust
            and toss the gauntlet before the feet of tyranny
            and I say segregation now, segregation tomorrow,
            segregation forever."

A Quick Flow of Brilliance
February 11

    It took the tight-wound Beatles just 12 hours
        at EMI studios in London
            to cut their first 2 singles
                plus the ten tunes on their first album *Please Please Me*

February 11
> Sylvia Plath had moved with her 2 children
>> to a London apartment
>>> low on cash & food

> In January of '63 *The Bell Jar* was published
>> under the pseudonym Victoria Lucas

> Then, on February 11, she put a plate of bread & butter
> for her sleeping children
>> on the kitchen table, & glasses of milk too

>> then placed her head in a gas oven & passed away
>> age 30

>> to leave behind the poems of *Ariel*
>> & a much-studied life of anguish & wrath

March 1
> the voter registration drive began in Greenwood, Mississippi

March 4
> the great William Carlos Williams
>> passed from a cerebral hemorrhage at 79

March 15
> Buckminster Fuller received a patent for
>> an "underwater submarine base"

—————————— **Attorneys for All Defendants** ——————————
March 18

> a prisoner in Florida named Clarence Gideon
> had been given 5 years for breaking into a pool hall
>> and stealing a 6-pack, some wine
>>> & change from a c-stick machine

> He then sent a handwritten letter
>>> in neat block letters
>> to the Supreme Court
>>> on an *in forma pauperis* petition
> asking for a new trial
>> because he had been denied an attorney
>>> even though he had asked for one

The Court took the case for decision & agreed
with Mr. Gideon
after which
states were required to appoint and pay for lawyers
should the accused not be able to pull together the money

It was a moment for America

—that even the lowly could expect
the high court to stamp its
justice and mercy
on a hand-written case

March 22
A human named John Profumo,
the Secretary of State for War in the Conservative British gov't
said no no no
to whispers
he'd been fucking the same "model"
as an attaché at the Soviet Embassy in London

March 31
a 100-day newspaper strike in NYC ended

———————— **A Sleazesome Gift for Fidel** ————————
early April

The man named James Donovan
who'd negotiated the release of the
Bay of Pigs prisoners
along with RFK aide John Dolan
were in a yacht
on the way to meet Castro
who was sportfishing off a beach east of Havana

Donovan was seeking the release of
some remaining Bay of Pigs prisoners
plus 3 CIA guys in Cuban jails

He had purchased a gift for Castro
an expensive skindiving suit which
unknown to Mr. Donovan
the CIA's Sidney Gottlieb, who loved
to slip LSD on unsuspecting victims

had smear-dusted on the inside
with what one book, *Deadly Secrets,*
described as a fungus to cause a chronic skin disease
plus, the germy Mr. Gottlieb
had contaminated the breathing apparatus with tuberculosis.

This stealth-smear was done on the orders
of one Desmond FitzGerald (who had taken over
the Mongoose/Operation W Castro-killing program
                  from William Harvey
                  who'd been shipped off to be
                  the Station Chief in Rome)

FitzGerald had also asked Gottlieb's death-lab
to rig some clams with explosives
            to be dropped where Fidel frequently dived

       —the sleaze sleazes in the sleaze

Perhaps Mr. Donovan was hip to the stealth-smear
because he purchased another skindiving suit
                 to give to Fidel

April 10
    The USS *Thresher* submarine went down with 129 men aboard
8,400 feet deep
        while diving 200 miles east of Cape Cod.

———————— The Institute for Policy Studies ————————

That spring some Kennedy administration liberals
Marcus Raskin, Richard Barnet & Arthur Waskow
founded the important, privately funded IPS

which grew during the '60s
as its participants published influential books
                on American policy

    such as the 1965 *Vietnam Reader*
    by Marcus Raskin and Bernard Fall
    which helped inspire the anti-war teach-ins that year

Hail to the Institute for Policy Studies
in the Time-Flow!

The Birmingham Campaign

April–May

Birmingham was
infamous the world o'er
for pictures of mob-sleaze
             attacking the Freedom Riders back in '61

& now the Steel City with its 340,000 inhabitants
             had closed its 38 playgrounds
             8 swimming pools & 4 golf courses
                          rather than integrate.

Martin Luther King Jr. announced early in '63
that he would lead rallies there till
             "Pharaoh lets God's people go."

The man with the power was named Bull Connor
the "independent" police commissioner
             elected with 61% o' th' votes
who could be truly said to be touched with evil.

             Day 'pon day they demo'd
             and day upon day were arrested.

Martin Luther King refused bail on April 12
& the next day he read an article in his cell
from the *Birmingham News* under the headline
             "White Clergymen Urge Local Negroes to
             Withdraw from Demonstrations"

King felt a kind of nonviolent fury & began writing his famous
             20-page
             Letter from Birmingham Jail

which has made its mark now for decades with lines such as

"when you have seen vicious mobs lynch your mothers and fathers
at will and drown your sisters and brothers at whim;
when you have seen hate-filled policemen curse, kick, brutalize and
even kill your black brothers and sisters with impunity;
             when you see the vast majority of your
             twenty million Negro brothers smothering

in an air-tight cage of poverty
in the midst of an affluent society;
....when your first name becomes 'nigger' and
your middle name becomes 'boy'
(no matter how old you are)
and your last name becomes 'John,' and when
your wife and mother are never given the respected title 'Mrs.'....
then you will understand why
we find it difficult
to wait."

It was a moment for America

April 15
A big rally by 70,000 in London
followed by the Aldermaston Peace March
sponsored by the Campaign for Nuclear Disarmament
from London to the "nuclear research center" at Aldermaston

———————— American Hero William Moore ————————
April 23, 1963

a white postman from Baltimore
named William Moore
was walking from Chattanooga, Tenn., to Birmingham
on his 10–day vacation
for peace & integration
pushing a postal cart

Near Attala, Alabama, on Highway 11
someone shot him to death
It was a lightning bolt to the Kennedy-era protesters
& it steeled the resolve of those in Birmingham
marching to change the City of Steel

to whom William Moore became
An American Hero

May 1
Winston Churchill at last retired from Parliament

He'd been in the Commons
for much of the century

and was PM of course during the war years
& then from 1951 till Anthony Eden in '55

———————————— **The March of the Children** ————————

Over a thousand children
on May 2 & 3
marched for freedom
in Birmingham

They came out of the 16th Street Baptist Church
2 by 2
singing "We Shall Overcome"
with high-energy clapping

some as young as six

Bull Connor sent out German shepherds
biting & snarling
like the days of the Nazis
to worldwide revulsion and derision

The police sprayed the children with Monitor Guns
which linked 2 hoses through a single nozzle
mounted on a tripod

and gave such force as to
roll innocent children down the street
as if from a flooded creek.

It was a time of evil.

———— The CIA Sends Up U2s Above Birmingham ————

As reporter Stephen G. Tompkins wrote in an article
resulting from a 16-month investigation for the
Memphis Commercial Appeal on March 21, 1993:

"Portions of the month-long Birmingham disturbances were recorded by
U2 spy planes taking off from the supersecret 'Site 98' outside
Nellis Air Force Base in Nevada. Over the next seven years,
at least 26 other such domestic spy flights by U2s and at
least two involving the more advanced SR71 were requested by
Army commanders and flown by the Air Force, according to
classified documents reviewed by *The Commercial Appeal*.
These expensive spy flights illustrate Army commanders' growing fear
of domestic upheaval as King's influence grew."

May 5
It's sometimes difficult to substantiate the word "first"
such as the first liver transplant which occurred on this day
at the University of Colorado health sciences center
in Denver
by Dr. Thomas Starzl

whereas the first successful liver transplant
was to await the year '67

——————— Censored in Early May ———————

Bob Dylan was set to appear on "The Ed Sullivan Show"
but hours before airtime
CBS attorneys riled Dylan's fury
when they told him
he couldn't sing the satiric
"Talkin' John Birch Society Blues"

nor wd the censorious CBS records allow the tune
on Dylan's next album

My friend Izzy Young, who operated the Folklore Center
on MacDougal Street
led a picket line at CBS against the censoring

May 9
    the ultrarightist Ngo Dihn Diem
            assented to the spending of $17 million
            on the Clio-cursing concept of "strategic hamlets"
            where villagers were rounded up into
                barbed-wire villages
                        to separate them from the Viet Cong

—— **Kennedy Orders Federal Troops to Birmingham** ——
May 12

Down in Birmingham
the white establishment
        especially those w/ downtown stores
      & those promoting industry
had worked out a deal
        w/ the black community
        (with its many ministers & leaders
        such as the cool-under-fire Andrew Young
        & the great Martin King)

for a time-table
      to integrate the schools
           the lunch rooms
              & public conveniences

Those with a klanmind
wanted chaos
& for the race-toothed Governor Wallace
              to militarize the state

(You can sort out these days by reading the beautiful book
Parting the Waters by Taylor Branch
           say around pp. 779 to 800)

On Saturday evening May 11
racist sleaze bombed Rev. A. D. King's parsonage
                   in Birmingham
and the same night
the Gaston Motel,
      Martin King's headquarters
               also bombed

and the streets filled up with angry protestors

whereupon Colonel Al Lingo of the State Police
led 250 troopers and irregulars

on a murder-bent rampage against blacks

the blacks responded

& there were businesses and houses and at least 24
autos
   burned to nothingness
       by the dawn

Emergency meetings at the Pentagon and Justice Department
ate the Sunday

JFK flew in from his weekend at Camp David
and they debated what to do
   w/ the heroic Burke Marshall
    calling Martin King directly from the White House

  In the end JFK ordered 3,000 US soldiers
           to Birmingham
  in what they called Operation Oak Tree

& then at 8:48 pm JFK
   went before a packed awaitingment of reporters

"The Birmingham agreement was and is a fair and just
      accord. . . .
The federal gov't will not permit it
     to be sabotaged
     by a few extremists
       on either side"

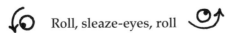 Roll, sleaze-eyes, roll

May 21

There were 6 civil rights cases bundled together
before the Supreme Ct, one where
        10 protesters were arrested trying to
        eat integratedly at the Kress dime store
                in Greenville, SC
    & were convicted

    plus a similar sit-in case from Birmingham
    and one from Maryland when 2 blacks boarded
             a carousel in a white-only park

    and on this day the Supreme Court
        reversed the convictions
            & tossed out the crackerly laws
                that had done them

——————————————— **Quang Duc** ———————————————
June 10

In an image of horror that stunned a generation
a Buddhist monk named Ngo Quang Duc
burned himself to death in the lotus position
    in Saigon
    as the ultimate statement

against the persecution of Buddhists
by the right-wing Catholic Diem

'Tween June and October
7 monks, known as bonzes,
                                burned themselves

Madame Nhu, wife
of Ngo Dinh Diem's brother

liked the blazes
She called the immolations "barbecues"

June 10
    in a speech at American U in DC the President
    said his nation would not nuke-filth the atmosphere
                        as long as other nations also refrained.

June 11
    2 black students, escorted by National Guard soldiers
    enrolled at the University of Alabama

    & Governor Wallace
                was forced to eat a northern liberal quiche
                        made out of a chopped-up Confederate flag

            as Kennedy sent National Guardsmen
            to force the hate-hearted Democrat twerp to
            allow Vivian Malone and James Hood
                into Foster Auditorium
                        to register

———————————— **A Sudden Speech** ————————————
June 11

In a sudden decision of the sort
                that makes advisors tremble with angst
JFK decided to make a civil rights speech
He asked for 15 minutes
                on the networks
                        at 8 pm

Ted Sorenson had two hours
           to put the speech together
during which the President
           who after all had won a Pulitzer Prize
           for his writing

     worked & reworked it

In the speech he outlined his proposed civil rights legislation
& showed the best of his heart with sentences such as

"We preach freedom around the world, and we mean it.
And we cherish our freedom here at home. But are we to say
to the world—and much more importantly, to each other—
that this is the land of the free, except for Negroes, that we have no
second-class citizens, except Negroes,
           that we have no class or caste system, no ghettos,
               no master race, except with respect to Negroes?"

           It was a moment for America

The very night of Kennedy's spontaneous speech
NAACP field secretary Medgar Evers was at a strategy session
                         in Jackson, Mississippi
His kids were allowed to stay up after midnight
           to greet their dad
               after Kennedy's talk

Evers drove home
           & got out of his Olds
               with a stack of
           "Jim Crow Must Go" sweatshirts
                   in his arms
when a nightmare evil from the Ku Klux Klan named
           Byron De La Beckwith
               shot him in the back
                   with a 30.06 rifle bullet

His children rushed out and
pleaded "Please Daddy, please get up!"

On the desperate trip to the hospital
Evers tried to sit up & his final words were
                   "Turn me loose"

then thanatos.
He was buried in Arlington National Cemetery

The quick-worded Klan sleaze
          got away with it for over thirty years
                    though finally was sent away for life
                              after a trial in early 1994

───────────── **Another Prayer Decision** ─────────────
June 17

The Supreme Court
banned forcing students to hear, read
or recite the Lord's Prayer and/or Scripture sections
                              in public schools

───────────── **The Patsyization of Oswald** ─────────────
Summer o' '63

Using the office of the viciously anti-Castro
activist named Guy Bannister as his headquarters
a guy named Lee Harvey Oswald passed out
                    pro-Castro pamphlets
                              in New Orleans

───────────── **Crackdown on Right-Wing Cubans** ─────────────
Spring-Summer '63

The Kennedy forces
          cracked down on the
                    rightist Cuban movement
                              in the USA
          that spring and summer

For instance on June 14
a human in Miami told the FBI
a bunch of Cuban exiles were going to
                    bomb the Shell refinery in Cuba

so the next day customs agents
raided an abandoned airfield near Miami
as a plane was about to be loaded with two 250-lb bombs
300 sticks of dynamite, 55 lbs of napalm, some grenades
                    and M-1 rifles

Further research by the FBI led to a raid July 31 on
a house near Lake Pontchartrain
which seized a ton of dynamite, bomb fuses, 50 lbs of Nuodex,
            and materials to make napalm

The grrr-ing right-wing exiles
went around the gov't to get help from the Hunger Heads

i.e., the American mafia
            which hungered to get back its
                        Havana casinos

& right-wing oil-oids such as the Hunt family
            who hungered to
                        extinguish the burning oil-slick of
                                    nationalization

& Kennedy-hating elements of the CIA which hungered
                                    to set up oligarchies

& investment bankers thirsting
                        for ownership
                        & ᴀᴧᴧ of cash

            and some of them hungry
                        to write Cuba's name
                                    with Kennedy's blood.

The South was aswirl with violent sleaze that summer
eager to kill the man
            who wouldn't let them kill

─────────────────── **Operation 40** ───────────────────

Lurking behind a good part of the Cuban exile movement
            was an entity known as Operation 40
            which murkily sleazed in the sluice
                                    of the sixties
            from 1960 till '70.

The CIA created Operation 40 in 1960
to set up what *The New York Times* wrote was
"described by Cubans as a CIA-devised

plan to set up a parent intelligence agency in Cuba after the
expected overthrow of the Castro Government"
                                                    after the Bay of Pigs

It had a murderous & evil side to it too
which was to kill elements in the post-Castro Cuba
believed to be too liberal, or
                    shudder shudder, too left

According to the interesting book *Deadly Secrets*
                    by Warren Hinckle & William Turner

Operation 40 had "another political function—to purge the Cuban
exile ranks of the anti-Castro left, the exponents of *Fidelismo sin Fidel.*"

                    Even after the '61 invasion failure
                    Operation 40 sliced onward for 10 years
                    in CIA supersecrecy
                                headquartered in Miami

Deadly Secrets (p. xliv) describes how
Operation 40 "was hastily shut down by the CIA in 1970"

                    after 10 years of fascist, totalitarian
                                            surveillance and thrill-kill

                    "when an Operation 40 plane carrying a cargo of heroin
                    & cocaine crashed in Southern California."

                    Elements of Operation 40
                    as we shall see
                                may have helped assassinate John Kennedy
                                        the man who was cracking
                                        down that summer
                                        on exile raidings

Sex Scandal in England
——————————— Shock-Thrills the US ———————————
June

The conservatives were in charge of England
       & their secretary of war one John Profumo
         was charged with fucking a 21-year-old beauty named
                                      Christine Keeler
         who at the same time was balling
              a Soviet naval officer in London

An osteopath named Dr. Stephen Ward was
accused of introducing Keeler to Profumo
On June 5 Profumo was forced to resign
           when a tabloid front-paged his eros
and on the 17th o' June "it" nearly toppled the conservative
           Macmillan gov't

For some reason John Kennedy was fascinated with the case
& asked for the latest intelligence reports on it
             to be delivered immediately

——————————— A New Civil Rights Law ———————————
June 19

Fresh upon the images of Birmingham's biting dogs
Kennedy asked Congress for a new and more powerful
                    civil rights law

It was to cause the fiercest debate, they said,
       since the union-mugging Taft-Hartley Act of '47

"We face a moral crisis," said John Kennedy
"It cannot be met by police action
It cannot be met by increased demonstrations
                in the streets
It cannot be quieted by token moves or talk
It is time to act in the Congress
in your state and local legislative bodies
and in all our daily lives."

Ping!

June 21
De Gaulle removed France's naval fleet from NATO

the same day
            Bob Hayes
                        went the 100-yard dash in 9.1 seconds

June 22
Martin King was invited to the White House
                                    for a private meeting with JFK

While he was waiting to go into the Oval Office
Robert Kennedy & Burke Marshall
(a senior Justice Department official)
separately told King he had to cease working
with Stanley Levison & Jack O'Dell
both of whom
            they averred
                        were communists
—Marshall went so far as to tab Levison
as a "paid agent of the Soviet communist apparatus"

                        King didn't believe it.
                        Marshall then took King to RFK
                        who said the same thing
                        but King asked for proof

as the quick-thinking leader pointed out that people in the South
were calling RFK himself a commie

Then King went into the Oval Office
JFK asked him to take a stroll in the Rose Garden
"I assume you know you're under very close surveillance,"
                                            the President said
and then put his hand on King's shoulder
and said he had "to get rid of" Levison and O'Dell

"They're communists," said Camelot

King replied he was not sure what the President
was talking about. Hoover, after all,
thought many people Communists

Kennedy replied that O'Dell was a "ranking member of
of the national committee of the American Communist Party"

As for Mr. Levison, Kennedy said that
Levison's role was too highly classified
                                        for details
but that Levison was O'Dell's handler

O'Dell, Kennedy putatively said,
was the "number five Communist in the United States."

Kennedy then mentioned the Profumo scandal
—then washing across the front pages—
            and the dangers of friends remaining loyal to friends:
            "Macmillan is likely to lose his gov't
            because he has been loyal to a friend"

Kennedy said "If they shoot you down, they'll shoot us down too. So
            we're asking you to be careful."

King demanded proof on Levison
            but no one ever gave it to him
                        because there was nothing to give.

            It was a J. Edgar Hoover scam.

Then JFK took King back into the Oval Office
for a fairly large gathering
of civil rights leaders

            after which the ever-seething President flew off to Europe
            & a greeting of one million people
                        in Frankfurt

───────────────── **Ich Bin Ein Berliner** ─────────────────
June 26

He toured West Germany for a few days
with a famous stop at the Berlin Wall
            & he spoke to a throng of 150,000
            at the Berlin City Hall
                        to utter some famous words

"All free men, wherever they may live, are citizens of Berlin,
and therefore, as a free man, I take pride in the words
Ich bin ein Berliner."

July 1
Kim Philby was revealed as the famous Third man
who had warned Soviet spies Guy Burgess and Donald Maclean
                    enabling them to hasten to the Soviet Union

(Philby was the British Intelligence link to the CIA
which must have caused many a shudder in the
                    National Security Grouch Apparatus)

On July 30 Philby was given asylum in the USSR

In the USA the same day
    the ZIP code system (Zone Improvement Plan) was put in place

———————————————— **The Moscow Talks** ————————————————
July 15

In a move that might have been a factor in JFK's shooting
the US and USSR began serious work in Moscow
                    on a test ban treaty

July 26 Kennedy called the test ban treaty "a victory for mankind"

———————————————— **Test Ban Treaty Signed** ————————————————
August 5

Right-wing grrr-heads
    and hard-edged national security grouches
thought Kennedy was veering close to treason
when the US above-ground test ban treaty was signed

but the great majority was pleased
                to have the nuke-fear eased

when the USA, Britain & the USSR signed the treaty
                and then 96 others
                but not France
                before it went into power October 1

63

(The treaty was only preliminarily approved & had to
be ratified by 2/3 of the Senate
   which was accomplished in September)

     Ping! Ping!

Kennedy didn't dare buck the Military-Industrial-Surrealists
  and go for an underground test ban also

  Grrr Grrr Grrr

──────── **Joint Chiefs Support Atmospheric Test Ban** ────────

As Gen. Maxwell Taylor points out in his book
      Swords and Plowshares
the Joint Chiefs, to their credit, testified before the Senate
in support of the atmospheric test ban
but, not to their credit, they had insisted on
      a "vigorous" ongoing
      underground test program

August 8
  Jackie gave birth to Patrick Bouvier Kennedy
  5 1/2 weeks premature, on August 6
    but today he passed away from respiratory distress

  The terrible grief of the loss
  brought husband and wife closer

     so close that the beautiful Jackie wd agree
     in a few weeks to accompany him to Dallas
      (her first political trip with him
        since the 1960 campaign)

August 12
  the US informed the UN
    the US will halt arms sales to South Africa

     Ping! Ping!

The Speech that Helped Save the Century
August 28

200,000 came to Washington for the
   March for Jobs and Freedom
      on a hot August day
I was one of them
  standing in the shade of an American elm
      with members of the Living Theater

One guy had rollerskated all the way from Chicago
Josephine Baker had flown in from Paris
     "You are on the eve of a complete victory"
         she said
& Marlon Brando held up a cattle prod
     used in Gadsden, Alabama

  Dylan sang his song about Medgar Evers
  Mahalia Jackson her "I've Been 'Buked & I've Been Scorned"
  Joan Baez sang "We Shall Overcome"
  & Peter, Paul and Mary sang "Blowin' in the Wind."

SNCC leader John Lewis was allowed to speak to the big crowd
though they forced him to modify his rhetoric
when he criticized the Kennedy administration for its failure to
         defend black rights.

The genius, of course, was brought from Martin King's speech
which he had polished in the Willard Hotel the night before

Most people have some of it memorized by now, but here are
some sentences:

"I have a dream that one day on the red hills of Georgia
the sons of former slaves and the sons of former slaveowners
will be able to sit down together at the table of brotherhood. . . .

"I have a dream that my four little children will one day live in a
nation where they will not be judged by the color of their skin
but by the content of their character. . . .

"I have a dream that one day the state of Alabama. . .
will be transformed into a situation where little black boys

and black girls will be able to join hands with little white boys
and white girls and walk together as sisters and brothers..."

It was utterly and totally engrossing
      & still is, heard on a tape 40 years later

John Kennedy
      watching King's "I Have a Dream" on TV said
                    "He's damn good."

———————————————— **The Hotline** ————————————————
September 1

A 4,883-mile duplex cable
allowing simultaneous communications
                    in both directions

DC ⇄ Kremlin

——————————————— **A Warning from Fidel** ———————————————
September 7

There was a party at the Brazilian Embassy in Havana
Fidel Castro was there and sought out Daniel Harker of the
                          Associated Press

to warn about hit plots:

"United States leaders should think if they assist in terrorist plans
to eliminate Cuban leaders, they themselves will not be safe."

September 10
JFK stopped the draft for married men

           Ping!   Ping!

——————————————— **Evil in Birmingham** ———————————————
September 15

That night some men of utter evil from the Ku Klux Klan
planted a bomb by a window beneath a magnolia bush

at the very church where the children had marched out that spring
singing hymns
& hopeful of better times

& then in the morning young women in the basement
of the 16th Street Baptist Church
were getting ready for youth services upstairs. . . .

Then a blast!

& four lay dead in their choir robes:
Cynthia Wesley, Carole Robertson, Addie Mae Collins, all 14
and Chris McNair, 11.

It was 10:22 am

The damage was terrible
A stained-glass window somehow survived
only the face of Jesus was missing

There were 28 unsolved bombings in Birmingham, Alabama
that year

Within months the FBI's Birmingham office
identified 4 of the Ku Klux Klanners
who had bombed these children
& urged J. Edgar Hoover, head of the FBI,
to present this information to the Justice Dept
but Hoover blocked it

a disgraceful lack of character which demands
that Hoover's name be taken off the
FBI building in Washington

September 16
  Malaysia was founded
      —Singapore, Sarawak and North Borneo
                        became one

    then on the 18th in Jakarta, Indonesia
    the great island chain to the south of Malaysia
    10,000 humans burned the British embassy
                  in ire o'er Malaysia's creation

The Right Tosses Out an Elected Government
———————— in the Dominican Republic ————————
September 25

    The Dominican Republic
    had been ruled since 1930
          by a dictator named Rafael Trujillo
          who was killed in '61.

  In December of '62
  a writer/politician named Juan Bosch
                was elected President

  Bosch angered the right
          with a program to improve the rights and lives of
                  farm and industrial workers

          and the constitution was revised to
                  limit the disparity-delighting curse
                  of ever-increasing ever-impoverishing
                  ever-mooching landholdings

          always a source of grrrrrrs

          among rt-  land-mooches

  so that on September 25, 1963
  right-wing military officers
          tossed out Bosch and his cabinet.

  To its credit, the Kennedy administration
  suspended financial aid &
  refused to recognize the
          rightist cabal then seizing the Dominican Republic

but Kennedy had but 5 weeks
before his own cabal
erased him in a slowed-down caravan in Dallas

(and when in 1965 it seemed as if the elected Bosch would
come back to power
cabal-product Johnson
sent in the Marines
to prevent the sharing
of the Dominican Republic's
resources
with all its people)

———————————— **The McNamara-Taylor Mission** ————————————
Late September

The President sent McNamara and General Taylor
to Vietnam in late September, 1963

Kennedy, in the words of General Maxwell Taylor,
"wanted to be reassured about the course of the war
and to know the truth about the reports that
[Ambassador] Lodge and [General] Harkins
were not communicating with one another,
and that the CIA was out of control. . . ."

There were classified sections and nonclassified in their report,
parts of which the White House made public on October 2

The McNamara-Taylor Report said that by the end of '63
about 1,000 Americans could be withdrawn

with the overall goal, as Gen. Taylor later stated it,
to reduce the Viet Cong to a "state approximating
low order banditry" by 1965

It was a good sign since the # of troops & personnel
had jumped from 11,300 in '62
to 16,300 in '63

Don't worry, Mil-Ind-Surr's, war-willing LBJ is on the way!

Ping! Ping!

September 26 & October 3

The CIA later claimed that on these dates
Lee Harvey Oswald visited the
           Cuban and Soviet embassies
                    in Mexico City

but, to quote the great Christian singer

"That was just a lie"

September 27
     a Mafia hit man named Joseph Valachi
     appeared before the Senate Investigations Committee
     and fingered Vito Genovese as
                   the boss of bosses
          in mobland
          and fingered Carlo Gambino
          and Thomas Lucchese
               as mob-family leaders

Families, he said, are known as borgatas
and he listed bosses, lieutenants and soldiers
in a system of mobs he called
                Cosa Nostra

        —riveting bits of Americana to the millions
        watching the hearings on television

——————————————— **The Q** ———————————————

Was Kennedy going to pull from Vietnam?
The repressionists of the Secrecy State still
as of this writing
           have not released all the documents

but clearly the cap-eyes were rolling to own
the lush wealth of Indochina

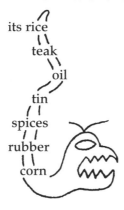

its rice

teak

oil

tin

spices

rubber

corn

like an ancient Demon of Conquest!

October 3

Arthur Krock in '63 was a powerful writer
for *The New York Times*
& in a column published today quoted a "very high official"
that the CIA's growth was like "a malignancy"
which the official "was not sure even the White House
could control... any longer" and "if the United States ever
experiences (an attempt at a coup to overthrow the government)
it will come from the CIA and not the Pentagon."

October 17

At Abbey Road in London
the Beatles used a 4-track tape machine for the first time!
as they recorded "I Want to Hold Your Hand" 17 times
with the final take the one used
on the record

October 24

US UN Ambassador Adlai Stevenson
spoke that evening in Dallas
after which he was spat upon, jostled & jeer-sneered
by Birch-brained crackers
outside the Dallas Memorial Auditorium Theater

The question then was raised
                    would JFK still come to Dallas in November?

October 26
    The President spoke at the groundbreaking of a library
        in honor of Robert Frost
                    in Amherst, Massachusetts:

        "Robert Frost. . . . saw poetry as the means of
        saving power from itself. When power leads man
        toward arrogance, poetry reminds him of
        his limitations. When power narrows the areas of
        man's concern, poetry reminds him of the richness
        and diversity of his existence. When power
        corrupts, poetry cleanses.
        For art establishes the basic human truths which
        must serve as the touchstone of our judgment."

October 31
    the Conservative gov't in England
                    ceased its aid to Indonesia

———————————— **A Coup Against Diem** ————————————
November 1

There was an Army coup in S Vietnam
        Ngo Dinh Diem was assassinated &
            succeeded by Gen Duong Van Minh

Some of JFK's civilian advisors had eagerly sought Diem's ouster
and some had argued against it

The Joint Chiefs of Staff were, by some accounts,
                                angry
and it seems clear that all the chiefs had opposed the coup
(though LeMay later claimed he had no inkling of it)
and then, during the 3 weeks left to JFK
    as Army historian H. R. McMaster wrote in his book
    Dereliction of Duty (p. 46):
    "Rather than relieving tensions between the JCS
    & the Kennedy administration, the 'Asian Bay of Pigs'
    exacerbated them and made cooperation even more difficult"

November 7
    US recognized the "new regime" in Saigon
    while the Military-Industrial-Surrealist complex kept grrring
    plus, by now, there was a new sound in the time-track:

                        Ping   Ping!

November
    The FBI hired a Ku Klux Klan informant
                    named John Wesley Hall
                    even though lie-detector tests
                    had convinced agents
                                that he had been involved in the
                                bombing of the 16th Street Baptist Church

            Hoover knew it,
            knew the connection
                        but kept it out of the flow of Justice

                        Nope

—— **White House Cooperates with Seven Days in May** ——
                    Mid-November

JFK himself urged director John Frankenheimer
to make a movie of the political thriller
                        Seven Days in May
            "to the dismay of the Pentagon"
            as Arthur Schlesinger Jr. wrote in his
                                book on RFK

Seven Days told of a military takeover in 1974
against a young president
who was making a disarmament treaty with the Soviets

The movie starred Burt Lancaster, Kirk Douglas,

Ava Gardner and Fredric March to a script by
Rod Serling, the author of the "Twilight Zone" TV series

Filming was completed in the days before
                              Kennedy's voyage to Dallas &
Look magazine, with a circulation of more than 7 million
published mid-November an article tracing how the

Pentagon had grrred "no" to requests by the director
              for a visit to the office of the Joint Chiefs of Staff
but how the President had allowed John Frankenheimer and crew
to tour the White House and to film the entrance ways

and then also to film a mock riot
between pro-President and Pro-Coup partisans
outside the White House on Pennsylvania Avenue on July 27
              ironically very near the day
              the Test Ban Treaty was inked in Moscow
                              pending Senate approval.

After Kennedy had read *Seven Days in May*
he commented to a friend that a military coup
was possible under certain circumstances
              "but it won't happen on my watch"

———————— **JFK Explores Rapprochement with Fidel** ————————
Fall of '63

Through the National Security Agency
by early May '63, the CIA had obtained a transcript of
a long, apparently 10-hour interview
              that ABC television reporter Lisa Howard had

with Fidel Castro

in which Fidel Castro declared his desire
              for a rapprochement with the USA

(The history of this is traced in James Bamford's history
of the National Security Agency, *Body of Secrets*)

Kill-heads by the multi-score
in the haunts of the Military-Industrial-CIA-Surrealists

were still unrespitedly plotting to kill Mr. Castro
                        that spring-summer-early fall

but a Peace Track was opened up
            which John Kennedy gingerly explored

using a man named William Attwood
who worked with UN ambassador Adlai Stevenson

(History surely will honor Adlai Stevenson
            for facing the fierce scorn of the
                        kill-heads during the years
                        '62 till his death in the summer of '65)

As James Bamford traces,
"President Kennedy began to explore
                Castro's apparent olive branch.
He approved a quiet approach by Attwood to Dr. Carlos Lechuga,
Cuba's ambassador to the UN, using ABC's Lisa Howard
                                as a go-between."

Attwood thought Castro was in a mood to talk
but RFK did not want Attwood to go to Cuba
but "that the meeting take place either in New York,
during a visit by Castro to the UN, or in a neutral country,
such as Mexico." (See *Body of Secrets*, p. 129)

Negotiations continued through
                    the tick tick tick
                            of the doom-drum fall

in as much secrecy as a doomed President
                under the full monitoring
                        of the Military-Industrial-CIAists
                            could garner.

    The morning JFK was in his final motorcade
    word came from a trusted associate of Castro
    that specific proposals
            for a meeting with Castro
                        were forthcoming

                    Ping!

Bye Bye, Lyndon

Evelyn Lincoln, the President's secretary
wrote in her memoir *Kennedy and Johnson*, of a conversation
she overheard on November 19, 1963
                in which JFK said
"I will need as a running mate a man who believes as I do."

Who would that be? she asked

"At this time I am thinking about Governor Sanford
                of North Carolina,
                        but it will not be Lyndon"

                And so the ancient Fates
                Clotho, Lachesis & Atropos
                began their ancient ritual

                spin spin, measure measure, cut cut

Bye Bye, Nam

In his book *Johnny, We Hardly Knew Ye*
key aide Kenneth O'Donnell
said that the President had told Senator Mike Mansfield
in the spring of '63
that he would order all troops out of Vietnam in 1965
                "But I can't do it until 1965—after I'm reelected."
                (Mansfield later confirmed the quote)

Randiness Around the Pool

A Secret Service agent named William McIntyre, age 28,
came to the JFK protection detail in the fall of '63
                & was placed on the midnight shift

Over 3 decades later he
told writer Seymour Hersh he saw women
                coming into the White House

McIntyre spoke of being on duty when Jackie wanted a swim
when JFK was in the pool,
                putatively sporting with 2 women

Jackie was halted at the door & fuming with anger
she summoned her personal Secret Service Agent

According to McIntyre when Jackie got to the pool
there were one big and two small pairs of wet footprints
leading toward the Oval Office.

However randy the President seemed to wend
I don't think the time-track provides the proof
for the accusation that he ever
—to borrow an ancient Egyptian hieroglyph—

thought with his

Secret Service Partying
——————— *sed quis custodiet ipsos/custodes?* ———————

The hunger to party can insinuate itself
into the fiercest dedications & so
according to Seymour Hersh's book
The Dark Side of Camelot
(try around p. 244)
"Some of the agents and military aides who traveled with Kennedy,
surfeited with available women, soon found themselves doing what
the president was doing. Drinking and partying became a constant
feature of presidential travel, especially on the weekend trips to
Hyannis Port and Palm Beach."

Hersh wrote that by the time of Dealey Plaza
"a few members of the presidential detail were
regularly remaining in bars until the early morning hours."

—————————————— A Trip to Texas ——————————

There was considerable anger at JFK in the South
because of enforcing integration
&, among some, because
of his liberal image

The spittle against Adlai Stevenson
was not long dried.

The concept, it has been written,
was to "take his case to the people"

& so he had chosen to go to Texas & also to Florida
to dazzle them with his "Ich bin ein Berliner" pizzazz
          —Florida had gone for Nixon &
                    apparently only having Johnson on the ticket
                    won him Texas.

———————— **Marita Lorenz & the Plot to Murder JFK** ————————

          What seems believable is that
          elements of the CIA &
          some highly placed members
                              of the military

          flamed with hatred of JFK enough
                              to scheme his demise.

The testimony of CIA operative Marita Lorenz
has seemed to me believable
on the question of who killed John Kennedy
(although a writer I respect, Anthony Summers,
                              doubts her story)

Marita Lorenz was the former lover of Fidel Castro
with whom, early in the revolution,
                    she'd had a child
& who later defected from Cuba
& became an anti-Castro activist
after the CIA had fibbed to her that Castro
                    was going to kill her and her baby

(a lie she only discovered years later)

During the early 1960s she worked to overthrow Mr. Castro
with the CIA group called Operation 40
for whom one of her jobs was transporting weapons

On November 21, 1963
          according to her sworn deposition at
               a trial (E. Howard Hunt suing someone about
                    an article linking him to events in
                                        Dallas, Nov 22, '63)

Lorenz went with Frank Sturgis (who would be one of
    the 1972 Watergate break-in group) from Miami
                in 2 cars to Dallas

    They brought with them rifles, cases of machine guns,
    thirty-eights, forty-fives.

        She and Sturgis checked into a motel
        She would have been about 22 years old
                        and was famously beautiful

        E. Howard Hunt, she testified,
        brought cash to Sturgis
                in the motel—
                Sturgis pulled it out and counted.

        There were others in the car
        whom she identified
                    in her testimony

Marita Lorenz testified she wanted to
get out of Dallas and back to Miami:
            "I knew that this was different from other jobs.
            This was not just gunrunning. This was big,
            very big, and I wanted to get out. I told Sturgis
            I wanted to leave. He said it was a very big
            operation but that my part was not dangerous.
            I was to be a decoy. Before he could go further,
            I said please let me get out. I want to go back to
            my baby in Miami. Finally he agreed and drove
            me to the airport."

        Later in the same testimony, Marita Lorenz said
        that when Sturgis later tried to recruit her for another
        CIA project, he told her that
                    she had missed
                        "the really big one."
        He said to her, "We killed the president that day. You
        could have been part of it—you know, a part of history.
You should have stayed. It was safe. Everything was covered
in advance. No arrests, no real newspaper investigation. It
            was all covered, very professional."

In 1977 she testified before the
House Select Committee on Assassinations
and said she'd been at a meeting in Sept. '63 at Orlando
Bosch's attended by Lee Harvey Oswald,
whom she then apparently already knew,
having met him earlier at an Operation 40 safe house. Also present
were Sturgis and a Major Pedro Díaz Lanz.
"The discussion concerned a trip to Dallas," she said

Her 1977 testimony is in
The House Select Committee on Assassinations, Vol 9 (p. 93)

Frank Sturgis, who died of lung cancer in December of 1993
denied he was involved in JFK

The same goes for E. Howard Hunt
who later sought to prove that he was in
DC on doom-day

—————————————— **The Final Trip** ——————————————

The President flew to Texas on November 21
first to Houston
where Camelot got huge ovations
& then to Ft. Worth
for more palm–thunder

& then on the 22nd to Dallas
where he landed at Love Field w/ Jackie

—————— **A Sleaze-o-Gram from the Scythy Right** ——————
November 22

Waiting for JFK that morning was a welcoming ad in the
Dallas Morning News with a sequence of rightist moans
such as:

"WHY have you ordered or permitted your brother Bobby, the
Attorney General, to go soft on Communists, fellow-travelers,
and ultra-leftists in America, while permitting him to persecute
loyal Americans who criticize you, your administration, and
your leadership" and

"WHY are you in favor of the US continuing to give economic aid
to Argentina, in spite of the fact that Argentina has just seized
almost 400 million dollars of American private property?"

                                                      et alia loonia

According to the book *Contract on America*
right-wing oil man Nelson Bunker Hunt
                              paid for the greeting.

"You know," the President joked to Jackie
as he skimmed the ad that morning
            in their hotel room
                    "We're heading into nut country today"

In the speech he was on his way to make
JFK was going to chastise
                    right-wing conservatives.

They showed him.

——————————— **"Take Off the Bubble Top"** ———————————

A reporter named Jim Lehrer
who years later ran a national news show
                    over the Public Broadcasting Service

was that day a reporter for the Dallas *Times Herald*
an afternoon newspaper
            & was covering Kennedy's arrival & departure
            from the Dallas airport

Mr. Lehrer wrote in a memoir that a rewrite man asked
him to find out if the bubble top was going to be on
                                    JFK's limousine

Lehrer then walked to the ramp where the limousines were waiting
& noted that the President's bulletproof bubble was on the limo

He asked the Secret Service agent in charge of the Dallas office,
Forrest Sorrels
            "Rewrite wants to know if the bubble top's going
                    to stay on?"

Sorrels looked skyward, Lehrer later wrote,
then asked another agent about the weather
                    in downtown Dallas
after which, assured, ordered "Take off the bubble top"

──────────────── **The Final Procession** ────────────────

Trapped in a hostile city
where so recently the lunchmeat necks
            had spat upon
                    the UN ambassador

the man of Camelot
wended to his doom.

The Secret Service had allowed open windows
in upper stories, for instance
        the 6th floor of the Texas School Book Depository

And it did seem odd that
immediately in front of JFK's limousine
as the shots were being fired
                    a man raised his umbrella aloft
                    as if to say "Now!'
(from frame Z-227 of the Zapruder film):

────── **And Then the Famous Tramps—Who Are They?** ──────

There was a series of 6 photos taken within minutes of the hit
showing 3 casually dressed men, later identified only as "tramps"
who had been pulled off a freight car & were
            being escorted by uniformed officers,
                    very casually & without handcuffs,
                    from the area behind the grassy knoll
                                through Dealey Plaza

Some say their names are known
Some say hidden
Some say they were actual tramps
Some say bidden

Air Force Colonel Fletcher Prouty was Chief of Special Operations
for the Joint Chiefs of Staff during the Kennedy years.
A few years after the assassination he was shown the six photos,
and noticed in photo number 1 a person he knew walking in
the opposite direction.

"Here he is," Prouty later told an interviewer, "during one of the most
important events in our history, casually walking past two police
with guns and the tramps, not even
looking at what could've been the killers of the President"

————————— **The Stun of an Ancient Play** —————————

Ancient plays were known for their moments of sudden gnosis
or sudden stunning knowledge
& so it was when Colonel Prouty recognized a friend in the photo:
"I was stunned to realize that this unconcerned
bystander was none other than my long-time friend and associate
Ed Lansdale.
...I just knew that he must be concerned with
the cover story. That was

his gift…his specialty.
I personally have no doubt that the photo is of Lansdale. I knew him
from 1952 in the Philippines to the time of his death.

He was one of my neighbors."
Same haircut, the twisted left hand, the big class ring, the stoop
General Lansdale
Dealey Plaza
Doom Day

The Bay of Pigs Got Even

The Joint Chiefs of Staff
——————— at the Moment of the Assassination ———————

Chairman Maxwell Taylor had just returned from a
3-day jetlag trip to Honolulu
to meet with Rusk, McNamara,
Ambassador Lodge & General Harkins
to come to commonality
on a plan for Vietnam.

That morning the Joint Chiefs were entertaining
the West German chief of staff and his successor
at lunch
just as JFK left Love Airport
for downtown Dallas.

As far as I can tell all the Chiefs (except Curtis LeMay)
were on hand:
Marine Commandant David Shoup
Chief of Naval Operations, Admiral David McDonald
Army Chief of Staff, General Earl Wheeler

Air Force Chief of Staff Curtis LeMay
to whom bombing was the whole thing
& who liked to blow his cigar smoke
in Taylor's nonsmoking face
told a biographer he was in Michigan
on Dallas day.

The meeting broke till 2
& the weary General Taylor was
taking a nap in his office
at the moment of gunfire.

Taylor was told of the shooting
& brought the Chiefs to his office
            & put US forces on increased alertness.
The Chiefs went back to the conference
                          with the Germans
who were told that Kennedy had been shot
& that the conference would go on.

Taylor was handed a note that Kennedy was dead
which he passed underneath the table to the Chiefs
               & each Chief passed to the next.

Taylor waited till the end of the meeting
to break the news to the German officers.
In his memoir *Swords and Plowshares*
Taylor wrote how he'd rarely seen such
           "ashen faces. . . or spontaneous grief."

Let the Germans cry
& the Chiefs stay dry

———————————————— **Amlash** ————————————————

In a Paris hotel room
at just about the very moment that
JFK was murdered
a CIA officer handed over a fountain pen
rigged with a syringe & poison
to a human named Rolando Cubela
           with which to kill Fidel Castro

(whether the CIA used its
Artichoke robo-kill techniques
on Mr. Cubela can only be speculated)

Cubela had previously demanded a meeting
with Robert Kennedy before
               killing Castro
but CIA honcho Richard Helms
had told Desmond FitzGerald
the officer in charge of killing Castro
that it was not necessary to check with RFK
but that it was okay to say he was the
        "personal representative of Robert F. Kennedy."

All that morning Robert Kennedy had met
        with 40 Justice Department attorneys
        as they mapped out a stepped-up campaign against
                    organized crime.

During lunch he had driven to his
                home at Hickory Hills
took a swim, then joined Ethel
        & US Attorney Robert Morgenthau
                by the pool to eat

J. Edgar Hoover called Kennedy's office.
His secretary was weeping.
She did not want to break the news.

The Attorney General had just told Morgenthau
        "We'd better get back to that meeting."

        when

 telephoned

"It's J. Edgar Hoover," said Ethel.

RFK picked up the phone. Hoover: "I have some news
for you. The President's been shot. . . ."

        like a spit across time

———————————— **On the Plane to DC** ————————————

A weeping federal judge named Sarah Hughes
gave Johnson the oath of office
        on the plane back to DC

Earl Warren went to Andrews Air Force Base
and was stunned seeing Jackie

                    with pink suit stained in blood
        as the coffin was loaded
                            into the hearse

———————————— **Oswald Arrested** ————————————

Lee Harvey Oswald was arrested at the Texas Theater
where they were showing Van Heflin in
                            War Is Hell

The only public statement he ever made was
                    to reporter Seth Kantor:

            "I'm just a patsy. . . . I didn't shoot anybody"

———————————— **Military Men View the Autopsy** ————————————

There seemed to be a glut of military men
                            viewing the autopsy

which began around 8 pm at the
Naval Hospital at the National Naval Medical Center
in Bethesda, Maryland.

You can look up in the tracks of time the
various controversies surrounding the autopsy.

———————————— **Patsyization Complete** ————————————

The next day's *New York Times* had a
                    front-page article

LEFTIST ACCUSED

Figure in a Pro-Castro
Group is Charged—
Policeman Slain

November 24
    Jack Ruby killed Oswald
        —was he Artichoked?

He may have been programmed to shoot himself
as in a quote Ruby uttered in a magazine interview,
"I would have shot myself
if they hadn't grabbed the gun."

JFK Buried at Arlington

On a caisson drawn by six gray horses
the great President was borne
from the Capitol Rotunda to St. Matthew's Cathedral

As he passed by his young son John
the boy saluted his father
burning an image into the mind of a nation

and then the caisson
carried Camelot toward Arlington National Cemetery

The Warren Commission
November 29

Johnson pressured Chief Justice Earl Warren
to head a commission
to look into the murder

At first Warren refused,
then Johnson brought him to the White House
where Johnson told him the FBI had a Cuban
who said he'd offered Oswald $6,500
to kill JFK for Fidel

He pressured mightily
& wanted of course to banish any thought
            that he was involved in the murder
(which was one reason there were 5 Republicans
            and only 2 Democrats on the Commission)

Sen Richard Russell   Sen John Sherman Cooper
Rep Gerald Ford   Rep Hale Boggs
            former CIA director Allen "No one reads" Dulles
                & John McCloy

The blankets of cover-up
            were already on the bed.

December 1
    Malcolm X, still a Black Muslim,
    spoke at the Manhattan Center on
                "God's Judgment on White America"
        after which, during the Q & A, someone asked his response
            to the assassination & Malcolm replied that it was a case
            of "the chickens have come home to roost"

            words to rile many minds & to stir
            the strife that led to his leaving the Muslims

                a tale you can easily follow
                by consulting the chrono-tracks

December 9
    FBI said Oswald acted alone in the shooting

December 10
    Linus Pauling accepted the Nobel Peace Prize
    won the previous year for his historic work to force a
                            ban on nuclear testing

December 25
    In the 47 years since the first *poème simultané*
                        at the Cabaret Voltaire in Zürich
    Tristan Tzara devoted himself to good works
                and now, this day, he passed to the final poem

The Quiet Brain Trust
December

LBJ asked historian Eric Goldman of Princeton to put together
a group of professors & intellectuals
        to become his "Quiet Brain Trust"

They were supposed to operate in secrecy

The Trust included Margaret Mead of the
        American Museum of Natural History
Richard Hofstadter of Columbia
David Riesman of Harvard
Eugene Rostow of Yale
& Clinton Rossiter of Cornell

Bill Moyers became part of it in May of '64

In August o' '66 Goldman resigned and in '69
published *The Tragedy of Lyndon Johnson*

Studebaker Workers Cheated Out of Their Pensions
December

Studebaker was once such a beautiful shape
        on American roadways
but shut its plant in South Bend, Indiana

& stabbed its 8000-member
        pension plan
          to death

It was a hallelujah! from the cap-eyes

There was a scream
of protest from the honorable workers
        treated so evilly by the eyes

& it would take 11 safetynetless years till 9-2-74
        when Gerald Ford signed what they called ERISA
        the Employee Retirement Income Security Act

which took preliminary steps

to protect workers' pensions

Slowly the Unions shall rise
for the safety of Workers
Rise, Unions, Rise!

––––––––––––––––––––––– **Jackie** –––––––––––––––––––––––

Hundreds of millions were brought to tears
at the trembling grace Jackie Kennedy revealed
     beneath her long black veil
caught by Andy Warhol in his multi-paneled painting
        Jackie (The Week That Was)

Novum '63
 George Zweig and Murray Gell-Mann
   "independently" suggested the fact of quarks
 the cassette tape recorder
     instant replay
      a measles vaccine &
 th' USA scattered copper needles into orbit to test a system for
        global radio communications
 &"A-15"
  Louis Zukofsky's poem set at the time of the assassination

  Weight Watchers
     in the postmodern struggle against chub chub
    weekly classes, "Personal Action Plans"
      & the beginning
      of Taking It Off
      as big biz

  "Puff the Magic Dragon" from Peter, Paul & Mary
   "Surfin' U.S.A." from something called the Beach Boys
    "Louie Louie" by the Kingsmen

and don't forget The Pro Football Hall of Fame

Neil Simon *Barefoot in the Park*
Duchamp's *Box in a Valise, Series E*

Luciano Pavarotti's debut in London in *La Bohème*
  & bye bye to the *NY Daily Mirror* tabloid

Libri '63:
   Sylvia Plath's *The Bell Jar*
   James Baldwin   *The Fire Next Time*
                2 letters including 1 after a
                meeting with Elijah Muhammad
   Charles Bukowski   *It Catches My Heart in Its Hands*
   Gurdjieff   *Meetings with Remarkable Men*
   Maurice Sendak   *Where the Wild Things Are*

   Pictures from Breughel   William Carlos Williams

   Edward Sanders   *Poem From Jail*
      an exploration of the Demeter-Persephone myth
      in the context of
      individualist pacifist direct action
            & meditations on Herman Kahn's "Doomsday Machine"
            as outlined in his book *On Thermonuclear War*

   Hannah Arendt's *Eichmann in Jerusalem:*
                A Report on the Banality of Evil

      Betty Friedan's best-selling *The Feminine Mystique*
         how women were in despair, boredom and ghastly isolation
         as a result of living exclusively as wives and mothers
      Friedan dubbed their discontent "the problem that
                                 has no name"

   Pynchon's *V*   Mary McCarthy's *The Group*
   Also Hannah Arendt's *On Revolution*
   Milton Friedman and A. Schwartz
         A Monetary History of the USA, 1867–1960

   Beyond the Melting Pot by Nathan Glazer and Daniel Moynihan
            a sociological study of five ethnic groups
                  Blacks, Jews, Italians, Irish, and PRs
         contending that some groups tended to resist the so-called
                        "melting pot"

Sad Departures, '63
         Robert Frost 88 on Jan 29   Francis Poulenc Jan 30 at 64
         Patsy Kline on March 5 flying in wind
                  on the way back from a benefit in KC
         the great Georges Braque at 81 on Aug 31

W. E. B. Du Bois at 95 on Aug 27
Jean Cocteau 74 on October 10   Edith Piaf at 47 on Oct 11
Aldous Huxley 69 Nov 22

Films '63:
Hitchcock's *The Birds*   Fellini's *8 1/2*
Cleopatra with Taylor and Burton
Irma La Douce
The Silence
Tom Jones

and tubeward: "Let's Make a Deal."

Thus ended a trembling year
'pon which it could be said that
the ancient goddess Hathor

"the Great Cow of Heaven"
in Louis Zukofsky's "A-15"
glowered angry from between
the hills of infinity

1964 1964 1964

Like a swollen face after nightlong torment
a new year drifted past Hathor
bearing the guest-gift of a choleric
president from Texas with an imperious temper
& a skill at what might be termed
                    "phone-flaming"

that is, forging his will with phone-schemes
                    phone-cajolement, phone-flame

He was a twelve-hour man—
with meetings, phone-flame & paperwork from 7 am to 2 pm
                    then he donned his jam jams for a nap
                    showered & returned to work
                    4 to 9

            There was no "sense of fun"
            in the dreadful Johnson in-zone

———————————— **Eros at the Willard** ————————————
January 5–7

Martin King stayed at the Willard Hotel in DC
in order to view the Supreme Court arguments in
                    Sullivan v. New York Times

Hot dang! the FBI surveillance officers exclaimed
& planted microphones in his room

One dozen reels of tape were imprinted with King's conversations
and fun at the Willard

94

There'd been a party with King, some friends from SCLC
& 2 black women who were employed at the
                                    Philadelphia Naval Yard.

Apparently there was some fucking &
highlights of the tapes were played for sex-crazed Eddie Hoover

One of Hoover's comments, according to FBI Domestic Intelligence
honcho William Sullivan, was
                        "This will destroy the burrhead."

January 7
        Cuba purchased 450 British buses
                        miffing the US State Department
                                    but the British told them, in effect,
                                                to go boil some tea

War, Always War—
—————————— This One on Poverty ——————————
January 8

In Lyndon Johnson's first State of the Union Address
he announced that "This administration today,
                        here and now
                                    declares unconditional War on Poverty. . . .
                                    We shall not rest until that war is won."

                        Of course, that was not the war at all
                        the war was the War

                when just weeks after JFK was in the ground
                much of the National Security Grouch Apparatus
                including the so-called liberals
                suffered a testosterone & hostility attack
                                    on the issue of Vietnam

January 11
        the federal committee appointed back in October '62
        to investigate the rising US death rate
        from lung c, arteriosclerotic heart disease, chronic bronchitis,
        emphysema
                            issued its report *Smoking and Health*
                            to the 70 million US smokers

fingering "cigarette smoking as a much greater causative factor in
lung cancer than air pollution or occupational exposure."

Not many heeded the call

January 16
    Hello, Dolly! by Jerry Herman
            opened at the St. James Theater in NYC

January 23
    the 25th Amendment was ratified, banning poll taxes

February 1
    The Beatles' "I Want to Hold Your Hand" became #1
                in a nation so eager for innocence
                after the shudder of November
                & the dogs of Birmingham

─────────── **The Russkies Derail the Patsyization** ───────────
                    February 4

        Khrushchev had ordered an investigation
        to find out if Oswald was a KGB agent
        & was pleased to find that he wasn't

        A KGB man named Lt. Colonel Yuri Nosenko
            met up with a CIA guy in Zürich
            outside a movie theater playing *Dr. Strangelove*
            in late January

            & said he wanted to defect
            which he did on February 4.

            Nosenko threw a maddening monkey wrench
            into the CIA's attempts to blame Russia
                            or Cuba/Russia for the assassination

            when he told the US that the KGB thought
            Oswald mentally abnormal, possibly an
                                    American agent
            & never sought to recruit him.

The CIA kept Nosenko locked up for 3 years
at Camp Peary, Virginia
                    trying to break him

—a police state tale you can look up in the
                    tracks of time

February 6
    Emilio Aguinaldo
        who was the hero of the struggle for Philippine independence
        both from Spain and from the US

    and badly treated by the US
                    dead at the age of 94

———————————— **Beatles in America** ————————————
February 7

New York dj's helped drum-beat the throng as
25,000 said hello with scream-shrieks at JFK airport
                in town for "The Ed Sullivan Show" on CBS
                        and two shows at Carnegie Hall

The Beatles were not about to be upped
                    by the edgy NY press

Reporter: "What do you do when you're cooped up
                in your rooms
                        between shows?"

George: "We ice skate."

———————————— **One Human, One Vote** ————————————
February 17

        The Supreme Court voted 6-3
                in a case called *Wesberry v. Sanders*
        that congressional districts
                must reflect equal populations
                as much as possible

It came about in Georgia
where the Atlanta district was over twice
the population size as the other 9 Georgia districts

As a result of the vote above
Atlanta was given two districts
& the others redrawn

———————— **FBI Bugging King's Hotel Rooms** ————————
February

The sex-crazed Bureau-ites continued to try to bug
King's hotel rooms in Milwaukee, Hawaii
and then paydirt! or erosdirt!
at the Hyatt House in LA on Saturday February 22, 1964

The 48 hours in LA gave the dirt-o-manes
some of their most prized recordings of King

as described by David Garrow in his book
The FBI and Martin Luther King, Jr. (pp. 109–110):

"The treasured highlight was a long and extremely funny
storytelling session during which King (a) bestowed supposedly
honorific titles or appointments of an explicitly sexual nature
on some of his friends, (b) engaged in an extended dialogue of
double-entendre phrases that had sexual as well as religious
connotations, and (c) told an explicit joke about the rumored
sexual practices of recently assassinated President John F. Kennedy,
with references to both Mrs. Kennedy, and the President's
funeral. The tapes of King's remarks, along with some still photos
and 16-mm film of King and his companions, immediately were
sent to Washington."

———————————— **Cassius & Malcolm** ————————————
February 25–March 8

The 22-year-old Cassius Clay
saying he'd "float like a butterfly, sting like a bee"
beat up Sonny Liston who couldn't come out for the 7th

Malcolm X had visited Clay's training camp on February 20
& on March 6 Clay changed his name to Cassius X Clay

March 8 Malcolm X broke with the Muslims
He was going to form a new black nationalist party
which tolerated violence
to confront white supremacists

"There can be no revolution without bloodshed,
and it is nonsense to describe the civil rights movement
as a revolution," he said

Malcolm formed the socialist Organization of Afro-American Unity

———————————— **Important Libel Decision** ————————————
March 9

The famous case *Times v. Sullivan*
grew out of an ad in *The New York Times*
on March 29, 1960
to raise money
for Martin Luther King's legal expenses

The ad traced ghastly acts by Alabama crackers
against civil rights demonstrators
No names were mentioned
though there were some factual errors

The governor of Alabama & a city commissioner from
Montgomery named Sullivan sued
and a state court awarded the plaintiffs $3 million

The Times, to their credit, took it to the highest court
which basically rewrote the libel law
& brought more freedom to the First Amendment

—establishing that a public official could not be libeled
unless she could prove the putative libeler
had uttered out of "malice."

The public was now free to speak at will
against public officials

It was a moment for America

March 13

In a middle-class neighborhood in Queens, NY
Kitty Genovese was attacked & stabbed
        in the courtyard of her apartment

She shrieked and screamed
        for an hour and a half

Some neighbors clicked on their porchlights and peered
        but the killer crept away

And then when they shut off their porchlights
he returned in the darkness
        to finish the murder

        while still she shrieked

& none of the heartless American chumps in nearby buildings
        37 of whom actually witnessed the killing
            did a molecule to help her

        not even call the police
        till death brought silence

Not a good moment for America

March 14
Even though famous attorney Melvin Belli headed his team
Jack Ruby received a death sentence for
killing
    Lee Harvey Oswald

————————— **The Travails of Lenny Bruce** —————
April

By early 1964 there were not many places
the very controversial & brilliant comic
        could play in the USA

Nevertheless he was able to do 4 Easter '64 gigs
        at the Village Theater on Second Ave

By then he had placed in his routines
one of his most controversial pieces
inspired by strips from
the 20-second Zapruder film
                    in the Dec 6, '63s
which Bruce interpreted as Mrs. Kennedy
                    "hauling ass to save her ass."

(though in fact Jackie had reached out to help pull a
Secret Service agent aboard. Then went back
to cradle JFK)

After the concert gigs at the Village Theater
(Bruce had lost his Cabaret Card
& so could not play where liquor was sold)
Howie Solomon brought Lenny into his new
Cafe Au Go Go on Bleecker Street
        with skyscraper-voiced Tiny Tim as opening act.

———————————————— **Bust at the Go Go** ————————————————
                    early April

It was the third night of Bruce's run
at the Cafe Au Go Go—
A guy in a dark suit named Herbert Ruhe
from the Dept of Licenses
                    & formerly a CIA agent

plunked down $4.70 for a ticket
and during the show took notes

The next day Mr. Ruhe visited ADA Richard Kuh
and then on April 1
2 cops with a concealed Minofon wire recorder
                    stealth-taped Bruce's gig

Asst DA Kuh brought the tape & transcription
to a grand jury which indicted Bruce
            though the tape recording was
            somewhat garbled and noise-crackly

April 3
   Bruce and Howie Solomon were arrested
         in Bruce's Go Go dressing room

────────────── **Committee on Poetry** ──────────────

The great bard Allen Ginsberg formed the
Committee on Poetry that spring
         in good part initially to go up against
         the attack on the Lower East Side underground culture
               by the Dept of Licenses, the police, Robert Moses,
               real-estate sleaze, and Cardinal Spellman
                     who then was conducting an
                     anti-porn crusade

Two friends, Helen Weaver and Helen Elliot
         organized a petition to help Lenny
               under the auspices of COP and
               one of freedom's greatest champions
               the author of "Howl" & "Kaddish"

         which many important American intellectuals of the era
                                                        signed

(It was a post-assassination era of oppression.
Around this time Jonas Mekas was convicted for screening
         Jack Smith's *Flaming Creatures* and Jean Genet's
         Chant d'Amour the former showing dongs
         the latter brief homosexual images from prison cells)

────────────── **Rachel Carson** ──────────────

The great Rachel Carson kept up her Icy Fight
with the Scythe Man
         defending her book against the icy attacks
         of chem-sleaze & profiteers
               till by March of '64
               the cancer had entered her liver

         & then on April 14
         she passed away
               of a heart attack
                     at 56
         in Silver Springs, Maryland

most of her estate she gave to the Nature Conservancy
                                        & to the Sierra Club

April 13
    Sidney Poitier
            won an Oscar, the first black,
                        for *Lilies of the Field*

———————————————— **Censoring Warhol** ————————————————
                        April 16

    The Pop Artist named Andy Warhol
    had been commissioned (by the architect Philip Johnson)
    to do a mural for the American pavilion
                at the NY World's Fair

He painted a 20' x 20' work in black and white entitled
"The Thirteen Most Wanted Men"—with mugshots of criminals
& it was installed, along with works by Robert Rauschenberg,
Roy Lichtenstein and others. Governor Rockefeller was displeased
with the work, and wanted it taken down.
Rockefeller already was famous for such things—
he'd ordered a famous Diego Rivera mural in Rockefeller Center
painted over during the 1930s, and during World War 2
Rockefeller had censored a government-sponsored movie
                                        by Orson Welles.

    Andy was told to remove or replace in 24 hours
    so he went out to the pavilion
                and painted it over in silver

Soon thereafter Warhol painted his wildly successful
                                series of poppy flowers
some of which he donated for the opening of my
                Peace Eye Bookstore in the Lower East Side

April 17

the Ford Mustang
just $2,368
at the New York World's Fair

April 21
    A rocket taking a US Navy satellite
    with a plutonium power supply
             blew up in the upper atmosphere
    after taking off from Vandenberg Air Force Base in California

    and dispersed 2.1 pounds of plutonium
             almost unbelievably carcinogenic
     down upon the earth

     possibly adding to the scourge of multiple myeloma
     that would claim my father
            & the American bard Robert Duncan
     or perhaps it helped give
     my cousin Denny his melanoma

April 22
    at the opening of the World's Fair in NYC
          civil rights demonstrators heckled
              war-maddened Johnson's speech
          and the fuzz arrested 300

──────── **The Great Society** ────────
April 23

     The words "Great Society" were first used by
     LBJ at a Democratic fund-raiser in Chicago

"We have been called upon—
are you listening?—
to build a great society
of the highest order
a society not just for today or tomorrow
but for three or four generations to come"

April 1964
President Goulart was toppled
by the Brazilian military
(with the help of the Great Society)

The CIA station in Rio
had financed huge big-city demos against Goulart
in their decades-old permabattle
against any kind of Nationalization.

Back in '62 President Goulart
answered a study that showed that
"20 of Brazil's 55 largest economic groups
were controlled by foreign companies"

by setting up a program to "promote
Brazilian ownership."

Carefully, consistently
the secret US forces
worked to snuff Goulart from power
since the '62 election

"(CIA) headquarters has begun to generate hemisphere–wide
propaganda in support of the new Brazilian gov't and to
discredit Goulart" wrote CIA officer Philip Agee on April 1

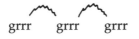

grrr   grrr   grrr

—————————————— **Ho Chi Minh Trail** ——————————————
Spring

The Ho Chi Minh Trail began, a supply line twisting
for 500 miles from the North into South Vietnam
and which cut into Laos north of the DMZ

then back out of Laos into South Vietnam
south of the DMZ
at various points 'tween the DMZ
& the Mekong Delta

The Trail had underground barracks, workshops,
hospitals, storage zones
all underground
to escape the scornful bombers of America

──────────── **Mississippi Freedom Democratic Party** ────────────
April 26

The Student Nonviolent Coordinating Committee
organized the Mississippi Freedom Democratic Party
at a meeting in Jackson on April 26

The Party ran candidates in the June 2 Democratic primary
for Senator & 3 House seats:
Fannie Lou Hamer, Victoria Gray, John Houston,
and the Rev. John Cameron

They lost
& filed petitions to be on the Nov ballot as Independents

The Board of Elections laughed them away.

Then the Party decided to conduct a mock election process
to challenge the Mississippi delegation at the upcoming
Democratic Nat'l Convention in Atlantic City

They freedom-registered 80,000 voters
held mock precinct, county & district caucuses & finally August 6
a state convention that
sent an MFDP delegation to Atlantic City
headed by Fannie Lou Hamer
to try to unseat the racist Mississippi delegation

They were counting on LBJ.

──────── **US Bombing of the Plain of Jars Begins** ────────
May

It will be recalled that, to his credit, John Kennedy
had decided that Laos was not a place
                    where America would risk its troops
                    to force a Vietnam-style right-wing gov't

but with Kennedy safely dead
the US military could begin that May
a kind of warfare which could be called
                    "Layered Robo-Kill"
on a place called the Plain of Jars in northeastern Laos
—a prosperous farming area for rice, bananas, cane, peaches
where 50,000 people lived—

The Layered Robo-Kill was
          described by Fred Branfman in his book
                    Voices from the Plain of Jars:

"Every day, for five and a half years, man's most sophisticated machines
of war were sent to hover in multi-layered orbit over the towns &
villages of the Plain of Jars: light spotter planes at 2,000 feet;
prop bombers, gunships and flareships at 5,000 feet; jet bombers, photo
reconnaissance, and electronic craft at 10,000 feet; super-tankers at
20,000 feet; and computerized electronic Command and Control aircraft
at 35,000 feet, coordinating the bombers
                    and gunships below."

          The 5 and 1/2 years of almost daily bombing
          were done in total secrecy

──────── **The Palestine Liberation Organization** ────────
May

Gamal Abdel Nasser of Egypt
had proposed creation of an umbrella organization
for the various guerrilla fighter groups
                    active in Palestine
                        and it was set up in May at a conference

A force within the PLO was the Movement for the
Liberation of Palestine, Al-Fatah,
co-founded by Yasir Arafat

May 14
Nikita Khrushchev
opened the Aswan Dam
in the United Arab Republic

May 19
The USA voiced their miff to the Commies
for the microphones
found in the US embassy in Moscow

June 2
Cuba executed 3 men as CIA spies

June 4
Fred Hansen legged down the track
clunked the pole into the slot   then up   twist   strain
push at the pole and arc over! with just a tiny rub
so that the bar quivered
& viewers shivered
but it stayed on the pins!
for the new world pole-vault record
17′ 1″ at the US championships

Then on July 25 Hansen went to 17′ 4″

Up and over, o Muse of Vaulting!

───────────────── **Quarks & Hadrons** ─────────────────

The bluster of what Dylan Thomas once called
"birth, death, sex, money, politics & religion"
is reflected in the confusion below
where by 1964 some 200 subatomic particles
had been identified

This was the year that American physicist Murray Gell-Mann
enhanced his
Eightfold Way of classifying hadrons

(Hadrons are a class of particles which include protons and neutrons
& are formed of various kinds of quarks and anti-quarks
whose name he borrowed from a line in *Finnegans Wake*)
"Three quarks for Muster Mark.")

The Quark Theory was proposed independently in '63
by Mr. Gell-Mann & George Zweig of the
California Institute of Technology.

Quarks have fractional rather than whole electric charges
and are proposed as the "basic constituent of matter"
more basic than the proton & neutron
which not so long ago were thought
to be the "elementary" particles

The new model of reality: there are atoms, there
are nuclei, there are baryons,
there are mesons, there are pions,
there are kaons, there are quarks

as the micro-slicer slices ever more microtically

so that even quarks themselves
may someday seem the progeny
of smaller yet quarkogeny

─────────────────── **Freedom Summer** ───────────────────
early June–late August

Love, persuasion, fortitude & a thirst for justice
came together
inspired by the Freedom Rides & Birmingham
& the era of Kennedy hope
when more than 1,000 college students
mostly white and mostly from the north
went to Mississippi
to work in 44 local projects
sponsored by the
Student Nonviolent Coordinating Committee

They lived in what were known as Freedom Houses
or with local black families

Their main task was to register black voters
& to work in what were known as Freedom Schools

A Summer to Show the Best & Worst
of a Great Nation

Johnson's Sham-Draft
June

The President had a Resolution already prepared
giving him *carte blanche*
to do anything he wanted in Vietnam

a couple o' months BEFORE
the Gulf of Tonkin attacks

All that was needed was to forge a crisis
& force it on Congress

A Climate of Evil in a Summer
of Moral Witness

There was an invisible muscle-structure of
militarism & race-hate on the rise

traced that summer by the bard Robert Duncan
in his poem "Passages 13"
in lines such as

"Satan looks forth from
men's faces:

Eisenhower's idiot grin, Nixon's
black jaw, the sly glare in Goldwater's eye, or
the look of Stevenson lying in the U.N. that our
Nation save face...."

He had his bard-eye focused on the Evil fully awake and at work
in
Freedom Summer

June 7
  Earl Warren and others
      interviewed Jack Ruby
          in the Dallas city jail

  Warren came away apparently convinced that
          Ruby acted alone
              & on the spur of the moment

  though Ruby was delusional
  "He took me aside," Warren said,
      "and he said, 'Hear those voices? Hear those voices?'
  He thought they were Jewish children &
      Jewish women
          who were being put to death in the building there."

      Of course they might have doped or Artichoked Mr. Ruby

June 10
  Senator Barry Goldwater voted against the new Civil Rights Bill
              which upset former President Eisenhower

───────── **Further Power for One Human/One Vote** ─────────
                  June 14

  The Supreme Court
          decided that both houses in State legislatures
          had to be apportioned on the basis of population

  in a strengthening of democracy.
  "Legislators are elected by voters, not farms
                  or cities or economic interests"
          read the opinion

──────────────── **Lenny on Trial** ────────────────
                  June 16

      Lenny Bruce went on trial in NYC at the age of 37
      at the court house at 100 Centre Street
          His attorney was the well-known Ephraim London
              assisted by Martin Garbus

Two days before the trial around 100 demonstrators gathered
                                    to show Bruce support
            but NYC has a mean, freedom-squelching side
            that erupts now and then

Testifying for the prosecution were
John Fischer, editor of *Harper's*, Robert Sylvester of th' *Daily News*

columnist Marya Mannes and rightest professor
                            Ernest Van den Haag

November 4
a 3-judge panel, with Judge Creel dissenting
                    found Bruce and Howie Solomon
                    (owner of the Cafe au Go Go
                    on Bleecker Street, where Bruce
                        had performed)
                            guilty

December 21
the repressionist ADA Mr. Kuh
        won his way
        & disgraced the Constitution at the same time
        as Judge Arthur Murtagh sentenced Lenny
                        to four months in the workhouse

Not a great moment for freedom

———————— **Chaney, Goodman, Schwerner** ————————
June 21

In Neshoba County, Mississippi
                where klanmind ruled
        a Freedom Summer volunteer named Andrew Goodman, 21,
        went forth in a station wagon with James Chaney, 21
        & Michael Schwerner, 24
                    to investigate the burning down of
                    Mt. Zion Baptist Church near a town named
                                            Philadelphia

    (It had been arsoned by the Klan
            because it was to be a Freedom School)

They were arrested that afternoon on a traffic charge
& held till nightfall
                    then released into the coils of klanmind

Their station wagon was found burned and charred
                    near Bogue Chitto swamp the next day.

The image overwhelms me 37 years later
of the slender, nervous, newly-wedded Rita Schwerner
as shown in the book *Freedom Summer* by Doug McAdam
urging that Freedom Summer surge ahead
                    even though
                        the fate of her husband Michael
                                    & his companions
                    would not be known for weeks

───────────────────────── **Hoover** ─────────────────────────

            If J. Edgar Hoover knew the identities
            of the Birmingham bombers
                        & then did nothing

            the deaths in the dam
                        are owed to his
                                criminal negligence

            —when top sleaze sleazes
                        bottom sleaze slimes

June 24
        the FTC announced that health warnings
                        had to be placed on all cig packs
        and cig ads, beginning in '65:
                    "Warning: the Surgeon General has determined
                    that cigarette smoking is dangerous to
                                your health."

            (leading to the 1971 ban of c-stick ads on tv)

June 25
        LBJ ordered 200 Navy personnel to help in the search for the 3
        missing civil rights workers

Freedom High
June 30

There was a meeting where SNCC leader Bob Moses
was sharing w/ the Freedom Summer volunteers
      the tremble-handed dangers of death
      and the great burden he was feeling
            for bringing them to Mississippi.
        Suddenly a girl began singing
        "They say that Freedom is a long, long struggle"

and all the room stood arm in arm to join her
        It was a time of courage and yes even joy & grit
        It was a time for a feeling of "Freedom High"

and it IS a long, long struggle

The Civil Rights Act of 1964
July 2

Johnson signed the Act on television
confiding to his aide Bill Moyers
      that the law had
      "delivered the South to the
        Republican Party
          during your life and mine."

Racistcrats & conservatives tried to begrunge the bill
      with over 500 amendments
      & they filibustered too
        but it passed

& set up the Equal Employment Opportunity Commission
preventing discrimination in employment on the basis of
      race, religion or sex

(the sex provision had been inserted by opponents
          to kill the bill)

      Many if not most restaurants and hotels complied
      right away

It was a moment for Johnson
and a moment for America

Nobody Reads
July 9

There was some concern on the Warren Commission
that Americans would get riled up
                about a conspiracy

"But nobody reads," said ex-CIA chief Allen Dulles
"Don't believe people read in this country.
There will be a few professors that will read
                                the record. . . .
The public will read very little."

July 11
        Johnson lifted one of his pet beagles
                        by the ears
        during a session with guests
                        on the White House lawn

                which offended some of us
                at the time
                        who started calling him Ear Grab

The Republican Convention
July 14–16

To the historic Cow Palace in San Francisco
                —built as a public works project by the New Deal—
                        came the Party of Lincoln

                now seized by right-wing railers
                like something concocted by Jonathan Swift

On Tuesday, July 14
        Ike Eisenhower spoke
                        to big applause
                after which there was a 90-minute reading of the platform

                Then Governor Nelson Rockefeller of NY came to the mike
                —it was already pretty late—
                to propose some amendments to the platform

                He was given 5 minutes
                to argue for a resolution against extremism

(he had in mind
                the vicious nuttery of the John Birch Society)
        and another 5 for civil rights

The convention had been almost totally seized by nuts
& replied to the centrist Republican
                        with moans and shrieks of hatred

As if he'd read the Futurist manifesto, *The Pleasure of Being Booed*
the Governor bucked the boos and taunted them back.
        He seemed to be enjoying the rudeness
"This is still a free country, ladies and gentlemen," he said

but the wailing wing-nuts wouldn't let him speak
forcing the Governor's allotted 5
                        to stretch to 15 minutes of televised hiss

Wednesday, July 15
    Barry Goldwater announced that his VP choice was
                the very conservative Congressman William Miller
                                        from upstate NY
        & then that evening Goldwater was nominated

——————————— **Goldwater's Famous Speech** ———————————
Thursday, July 16

Goldwater no doubt believed he was tying the casket of history
                with the threads of right-wing raillery
                in his acceptance speech
                which he ended with words far-famed in their era—

            "I would remind you that extremism
            in the defense of liberty
            is no vice

        and let me remind you also that moderation
                        in the pursuit of justice
                                    is no virtue!"

        —true enough in certain limited circumstances
        not from the nuke-friendly lips of someone
        who'd voted against the Test Ban Treaty

116

& the Civil Rights law
& who wanted to resume
                    cancer-spreading open-air testing.

Blinded by folly, the hissing right was sure the
nation would vote a quick passage from New Frontier
                                        to Old Fortress

                    —they were wrong,
                    for the moment

———————————— **Riots in Harlem** ————————————
July 16–18

a policeman named Lt. Tom Gilligan
shot a 15-yr-old black
named James Powell
—the Lieutenant later said Powell'd drawn a knife—

& then on July 18
the Congress of Racial Equality held a protest rally at
                              125th & 7th Ave.

Afterwards
a group went to
the local precinct station
& soon began hurling
            bottles & trash.

What they called the Tactical Patrol Force was called in
            & a riot ensued
                with what store owners hate very much:
                wide spread looting

————— **The War Machine Looks for an Excuse** —————

Lyndon Johnson and his generals
            were looking for an excuse
            to spill more blood &
                        drop more bombs

(& we have noted that they had a Resolution
already written months in advance

giving the president the power to
                 expand the war at pres-whim.)

As the Pentagon Papers later noted
                 (Vol 2, Gravel Edition, pp. 328–329)
the South Vietnamese that summer of '64 badly wanted to
                 attack cross-border into North Vietnam

             & also to bomb the North

The Pentagon Papers (in the same pages noted above)
depicted how new Vietnam Ambassador Maxwell Taylor
had been authorized to tell the Vietnamese the US was
pondering attacking N. Vietnam which "might begin, for example,
if the pressure from dissident South Vietnamese factions became
too great."

The Gulf of Tonkin

         The chance to begin a full-scale war
         came in early August

The Defense Department reported on August 2 that NV PT boats had
     fired torpedoes and shells at the destroyer *Maddox*
         while it was out "on a routine patrol"
            in Tonkin Gulf

     The *Maddox* patrol was not routine
            but rather it was on an electronic spying caper
       and was in Vietnamese territorial waters
       —and no torpedoes were fired at it
            as McNamara had fibbed

The Putative Attack
According to the Pentagon Papers

"Within a week (after Taylor and Kranh discussed bombing the
North) North Vietnamese PT boats attacked the US destroyer
Maddox, in admitted retaliation for an attack by South Vietnamese
boats on two North Vietnamese islands. Then a disputed further
attack of North Vietnamese PT boats on the *Maddox* and the
Turner Joy on August 4 provoked a US retaliatory raid on
the main North Vietnamese PT boat base and its support facilities.
     The raids lifted GVN's spirits, as expected, and

encouraged Kranh to clamp down internally.
On August 7, he proclaimed a state of emergency,
the idea he had been discussing for some time
              with both Lodge and Taylor.
He reimposed censorship and restricted movement;
but he left politicians and potential coup-plotters alone.

Also on August 7, the US Congress in joint session
passed the Gulf of Tonkin Resolution."

August 4
    They back-hoed into a fresh earthen dam
        to discover James Chaney, Andrew Goodman and Michael
           Schwerner in Philadelphia, Mississippi

─────────────── **The Gulf of Tonkin Resolution** ───────────────
August 7

The United States Congress in joint session
voted the Gulf of Tonkin Resolution
to give Mr. Johnson full powers
        to stomp down North Vietnam
        on behalf of S E A T O

Thus began Mr. Johnson's war
borne aloft on a lie

      Only Senators
      Wayne Morse of Oregon
      & Ernest Gruening of Alaska
              voted against it

It took the publication of the Pentagon Papers to
show Johnson's duplicitous war-batty mind

    Actually the 2 American ships had made attacks on North
Vietnam

    but there was no American Zola
    with enough power & knowledge
             at the time

to do a

─────────── **The Bravery of Wayne Morse** ───────────

The time-track tends to ignore
                    in the Current Mind
          the brave acts of those
                    who stand for the best of America.

"I am pleading that the American people
          be given the facts about foreign policy,"
                    Senator Morse said to a reporter
                    on CBS's "Face the Nation"

          He was challenging the morality
          as opposed to the winability
                    of the war

The coarse LBJ, of course, became Morse's enemy.

─────────── **Johnson as Simulacrum** ───────────

          Robert Duncan put his bardic pen directly upon it
          in his poem "UPRISING   PASSAGES 25"
                    that summer, beginning:

"Now Johnson would go up to join the great simulacra of men,
          Hitler and Stalin, to work his fame
          with planes roaring out from Guam over Asia. . . .

          until his name stinks with burning meat and heapt honors"

—the full poem you can savor in Duncan's book *Bending the Bow*

Bombing North Vietnam

Immediately after the Tonkin Resolution
        the bombopaths in the sky
            began to scorch North Vietnam

& the number of US troops
        instead of falling as Kennedy had hoped
        would zoom to almost 200,000 through 1965

the US Air Force
        napalming women
            with the screams of jellied unstoppable gasoline

and telling the world the victims were Viet Cong

        so that the lies of Tonkin began to
        write ever largely
            on the harsh stones of time
                in gory red:
        Lyndon Johnson, slaughterman

        as the soul-wrenching unstoppable chant began
        against the human who could have been great

        "Hey, hey, LBJ
        How many kids did you kill today?"

Democratic Convention
August 22–28

LBJ wanted to sabotage the Mississippi Freedom Democratic
Party's challenge of the all-white Mississippi delegation

There was to be a vote of the
        convention credentials committee

Martin King stood fully in support of the MFDP
while LBJ's forces assisted the all-whites
        in a move that smells to this day
            like rotting tofu

Meanwhile, the FBI was wiretapping King's room
at the Claridge Hotel in Atlantic City

and feeding the transcripts
on the nonce
for Tonkin-hubris'd Johnson to read

helping him to shove his will
as the Freedom Party was defeated.

It has been pointed out that many
of the white Mississippians whose delegate seats
Johnson preserved would support Goldwater
in the fall

August 17
Johnson was nominated &
Senator Hubert Humphrey as VP

───────────── **The Economic Opportunity Act** ─────────────
passed August 11, signed August 20

Johnson signed the antipoverty bill, providing for
job training, low-income farmer loans & loans for business

───────────── **Wilderness Areas Act** ─────────────
September 3

Mine-grime had opposed the Wilderness Act
'neath the ancient bad human behavior equation
Extractive = Evil

but Johnson finally signed
a law that put 9.1 million Federal acres
into a National Wilderness Preservation System

In later years the system expanded to 91,000,000 acres
though always drooled upon
by land-ruiners & wildland-rapers

September 3
Robert Francis Kennedy resigned as Attorney General
to run for the US Senate in NY

September 4
Eduardo Frei Montalva was chosen president o'er
the "People's Front" candidate Salvador Allende

September 22
Fiddler on the Roof
        opened at the Imperial Theater in NYC
        based on Sholem Aleichem's *Tevye Stories*
           w/ lyrics by Sheldon Harnick
           & tunes by Jerry Bock

      it would run till 1972
         3,242 performances
            almost as many as *Grease*

─────────────────── **The Warren Report** ───────────────────
September 27

       Johnson pressured to have it out
            before the election

       so the 888-page report was made public

       Numbingly detailed
       it became a best seller
           & was generally accepted at first

       until the gaps, omissions & alternatives
       began to appear.

     Whatever its faults, the Warren Commission
     —as poet/sleuth Peter Dale Scott has pointed out—
     forever removed the scheme to paint Lee Harvey Oswald
     (& Jack Ruby too for that matter)
            as agents of Cuba or Russia.

"No one reads"
Allen Dulles had said

against which the implications of
"Oh my God! They've shot my husband.
I love you Jack!"
       holding him as the limo
       raced toward Parkland

           twisted like a thread of evil
           to the wall of conspiracy

October 10–24
    the media tended to view the Tokyo Olympics
    as a Cold War & cultural rumble
            —US 36 gold medals, Russkies 30, Japan 16 and others

        but it really comes down to the Pindaric thrill
        of the mighty individual

        as Bob Hayes won the 100 meters in 10 seconds
        or the contest 'tween Dallas Long & Randy Matson
                                    in the shotput
        or to watch Al Oerter spin & win
                            the ancient discus throw
                    as old as wheat on the Spartan plains

October 14
    Word of the Nobel Peace Prize going to Martin Luther King
    caused a rightist brain-flame in J. Edgar Hoover

grrr   grrr

────────────── **The Sneery Fall Campaign** ──────────

        Goldwater suggested, in campaign's midst,
                that the US blast and clear the Vietnam jungles
                                    with nuclear weapons!

        & mal-minded Milton Friedman
                        was Goldwater's economic advisor

        It was as if Goldwater had borrowed Khrushchev's shoe
        but not to beat on the tables of time
        but rather to fire a few slugs
                    from a Buntline Special
                        into its toe

124

The Shoe Man Shunted Aside
October 15

Speaking of the Shoe Man
Nikita Khrushchev was vacationing by the Black Sea
when the Central Committee of the Communist Party
               voted unanimously to get him out of there

& a human named Leonid Brezhnev
          took over as First Secretary
               after 11 years of the Shoe Man
               (who had also served as Premier)
   with Aleksei Kosygin becoming Premier

October 15
Labour won the general elections in England!

317 seats to the Conservatives at 304
& the Love Me I'm a Liberals at 8
so that Harold Wilson formed a Labour gov't

One of the first acts of the new Labour gov't
          was to give England's citizens
               free medical prescriptions!

October 16
China exploded an h-bomb, their first
It was above ground, on a "remote" desert called Lop Nor
      though death-clouds do not recognize the word "remote"

October 20
    Former president Herbert Hoover passed away in NY

November 3
    Johnson beat the mal-mental'd Barry Goldwater
            42 million to 27 million
    and the Democrats won 295 seats in Congress
                            to 140 for the Repubicans

    Robert Kennedy was elected Senator from New York
    & down in Georgia the activist Julian Bond
                        won a seat in the Legislature
                which voted not to seat him
                        (because he was black &
                        because he supported those who
                        refused to be drafted into the military)

November 18
    J. Edgar Hoover told a group of women reporters that
                Martin King was "the most notorious liar" in the USA
                & that "He is one of the
                        lowest characters in the country"

─────────────────── **The FBI Smut-Tape** ───────────────────
November 20

        To offset the impact of Martin King's Nobel Prize
        the FBI Laboratory was assigned
        the task of creating a "Greatest Hits" smut tape
        from the buggings & tappings
                        of King

        Then FBI Domestic Intelligence chief William Sullivan
        wrote an anonymous letter to King
        pretending to be an affronted black,
        accusing King of many things, including being
        "an evil, abnormal beast."

        The next day it was couriered down to Miami
        by a trusted Division Five agent
        where it was mailed from a post office to
        King at the SCLC in Atlanta

        Not a great moment for America

The FBI offered wiretap transcripts of King to *Newsweek* and
the *Chicago Daily News* was shown photos of King & a woman
leaving a motel and offered transcripts. *The Los Angeles Times,
Atlanta Constitution,* and others were likewise approached
                                        as the secret police went smut-batty

December 1
    Hoover met with King but not alone
    He had assistant Cartha DeLoach in the room & King had
    Reverend Abernathy, Walter Fauntroy & Andrew Young

            King expressed his dislike of communism and communists
            but, heh heh, left out democratic socialism!
            & stated he wanted better dealings with the Bureau

    Hoover went into a memorized monologue
    on the FBI's actions against the Klan going back to the '20s
    & said that there would be arrests soon
                        in the murders of Chaney, Goodman & Schwerner
            Totally unresolved & undiscussed was
                the matter of the FBI smut-flow against the great King
                        which continued thereafter in full flow-smut

————————————————— **The Killers** —————————————————

    As for the killers of Schwerner, Chaney and Goodman
    the FBI offered a $30,000 reward
    & so 2 guys came forward to point
                    where they had been buried

    & then on December 4, 1964, the FBI arrested 21 men.

    (A federal grand jury later indicted 18 of them
            beneath an 1870 statute
            for conspiring to violate the constitutional rights
            of the three murdered heroes

    In October of '67
    7 of them were found guilty
    8 were acquitted
            and the other 3 had a hung jury)

The military hungered to bomb bomb bomb
& made that point to LBJ like a drumming fist

They would never admit, in their severe proposals
that they were actually chanting
an early version of
what would later haunt the architect of the Great Society:

"Hey, Hey, LBJ   Please let us bomb some kids today!"

──────── **Free Speech Movement** ────────
fall '64

Freedom Summer had energized the colleges
For instance, a student at UC Berkeley named Mario Savio
was down in Mississippi that summer
                    working with SNCC

& went back to school
to witness and help lead what was known as
                    the Free Speech Movement
which came about from the racism of UC Berkeley officials who
wanted to stop civil rights activism among their students
                    especially by SNCC and CORE

On October 19, a young man named Jack Weinberg was arrested
at a CORE fundraising table on campus

& hundreds of students sat down around a police car
                    when they tried to take him away

After a 36-hour sit-down,
          Weinberg was released
                    and the Free Speech Movement began

          which used the civil rights tactics of sit-ins
          nonviolent confrontations & utilizing the media

          plus setting up the type of highly democratic participatory

organizational structure
they envisioned for the university itself

UC Berkeley Chancellor Clark Kerr
was a rather stiff & wall-hearted Cold War liberal
(against whom however J. Edgar Hoover &
the FBI campaigned without cease for years)

Within days there was a big student strike
whose banners were felt around the world.

The FSM analyzed how colleges were slave units
to train dutiful drudges for corporations
and demanded student participation in
how universities were run

On December 5
there was a large rally and occupation of Sproul Hall
against the suspension of Savio and other students

The frostocrats called in the police and National Guard
to arrest those sitting in
which resulted in a student strike and a walkout
of faculty

December 7
Mario Savio was dragged from the mike
in front of an audience of 13,000
on the Berkeley campus

In the end the university okayed
the demands of the Free Speech Movement
for campus political freedom

(It was the prototype for challenging authority
to be used when Ear Grab
foisted increases in the Vietnam War
just a few months ahead)

A great great apothegm arose from
those Berkeley years:

The Issue is not the Issue

December 10
On the plane to Norway
for the Nobel Prize
King sent a taped message to Socialist
Norman Thomas

"I can think of no man who has done more than you
to inspire the vision of a society free of injustice and exploitation. . .
Your example has ennobled and dignified the fight for freedom,
and all that we hear of the Great Society seems only an
echo of your prophetic eloquence."

 Roll, cap-eyes, roll

─────── **The Smooth Scandinavian Social Democracy** ───────

While J. Edgar Hoover foamed in racist-batty bile back home
Martin King was very impressed
by the smooth & successful Scandinavian social democracy
when he was there for his Nobel Peace Prize

(It's still smooth and successful
—go check it out for yourself)

King, of course, could never have uttered in public
that he was a socialist
though he apparently told close aides he was.
He termed himself, in public,
a "socialized democrat"

Charles Townes, Nikolai Basov and Aleksandr Prokhorov
won in physics for developing lasers
Dorothy Hodgkin the Prize in chemistry
for her work on Vitamin B-12
Konrad Bloch and Feodor Lymen in medicine for cholesterol studies.

───────────── **By Any Means Necessary** ─────────────
December 20

Malcolm X introduced
Fannie Lou Hamer
of the Mississippi Freedom Delegation

"Policies change, and programs change, according to time.
But objective never changes.
You might change your method of achieving the objective,
                    but the objective never changes.
Our objective is complete freedom,
complete justice, complete equality,
                    by any means necessary."

Around the same time Malcolm spoke on the roots of freedom:

"They'll label you as a 'crazy Negro,' or they'll call you a
'crazy nigger' —they don't say Negro.
Or they'll call you an extremist or a subversive,
or seditious, or a red or a radical.
But when you stay radical long enough
and get enough people
            to be like you,
                    you'll get your freedom"

December 20
    Princeton basketball star Bill Bradley
    decided to go to Oxford as a Rhodes scholar
                    before joining the New York Knicks

December 1964
    I opened the Peace Eye Bookstore on East Tenth
                                in the East Village
                in an small tile-walled kosher meat market.
                I left the words "Strictly Kosher"
                                on the window

            but converted the storefront into
                        a vegetarian Freedom Zone

        The poet Tuli Kupferberg lived next door
        above Lifshutz Wholesale Eggs
        & a few days later we founded the
        folk-rock satire group the Fugs

    The bard Allen Ginsberg lived just down the street
    & with him we founded the Committee to Legalize Marijuana
    or LeMar which operated out of Peace Eye

Within weeks we held the first public demonstration
to legalize it
        outside the Women's House of Detention
           then on 7th Avenue

       For years I had Allen's "Pot is Fun" sign
               on my bookstore wall

       Wish I still had it
       because to tens of millions it IS innocent fun
       & no multi-generation Drug War
              & prison-batty power structure
                     can erase it

—————————————— **Checkers Joins Gaia** ——————————————
late December

In a pet cemetery in Wantagh, Long Island
a headstone was laid for
        Dick & Pat Nixon's cocker spaniel
        "Checkers, 1952–1964"

Novum Sub Sole '64:
    John Coltrane's *A Love Supreme*

    Roy Orbison's "Pretty Woman"
        The Shangrilas' "Leader of the Pack"
    "The House of the Rising Sun" from the Animals

    The Beatles   "A Hard Day's Night"
    The Supremes   "Baby Love"

    Warhol's Brillo boxes
           and the Japanese bullet train

It was the year
>the ACLU reversed its ghastly 1957 policy
>which okayed the constitutionality
>of the sodomy statutes and the banning of gays
>>from federal jobs

>Op Art began to surge
>>with Vasarely & Anuszkiewicz
>Robert Rauschenberg won the Grand Prix at the Venice Biennale
>George Segal's white plaster mummies
>>at work or at play
>>& Claes Oldenberg's *Giant Soft Toothpaste*

Libri '64:
>Ernest Hemingway's fine *A Moveable Feast*
>*Last Exit to Brooklyn*   Hubert Selby, Jr.
>Richard Brautigan   *A Confederate General from Big Sur*
>*77 Dream Songs*   John Berryman
>Robert Lowell   *For the Union Dead*
>*Understanding Media* by Marshall McLuhan
>Herbert Marcuse   *One-Dimensional Man*
>Eric Berne   *Games People Play*

>Arthur Miller   *After the Fall*
>Harold Pinter   *The Homecoming*
>Peter Weiss   *Marat/Sade*
>LeRoi Jones   *The Dutchman*

'64 Births & So Longs
>>Marc Blitzstein at 58 Jan 22
>>Norbert Wiener March 1 at 69
>>Brendan Behan on March 20 at 41
>>Peter Lorre on March 23 at almost 60
>>Douglas MacArthur sunset at 94 April 5
>>May 1 Spike Jones at 52—oh no! Not Spike!
>>May 30 Leo Szilard at 66
>>Stuart Davis on June 24 at 69
>>August 3 Flannery O'Connor at 39
>>Gracie Allen! on Aug 28 at 58
>>Deirdre Elise Sanders born on September 4
>>September 5 Elizabeth Gurley Flynn
>>>inspiration for Joe Hill's "Rebel Girl," at 74
>>Sean O'Casey Sept 18 at 84
>>Harpo Marx on Sept 28 at 70

October 15 Cole Porter at 72
Edith Sitwell 77 Dec 9

Flicks o' '64:
Stanley Kubrick's *Doctor Strangelove*
        with Terry Southern's great screenplay
A Hard Day's Night from the Beatles
Zorba the Greek
Lord of the Flies
Goldfinger   *My Fair Lady*   *The Pink Panther*
            —not a bad flow of eyeball-thrills

and tubeward: "The Munsters"   "The Addams Family"
       "Peyton Place" plus "Gilligan's Island"
        the celebration of
            controlled weirdness

Get Ready for a Sneaky War
o Nation!

January 4
    in President Johnson's State of the Union speech
        he presented more of his Great Society vision—

• Head Start   • Medicaid and Medicare   • Model Cities
    • Aid for Families with Dependent Children

    I think it was part
          of his Grand Compromise
    with the military-industrial-surrealists
    & those foot-drumming the bleacher seats for war

January 4
    T. S. Eliot passed away, weakened by emphysema
            and leaving a gift of interesting poems with
                          complicated metrics

──────────── **Coretta Listens to the Tape** ────────────
January 5

Coretta King finally listened to the anonymous FBI tape
    sent back on November 21

    It had been forwarded unopened
    to the King house from
        the SCLC office

    She listened to part of it
    scanned Counter-Intelligence Chief Sullivan's smut-letter
            then called her husband.

    Martin, Abernathy, Young, Joseph Lowery & Coretta
    then listened to the whole compilation

    much of which was garbled
    with a good portion from the original Willard Hotel
                smut-surv

    The Smut Tape did not break up
    the King marriage
        which baffled the smut-batty
            authoritarians
            at the Bureau

January 20
    Johnson's second swearing-in
        on a cold DC day

January 24
    Winston Churchill passed
        into the place where there are no
        cigars or sherry
            or places to bomb

Agent Orange, made up of equal amounts of
                    2,4-D and 2,4,5-T
had its premiere death-dump
            from US warplanes
                    on the people & foliage of Vietnam

2,4,5-T has a contaminant—
a dioxin called 2,3,7,8 tetrachlorodibenzo-p-dioxin
known by the initials of TCDD
            perhaps the most toxic molecule
            ever fiended up in the
                    brains of greed

(Back in early '62
JFK had approved a program
                appropriately called Operation Hades
                later changed to Ranch Hand

which had death-dumped
            various mixtures of 2,4-D & 2,4,5-T
                        to kill crops & clear roads)

Agent Orange's effects?
cancer, deformed children, Jekyll-&-Hyde personality changes,
stillbirths, miscarriages, aches and weaknesses all over the body,
lumps and festering sores

                though, to hear the military-industrial-surrealists talk
                it was as safe as cotton candy

                till 1970, after 12 million gallons of evil
                there was shown to be a high rate of
                        stillbirths & birth defects
                                in South Vietnam

                    & the evil was halted

————————————— **Premiere Perf of the Fugs** —————————————
February 5

Andy Warhol made commemorative banners of his famous flowers
for the opening of the Peace Eye Bookstore
                    at 383 East 10th in the East Village

George Plimpton, Wm Burroughs, James Michener
& Warhol himself were among those packed in among the books

to hear the first performance of the poetry/satire ensemble The Fugs
as they crooned conga-backed renditions of "The Swinburne Stomp"
            "Nothing" & other creations of the
                        Age of the Happening

February 7
Some of the President's advisors, such as the ghastly
                                    McGeorge Bundy

chanted in memos and measured assurances
the harm-line of "Bomb bomb bomb bomb"

so that regular bombing of North Vietnam commenced
greatly enriching the military-industrial complex
                    and its legions of
                    money-mooching twerps

————————————— **Selma** —————————————

There were 29,500 humans in Selma, Alabama
west of Montgomery
            15,100 of whom were black
            —that's over 50 percent—
yet only 1% of voters were black

in a state where humans
had to give written answers
on a 20-page test on the Constitution &
                        local/state gov't
in order to vote.

For seven weeks that year
the great Martin Luther King

led hundreds of Selma's citizens
seeking to register

Sheriff Jim Clark led his troops
with billy-club bashes and the jolts of cattle prods
as 2,000 were arrested

Demonstrations spread to the nearby town of Marlin
where state troopers and crackers
attacked 400 nonviolent black demonstrators

A black youth named Jimmie Lee Jackson
was shot in the stomach
& died
to show yet again the unearned suffering
that evil brings to good

February 7–10
Martin King
& 770 were arrested
picketing the county courthouse in Selma

Sheriff Clark and his crack clutter of crackers
used cattle prods and smashing clubs
as they marched 165 children
to a "makeshift" jail

February 11
LBJ ordered the first air strikes from Navy carriers
on putative VC staging areas in southern North Vietnam

———————————— **Malcolm X** ————————————
February 21

There were constant death threats
when Malcolm X had been out on a speaking tour at colleges

He'd been dictating his autobiography to
Alex Haley
and didn't think he'd live long enough
to read it bound

He was right.

The week before his house had been firebombed
& his wife Betty Shabazz and four daughters
                moved to temporary safety
while Malcolm stayed in a hotel
from which he drove in his blue Oldsmobile
to the Audubon Ballroom in Harlem
                for an afternoon talk to around 400 at 2 o'clock

Five assassins nonchalantly walked into the Ballroom
One of them packed a .45, another a Luger
                    & a third a sawed-off shotgun

A fourth was to toss a smoke bomb
                and set up confusion
                        so as to allow the killing

Malcolm strode upon the stage
there was a scuffle in the audience
His bodyguards moved out to quell it
leaving X open to the hate
                of a shotgun blast

An undercover NYC cop who had infiltrated
Malcolm X's Organization of Afro-American Unity
tried, but could not resuscitate him

Some Muslims were convicted of the hit
    but Malcolm X himself was convinced that
            the assaults and pressure against him
            lay beyond the power of the Nation of Islam
                & could only have happened
                    with "governmental assistance."

———————— **The Hideous Rolling Thunder** ————————
March 2

The US began a hideous bombing campaign
                    named "Rolling Thunder"

Its targets were chosen at first for their
            psychological/political significance
& not so much for their military worth.

On an average day 800 tons of bombs were dropped
Think of it—800 tons!

Rolling Thunder was supposed to be an 8-week quickie
but the Fates wove else
          and the Thunder stretched timeward in a
                          skein of grief & evil
                                    for 3 dread years

The VC stood firm, against which
then there was "graduated pressure"
                    i.e., more slaughter from America

          But as US protestors sometimes chanted
                    "The people! united!
                    can never be defeated!"

& so 10 years of American explosions
                    floated past the looms of murder

─────────── **Vietnam as a Lab of Military Evil** ───────────

Few on the outside knew then what
          a lab of military evil that part of Gaia would become
& no one with inside knowledge
          was in a respected enough position yet to
          pull off a

but Vietnam became a torture zone for
          the military-industrial-surrealists

          with maiming devices & tiny mines,
          something called "carpet bombing"
          sensors to detect the VC
          & cluster bombs like a billion switchblades
                              to kill an ancient culture

                    that had never attacked America
                    and never would

March 4
  Syria nationalized some oil companies, 2 of 'em US owned.

——————————— **The First Selma March** ———————————
March 6

After the white sludge killed Jimmie Lee Jackson
Martin King inspired a march from Selma
                    to the state capitol at Montgomery
                                        50 miles away

        It must be remembered that
        the purpose was to get to vote

United States Attorney General Nicholas Katzenbach
advised that Martin King not actually take part in the walk
so that SCLC deputy Hosea Williams walked in his place

        They marched out of the city of Selma
        two abreast
                    toward the Edmund Pettus Bridge
                            o'er the Alabama River

        As they crossed the span
        200 state police with whips, tear gas
        and clubs
                assaulted them
                        knocked them to the ground

        It had the leathery look
                of something nazi.

        The grainy footage was like a lurching
        underground movie
        but told a grainy groan of despicability
                        on televisions
                            around the world

        It was an early example
        of footage-forged social change

March 7
 The next day in Selma
 James Reeb, a Boston Unitarian minister
  was beaten to death by crackers

 —a murder case still open & waiting for the
  Feather of Justice

———————————————— **Selma Two** ————————————————
March 8, Tuesday

 MLK led another march
  with 1,500 on hand
 but the marchers turned back
 because Dr. King
 sensed that the local power structure
 was ready to spring a violent trap
 on the marchers
  just beyond the bridge leading from Selma

March 8
 3,500 US Marines landed in South Vietnam
  and by the end of the month were sent out on patrol
  to protect an air base at Danang
   with orders to fight

 It was a big change.
 Up to now, though there were 23,000 American soldiers
 o'er there, they were supposed to serve as advisors to the SV military

  escalation escalation

The War Zone

"We Shall Overcome" Comes to Congress
March 15

President Johnson spoke to a
            joint session of Congress

        where, because of the Selma nightmare
        he could propose a successful Voting Rights Act

The good part of his psyche
                went aloft
as he spoke how all Americans
"must overcome the crippling legacy of bigotry and injustice."

Chief Justice Earl Warren in the front row wept
            in the sudden surge of applause
            & reconciliation as the man from Texas
            raised his arms and uttered the
            great healing words "We shall overcome"

        It was a moment for America

There was a great federal judge
                named Frank Johnson
who on March 17
                decided in favor of a federal suit
brought by the NAACP

against Governor George Wallace

Johnson found that the "march along
U.S. Highway 80 from Selma to Montgomery. . . . [was]

a reasonable one to be used and followed
in the exercise of a constitutional
                right of assembly and
          free movement within the state of Alabama."

Take that, creepy George.

March 18
    the Soviets had the first guy to walk in space
        Cosmonaut Aleksei Leonov for 20 minutes
                from the good ship *Voskhod 2*

    Then in May Edward White of the USA
        tethered to the *Gemini 4*
        floated above earth
        & gazed down upon the beauteous California coastline

March 19
    the Indonesian gov't nationalized 3 American oil companies
        plus Goodyear Tire and Rubber

        —get ready for the infamous CIA-assisted
                slaughter of a million leftists

———————————— **Selma Three** ————————————
March 21

MLK began March #3
    54 miles, 5 days
        joined by Joan Baez, Harry Belafonte, Ralph Bunche Jr.
        Sammy Davis Jr., Lenny Bernstein

Johnson sent federal marshals, 1,000 military police
and a slew (1,900) of "federalized" Alabama National Guardsman
            to protect the legal march

        "Segregation's got to fall. . .
        You never can jail us all"
                        the marchers chanted

            25,000 gathered in Montgomery on March 25
            for the closing rally

————————————— **The First Teach-In** —————————————
March 24

    Six weeks after daily bombing began
    the first Teach-In against the war
            lasted all night
                at the University of Wisconsin, Madison

The idea spread
            around the nation
                that spring
                    in the despair of an unjust war

    as 10,000, for instance, came to a two-day Teach-In
                            at UC Berkeley

(*The Vietnam Reader*
            by Marcus Raskin and Bernard Fall

    helped provide context for the Teach-Ins of '65
    It had been rejected by 11 publishers before it
                came out early in '65 from Random House.)

————————————— **Viola Liuzzo** —————————————
March 25

There was an FBI informant riding in a car
            full of klanslime
            as it drove alongside the car of
                    a Selma volunteer from Detroit
                    named Viola Liuzzo

and shot her to death
—4 were arrested the next day

The creepy smut-addict named J. Edgar Hoover
had little sympathy for Mrs. Liuzzo
telling Lyndon Johnson
　　　"She was sitting very, very close to the Negro
　　　in the car. . . .
　　　　　　It had the appearance of a necking party."

April 6
　　　the first commercial satellite, *Early Bird*,
　　　　　　22,000 miles 'bove Gaia
　　　to send down telephone calls & television

———————— **They Began Dropping Napalm** ————————
April 15

　　　Salute to evil, o Dow
　　　Salute to evil, o Monsanto

　　　as the US began dropping napalm
　　　on a wooded "Viet Cong stronghold"
　　　near the Cambodian border

　　　sizzling monkeys
　　　sizzling tree frogs
　　　sizzling sizzling
　　　　　　as evil as ancient Apopis

who tried to eat the sun each morning

April 17
   there was a big student demonstration
                organized by the SDS
   against Johnson's bombing, with 20,000 on hand
   for a March from the White House to the Washington Monument
                                    to Capitol Hill
   It was the demo where
                Allen Ginsberg coined the phrase "Flower Power"

April 23
   President Johnson clung to the prestigious
   Edward R. Murrow, the great journalist
                who had taken on Joseph McCarthy
   & now was the head of the US Information Agency

   not wanting him to retire
   but who today passed from lung c caused by
   smoking 2 packs a day
   just before his 57th birthday.

           He made a mark with his broadcasts
           during the Battle of Britain
           & who can forget his '45 words to the nation:
           "I pray you to believe what I have said about Buchenwald"

────── **A Populist Uprising in the Dominican Republic** ──────
                    April 24

   Juan Bosch was elected president in free elections in 1962.
        That year he introduced a constitution and
                reforms on behalf of workers & small farmers

   The military overthrew him in September 1963
   and a conservative civilian triumvirate
                supported by the US
                        came to power

   On April 24, Bosch's supporters arose to put him back—
   after all, he was the elected president.

The US Invades the Dominican Republic
April 28

The US Imperium waxed tremble-legged
at the activities of "fifty-eight trained communists"
who were allegedly
        working the bowels of the Dominican uprising

a kind of pitiful excuse
to use to invade a country
                but it prevailed

although Ear Grab used the old "protect Americans" excuse
            as he sent in first 6,000
                        then 20,000 American troops

        to restore the oligarchs

CIA officer Philip Agee, then stationed in Uruguay
noted in his diary how Cold Warrior Averill Harriman
held a press conference "in which," in Agee's words,
"he blamed those fifty-eight trained communists
                        for having taken over
the Bosch movement, thereby creating the need for intervention.
. . . . 'Fifty-eight trained communists' is our new station password
                and the answer is 'Ten thousand Marines.'"

Johnson gave a TV speech May 2 saying
"We must use every resource
at our command to prevent the establishment of another Cuba"

April 29
    for some reason, to the chants of public disapproval,
    Australia decided to send troops to Vietnam
                1,500 troops, later in 1966 increased to 4,500

May 3
    the US Supreme Court
            in *Zemel v. Rusk*
                with Justices William O. Douglas, Arthur Goldberg
                & Hugo Black dissenting

            oppressively upheld the right of the State Dept

to restrict the rights of US citizens to travel
                    —in this case to Cuba
          (from a 1-16-61
          policy which allowed visits to Cuba
          only by those deemed to be in
          the best interest of the nation

          Restrictions on travel to Cuba were at last partly
          lifted in 1977)

May 4
     Frances Perkins passed away
               the secretary of labor under Franklin Roosevelt '33–'45

May 8
     Randy Matson the first to heave over 70' in the shot put
               70' 7"
          I always loved the 4-second ballet
          of the shot putter's hop, hop, hop, heave!
                              in the spring glare

May 14
     Another cancerous outdoor nuclear explosion in China

May 29
     Ralph Boston at the California Relays
               a world record of 27 feet 5 inches in the broadjump
                         another American multi-second ballet

Important Decision Keeping
———— **Right-Wing Nuts Out of Bedrooms** ————
June 7

The case was called *Griswold v. Connecticut*
in which Estelle Griswold
head of Planned Parenthood of Connecticut
& Charles Buxton
     of the Yale Medical School

were arrested 10 days after opening a birth-control clinic
for violating a ghastly 1879 Connecticut law
               preventing the use of rubbers & contraception.

Written by the great Justice Wm O. Douglas
the decision tossed out that law
            & created a new area of freedom:
              the right to privacy
              to be left alone
              to choose for oneself—
        guaranteed by the Bill of Rights!

Right away the attitudes of many Americans
on the right to abortion began to change
        & *Roe v. Wade*
        was but 8 years ahead

June 8
    The bad components of the psyche of LBJ
              committed US soldiers to combat

    & the same day, 17,000 filled Madison Square Garden in NYC
                            against that commitment

—— **The White House Festival of the Arts & Humanities** ——
                  June 14

The President invited an assortment of
writers, painters, sculptors, actors, photographers
                    to the White House
for a one-day festival of the arts
mimicking JFK's of 2 years earlier

—Edmund Wilson, Saul Bellow, John Hersey among them

It was no doubt felt in the
                councils of power that
the creative types would be properly humble
                and lickative of boots.

After a bout of instability early in the year
the poet Robert Lowell
        had worked on a translation of Aeschylus' *Oresteia*
        —a fitting subject
                for the year LBJ went slaughter-batty in 'Nam

150

First Lowell agreed to read some verse
(Cassandra's song to Hecuba in *Agamemnon*
                    would have been appropriate)
then turned it down, sending LBJ a letter,
            which, being a bard conscious of ink,
                        he also sent to the newspapers.

    The New York Times placed the letter on its front page.

As for the festival, I read that writer Dwight Macdonald
                nearly got into a fist fight with
                            right-wing gun nut Charlton Heston

John Hersey was invited
                & announced he would read from *Hiroshima*
                and that he would augment his recitation with
                statistics on current nuclear weapons

                at which,
                in the parlance of the era, Lady Bird freaked out

She ordered fest organizer Eric Goldman
to tell Hersey not to read *H*
                    but to his credit in the time-track
                    Goldman, an historian,
                            refused

and Hersey, now and then looking directly at the glum Queen of the
                                                    Johnson Ranch
read what he had chosen
                to great applause

Mid 1965
    The Autobiography of Malcolm X
        with Alex Haley

    appearing around the same time as the English version of
        Frantz Fanon's *The Wretched of the Earth*.

Like the Communists he hated
      Johnson demanded a party line on the War
      & total loyalty from his
         tongue-lashed staff

'65	184,300 troops	636 killed
'66	385,300 troops	6,644 killed
'67	485,600 troops	16,021 killed
'68	536,000 troops	30,610 killed

————————————————— **Head Start** —————————————————
June 30

LBJ began th' Head Start program
to help some 561,000 pre-schoolers
from "disadvantaged backgrounds"
to get ready for school
         in the fall

July 8
   Maxwell Taylor resigned as US ambassador to South Vietnam
after a year of work there
      leaving just as Johnson was upping the war's intensity

————————————————— **Adlai Stevenson** —————————————————
July 14

The US Ambassador to the United Nations
Adlai Stevenson had been in San Francisco
for the 20th anniversary of the UN's founding

He'd gone out fishing in San Francisco Bay
with Chief Justice Earl Warren
      & Governor Pat Brown
         the morning of July 11

I wonder if he talked about
      coming out publicly
         against the Vietnam War
           with his fishing mates?

Two days later he flew to London
where on the 14th
as he was walking near the US Embassy
he was forced to the curb by a group of young people.

Then he passed the iron fence of the
                International Sportsmen's Club
                        and fell down dead
                        from an apparent heart attack

before he had a chance to speak out
(or perhaps even because of his intentions to speak out)
                against the ever-widening Vietnam nightmare

———————————— **Berkeley Poetry Conference** ————————————
July 12–23

It was one of those events
whose power seemed to move beyond itself
                        through invisible Platonic currents—
such was the Berkeley Poetry Conference that summer
when important poets gave readings and talks
with parties afterward & the chance to hang out by the
                                        hundred-hours
                bard with bard

Gary Snyder, Charles Olson, Robert Creeley, Joanne Kyger,
LeRoi Jones, Lew Welch, Jack Spicer, Robert Duncan,
John Sinclair, Lenore Kandel, Ted Berrigan, Ed Dorn,
Allen Ginsberg, and others (including the author of
                America, A History in Verse)

It was Charles Olson's bacchic/bardic reading
on July 23 at UC Berkeley's Wheeler Hall
                that stirred the greatest legend

A silent impact, as was his 1950 "Projective Verse"
that works its subtle
                enforcement
                even now

During the Conference Robert Duncan wrote his
fine anti-war poem called "Uprising" which ended:

153

"and the very glint of Satan's eyes from the pit of the hell of
America's unacknowledged, unrepented crimes that I saw in
Goldwater's eyes
now shines from the eyes of the President
in the swollen head of the nation."

July 25
Bob Dylan was "booed off the stage"
at the Newport Folk Festival
for utilizing electric instruments
It did seem to measure his switch
to the good-time yet anguished rock-and-roll center-right
—less protest, more electricity

(& he never would come out against the Vietnam War
though this was the year he gave Allen Ginsberg some money
to buy a Uher tape recorder
on which the poet composed his excellent poem
"Wichita Vortex Sutra")

July 28
Johnson sent 50,000 more troops to Vietnam
increasing the total to 125,000
and the monthly drafts to the army
would climb from 17k to 35k

It was just about now
the mantram
"Hey, Hey LBJ
how many kids did you kill today?"

began— to wreck his life

———————————— Goldberg to the UN ————————————
July 28

Johnson appointed Supreme Ct Justice Arthur Goldberg
as the US delegate to the United Nations

Goldberg was hesitant to leave the Court
where he was with that great majority
forging some decency in American life

154

but he reportedly hungered
to help bring an end to the Vietnam War
after which he felt he would
                return in triumph
                    to the Court

though Snip Snip   Measure Measure   Weave Weave
                    the Fates twisted else
                        their skein of pain

———— The Great Medicare Legislation ————
July 30

Acting like money-batty pain-shills
      the AMA fought Medicare
            by trying to toss great buckets
            of lemony water
                  like a thermos left over after a
                            church picnic

(not to mention the cadres of those in Congress
who seemed to love seeing Americans
            reduced to poverty
                when fighting an illness)

Johnson signed the Medical Care for the Aged bill
at the Harry Truman Library in Independence

Medicare, of course, had its glaring weaknesses
—it assisted only the aged
and it was not as strong as Truman's
           plan for National Health in '48

but it still had its greatness

The bill expanded Social Security
to provide "hospital care, nursing-home care,
home-nursing services and out-patient diagnostic services
to all Americans over 65"
           but not money for prescription drugs.

Medicaid was set up at the same time

155

─────────── **Lake Erie: Ooze-Target** ───────────
August 1–15

there were Public Health Service hearings
on Lake Erie pollution
  in Cleveland and Buffalo
  which traced in horror
    an ooze of evil from the paper mills
    the "technologically terrifying" sewers of Detroit
    the steel mills

Senator Gaylor Nelson
    who later helped found Earth Day
accused industries of turning the Lake
"from a body of water into a chemical tank"

  Around this time the brilliant Cleveland poet d.a. levy
  printed a poster of a target superimposed on Erie
    He called it "Shit Target: the Lake"

─────────── **Unearned Suffering Leads to Law** ───────────
August 6

Lyndon Johnson signed the Voting Rights Act
  which banned literacy tests
  & allowed the AG to send Federal Overseers
    into states with pervasive patterns of
      not allowing people to vote

  With this law
  federal examiners were sent to 7 southern states
  to help voter registration

 & within 12 months 450,000 blacks registered to vote

─────────── **The '65 Anti-war Strength** ───────────
August

  People sometimes forget the power of
  the urge to war on in South Vietnam

  such as August '65 when a Gallup Poll showed

61% backing the US war
& 24% saying no

———————————— **The Watts Riots** ————————————
August 11–16

The hostility had built up
                and burst forth
                              in the LA Watts ghetto
as it often does
                from a minor event
as when the police arrested a young black driver
and then clubbed a bystander

for which the people rose up—
there was looting & firebombing of stores

Police & National Guard used violence
34 or 35 were killed, most of them black
                           & 4,000 were arrested.

———————————— **King Against the War** ————————————
mid-August 1965

At the Southern Christian Leadership Council convention in
Birmingham
    Martin King proposed that he send personal letters
to the US, Sov, Chinese and North Vietnamese gov't heads
        appealing for a settlement of the Vietnam War.

When he began his stand against the war
the FBI used it to justify continued bugging & tapping

        (bugging & tapping: two different things)

August 27
    shapeman Le Corbusier
        one of a group of shapemen
        such as Frank Lloyd Wright and Mies van der Rohe
        died swimming in the Riviera at 77

—————————————— **The Rise of César Chávez** ——————————————
September

Farm workers were excluded from the
National Labor Relations Act of 1935

with no right to organize
no minimum wage
no federal work standards

Throughout the early '60s a great American named César Chávez
had struggled to form a National Farm Workers Union
(with Doris Huerta)

He settled with his wife & 8 kids in Delano, California
where the great portion of America's table grapes is grown

In September of '65, César's National Farm Workers Association,
with some 1,200 worker families, joined an AFL-CIO-sponsored
union of Filipino grape pickers
to strike against big Delano-area table and wine grape growers.

Showing himself a brilliant leader, Chávez put together a coalition
across the nation of unions, students, minority,
church & consumer groups
to forge a successful boycott of California grapes.

The strike and boycott lasted till '70
when the union was recognized
and became the United Farm Workers

Rise, o Unions, Rise

in a moment for America

September 24, 1965
President Johnson used the phrase "affirmative action"
for the first instance
in Executive Order 11246
which set up rules requiring federal contractors to
take "affirmative action" to make sure
there was no racial discrimination in employment

158

an issue that has made rightists
grrrr & grumble every year since

September 29
the National Foundation on the
Arts & Humanities
was founded

(Now the Foundation is composed of the
National Endowment for the Arts
the National Endowment for the Humanities
the Institute of Museum Services
& the Federal Council
on the Arts and Humanities

The Endowments
have separate councils
consisting of a leader & 26 members
appt'd by the Pres)

———————————— **On the Road with Che** ————————————
October 4

Revolutionary hero Dr. Che Guevara
author of the '59 *Guerrilla Warfare*
had departed from Cuba
"to fight imperialism abroad"
Fidel Castro noted today

(Che had gone to organize Marxist forces in the Congo)

Later he went to Bolivia
He was chanting the Revolutionary Catechism:

"No rest & no ceasing
till the thunder of Marx brings forth
die Diktatur des Proletariats"

October 18
David Miller, a member of the Catholic Workers
was arrested in Vermont by the FBI
for burning a draft card at a rally in NYC

the first arrested under a new federal law
Miller faced 5 years and $10,000
(& later served 2 years of a 3-year sentence)

October 29
the US exploded an h-bomb in the Aleutian Islands
equal to 80,000 tons of tnt

Thanks, Mr. Teller

November 8
Dorothy Kilgallen had the power,
so difficult to savor in later decades,
that comes from writing a national column

She was also a regular on Bennett Cerf's TV quiz show
"What's My Line?"

She had a fascination to understand the murders in Dallas
She'd attended Jack Ruby's trial in 1964
& apparently kept on sleuthing

She told a friend in early November '65
she was going to break the JFK case wide open

Then she died in her NYC apartment on the 8th
at the age of 52
they said it was drink & barbituates
but others said otherwise

November 9
there was Darkness for the East
when a switch failed in a station near Niagara Falls at 5:17 pm
& spread like an explosion of eery noir
through New York, PA, NJ and New England for 13 hours
as airliners faced dark runways
& fingers fumbled for candles
on kitchen shelves

Also in November
the Supreme Court
acting in unison
stomped down

a totalitarian provision of the
1950 Subversive Activities Control Act

which had required that Communist Party members
register with the US Attorney General

———————————— **Pollute Them Sites** ————————————
December

According to the excellent book
The Late, Great Lakes

there was a water-pollution conference in DC
sponsored by the US Chamber of Commerce

at which, to great applause,
Governor Bellmon of Oklahoma

assured the conference that one of
the main purposes of a watercourse
was as "a repository of waste"

December 3
In less than a month that fall
in the quick sessions that marked their genius
the Beatles recorded the great pop tunes of
Rubber Soul
such as "Norwegian Wood," "I'm Looking Through You"
"Think For Yourself," "Michelle"
released this day to
astounded ears

I had a friend who was close to the Beatles
& I had him ask McCartney how many
errors there were on *Rubber Soul*

—Two

At the end of '65
there were several attempts at ending the Vietnam war
but discussion of the unification of North & South
was not allowed
& so on it went

In a kind of Grand Powernoia
China accused Russia of somehow working with the USA
to defeat the Viet Cong
by pressuring North Vietnam to negotiate

and that the weapons Russia was supplying NV were out-of-date
It banned Russia from using Chinese bases to fly them to Nam

──────── **Merry Christmas! A Brief Bombing Halt** ────────
Christmas of 1965

With 154,000 at war (& 636 Americans dead that year)
Johnson celebrated the birth of Jesus
with a 37-day bombing halt
although the troops on the ground paused just 24 hours
before surging back to the hell of
napalm, leg-tomic mines, fragmentation bombs,
Agent Orange, and gun ships.

──────── **Standing Up to Mr. Mean** **Face** ────────

It's hard now to accept how few
stood up publicly
to the police-statist Hoover

One was the writer Rex Stout
whose '65 book *The Doorbell Rang*
angered J. Edgar Hoover
for its critical depiction of the FBI

Then Stout went on "The Today Show"
& called Hoover a "tinhorn autocrat"

He told the camera "The FBI retains dossiers on
thousands of individuals and through the
FBI's possession of these dossiers they have an
implied blackmail threat
against numerous citizens."

Hoovie boy was so angry
he probably didn't put on a dress
for at least a week

162

Novum Sub Sole '65:
       miniskirts
             the *Pieta* came to NYC to be gawked at
& when Pope Paul VI visited New York City
the artist Warhol flew helium-filled silver pillows
                     from his Factory roof
                 as a kind of pillow talk for the pontiff

Mark Rothko began his Chapel Paintings in Houston
Joseph Beuys
       How to Explain Pictures to a Dead Hare
Francis Bacon
       Study from Portrait of Pope Innocent X
Edward Kienholz
       The Beanery
            in the continuing fascination
            for startling images & 'glyphs

Also Novum was Minimalism
               —art stripped down like a
                  1950s Rail Job
Of course, to some it was a
       reductio ad risionem
       a reduction toward risibility
but to others it was a stark Zen Zone of clarified infinity

A kind of minimalist art song was
the angst-mantram
       "(I Can't Get No) Satisfaction"
            from the Rolling Stones
in the year of
the Temptations in "My Girl"
the Beach Boys' "California Girls"
& "Yesterday" the first clear evidence
            of Time's Wingéd Chariot
               from the Beatles
     (unless you count "I Want to Hold Your Hand")

Dylan's "Mr. Tambourine Man"
     & Seeger's "Turn Turn Turn"
            from the excellent Byrds
        with those beautiful 12-string riffs
     plus Roger Miller's "King of the Road."

In the zone of Thespis, Neil Simon's *The Odd Couple*
                                    oddly odded
Eero Saarinen's Gateway Arch
        a huge parabola 630 feet high
                above the Mississippi in St. Louis

            Many said it was a marvel
            though some that it looked like
                a huge needle head
                    jammed into the ancient riverbank

Libri '65: *An American Dream* by Norman Mailer
    Herman Hesse's *Steppenwolf* published in English
                    Sylvia Plath's final poems   *Ariel*

    77 Dream Songs by John Berryman the Pulitzer in poetry
        Henry Miller   *The Rosy Crucifixion*
            Dr. Timothy Leary's *The Psychedelic Reader*
                Herbert Marcuse's *One-Dimensional Man*

———————————— **Unsafe at Any Speed** ————————————

Ralph Nader's book this year *Unsafe at Any Speed*
exposed safety problems in
autos, especially the Chevrolet Corvair

        GM did not dig Nader terming the Corvair
                "one of the nastiest-handling cars ever built"
                & harassed Nader with private eyes
                (w/ Nader winning a big settlement later
                        in an invasion-of-privacy suit against GM)

            & just as Upton Sinclair's 1906 *The Jungle*
            had led to the Pure Food & Drug Act
                    & the Meat Inspection Act

        Unsafe at Any Speed also led to
        the Traffic Safety Act of 9-9-66

———————————— **The Demise of Deus** ————————————

        The voice of Nietzsche kept echoing
        as the theologian Thomas J. J. Altizer
        of Emory University said that year:

"We must recognize that
the death of God is a historical
event:

God has died in our time,
in our history, in our existence."

Not so fast, said billions of
Muslims, Buddhists, Christians, Jews,
    Hindus & aficionados of Pan-Soul

1965
    visits to aeternitas:
    Stan Laurel at 74 on Feb 23
    Lorraine Hansberry on Jan 12 at 34
    Nat King Cole, lung c from too many cancer sticks, at 45 on Feb 15
    February 22 Felix Frankfurter at 82
    David Smith on May 23 at 59
    Martin Buber the philosopher on June 13 at 87
    Bernard Baruch 94 on June 20
    Shirley Jackson on August 8 at 45
    September 4 Albert Schweitzer at 90
    October 11 Dorothea Lange at 70
    Randall Jarrell on Oct 15 at 51
    November 6, Edgar Varèse at 81
    November 11, the great Henry Wallace at 77
    Somerset Maugham at 91 on Dec 16

Films o' '65:
    Jean-Luc Godard's *Alphaville*
    The Sound of Music   Academy Award
    Doctor Zhivago
    Julie Christie in *Darling*
    The Beatles   *Help!*

Tube-stare: "Mr Ed" the talking horse

                Then came the kicks & tricks
                        of 1966

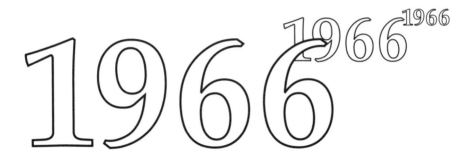

The Slaughter Begins in Indonesia
January 12

Today it was reported that 100,000 "communists"
had been killed the last 90 days in Indonesia

The reader will recall the program of nationalization
in Indonesia
        always a source of anger and urge-for-coups
        in the National Security Grouch Apparatus

& recall too how the CIA had tried to set up a conservative gov't
                back in early 1958
                but failed

(see *America, Volume 2,* pages 354–355)

but now the blood ran vile
as the CIA provided the names of leftists
        to a military bent on slaughter
    —as many as a million were destined
        to be murdered because of a belief
            in national sharing

January 12
    in his State of the Union speech, the President
        trembled the time-track like
            someone grinding his teeth in sleep:

"The days may become months and the months may become years
    but we will stay as long as aggression
            commands us to battle."

—did that include his own & the grrring members of his staff?

January 17
> for the new Dept of Housing and Urban Development (or HUD)
> Johnson chose the first black cabinet member, Robert Weaver
>
> & it was the day Britain's Labour gov't
> > nationalized the steel industry
>
> All right!
>
> but also the day an h-bomb dislodged & plopped in the water
> from a B-52 over Almeria, Spain
> when it collided with a K-C 135 fuel-supply plane in the air
>
> > (March 17 a small US submarine found the h-bomb
> > —it was important
> > > to keep the Russkies
> > > > from grabbing it up
> > > > > for a tech-mooch)

————————————— **The Trips Festival** —————————————
January 21–23

Everything wasn't so grim that Agent Orange winter
such as in San Francisco where the first Trips Festival was

> organized by Ken Kesey and the Merry Pranksters
>
> three days of LSD and partying
> trampolines, Day-Glo body paint
> and new-fangled closed-circuit tv.
> Martin Lee in his fine book *Acid Dreams*
> pointed out that era-framing moment
> in the Trips Festival when Kesey
> projected the following message onto the screen:
> "Anyone who knows he is God please go up on stage."
>
> The Grateful Dead was one of the bands
>
> Bill Graham had just begun his psychedelic rock shows
> & on the edge of the Golden Gate Park
> lay the Haight-Ashbury district

where the old Victorian houses
were perfect for acid-rock communes

The Haight became the center of the
"psychedelic lifestyle"

A youth named Augustus Owsley Stanley III
made acid by the far-famed oodle during those times

He was a Puritan, in the proud American tradition
of wanting the acid pure
& felt that the "vibes" at the moment of manufacture
were important in determining what
sort of trips the users would have

He had developed a technique so that the crystals
shone blue-white under fluorescence
& if they were shaken
flashed with the blue light
of piezoluminescence.

And speaking of Light
it was time now for the invention of
Light Shows!

those thrilling combinations of
slide projections &
projected images of every type
including swirls of colored paints
projected off a petri dish
plus snippets of films
poems & other text
overply 'pon overply of blobby simulacra
in honor of the
Great Cosmic Tapestry

and flashed upon the scrims o' th' the stage where a band was
performing, say, a 47-minute guitar break
in a tune with two minutes of lyrics!

January 31
the US began its hideous bombing of Nam again
after a pause of 37 days

February 3
    the Soviets brought *Luna 9*
    down for the first soft landing on
                           Selena the Moon
    The cameras of *Luna 9*
          sent back the first pictures

    (intercepted by those great codebreakers the British)

February was also the month that
       Senator J. William Fulbright
          the chair of Senate Foreign Relations Committee
          held televised hearings where

       George Kennan   Gen James Gavin   Gen Matthew Ridgway
       told how the war was going to be lost
          and might even lead to a battle with China

       Fulbright, a friend of the napalm-mental'd LBJ,
       had guided the Gulf of Tonkin Resolution to enactment
       back in '64
          but now was just about to criticize the nation's
                     "arrogance of power."

February 24
    Kwame Nkrumah was off to Peking on what was called a
    "Vietnam peace mission" when a coup occurred
          led CIA-style by the military
             then ahh,
             March 1
             Ghana tossed out its "Soviet advisors"

In March
    it was Charles de Gaulle's turn to toss
    as France left the military command of NATO
    & tossed NATO headquarters from France soil

       challenging US hegemony in Europe

March 4
    John Lennon said that the Beatles
          were more popular than Jesus

(I read once that the sick & afflicted
            sometimes waited at airports
                        wanting to be blessed or vibe-healed by the band)

Beatles records were then burned in the Bible Belt
            by the same sort of nope-heads who had once
                        torched "Hound Dog" & "Don't Be Cruel"

———————————— **CIA Snuffs Another Gov't** ————————————
March 11

Finally "triumphing" as it had in
Iran, Guatemala, Brazil, the Dominican Republic et al.
the CIA, on orders from the grrring American power structure,
                        chopped up another nation.

After well-organized demonstrations
            Indonesia's President Sukarno
                        turned over political power

to right-wing CIA flunkey-lackey General Raden Suharto
            who ordered the military to kill every vestige
                        of the Communist party

                        & who then looted his nation
                        for the next 30 years

March 22
            the head of General Motors, a human named James Roche
            apologized to Ralph Nader
                        for a GM investigation of Nader
                        where private dicks talked with 50 to 60
                        of Nader's relatives and pals to sleuth out data on
                        his sex life & political habits,
                                    & his attitudes toward Jews

March 31
            Labour won a 97-seat advantage in Parliament

March 31
            20,000 marched down Fifth Ave
            against the war

and there were also big marches in DC, Calif, and other cities

growing growing

April 14
in a blow against the freedom to experience
the Full Galactic Swirly-Swirly
and to take inner voyages known as Trips
Sandoz Pharmaceuticals in Switzerland
stopped sales of LSD
on pressure from authoritarians

Then on April 17
Tim Leary, former Harvard psychology professor

was arrested in Millbrook, NY
when fuzzies found a small amount of pot in a bedroom

There were about 30 there in the mansion
having fun
journeying through the universe
on the Good Ship Microgram

(The man who led the raid was G. Gordon Liddy
then with the Dutchess County DA's office
& later to help bring disgrace & downfall to Nixon
as part of the so-called Plumbers Unit)

——————— Mao's Proletarian Cultural Revolution ———————
April

Mao Zedong had retired in late '58
but surged back in '62
to breathe new force into his view of
Communism.

The "Little Red Book" called
Quotations from Chairman Mao
was published in '66
& was a big organizing tool of the Mao forces

calling as it did for the educational movement known as
Rectification:

"Rectification means the whole Party studying Marxism
through criticism and self-criticism" (*Little Red Book*, p. 4)

Of course, Mao outlined the fierceness of it
                                way back in '27:

A revolution is not a dinner party
or writing an essay or painting a picture
or doing embroidery
It cannot be so refined, so leisurely and gentle
so temperate, kind, courteous, restrained & magnanimous
A revolution is an insurrection
an act of violence in which one class overthrows another

And so in '66 he force-forged the
                Great Proletarian Cultural Revolution
                        to bring that '27 fervor to the Rev.

He called upon university students
to stomp out those trekking the "capitalist road"
                                and to rub out "revisionism"

This was followed by the fearsome "Fifty Days"
June–August 1966
when students took over campuses,
and teenage shock troops, known as the Red Guards,
went on a rampage
                like something out of *Lord of the Flies*
vowing to stomp out bourgeois "ghosts and monsters"

It was the slashsome side of Populism
—that the same masses who gather
                        at a stadium to pray
will rush, if roused, to watch a hanging
                —or worse,
                will slash and slice to thrill the Furies

April 28
        one year after the US take-over of the Dominican Republic
        US troops shot 7 protesters

May 5
    Senator William Fulbright of Arkansas
    said the United States in Vietnam was
            "succumbing to the arrogance of power."

                No kidding

May 9
    the Pope abolished the index of banned books

                Thanks, Pope

May 15
    the strange, thrilling sprup!-sound of a pole
                    sliding quickly in the launch-box
    as Bob Seagren lofted up to a pole-vault record of 17' 5 1/2"

———————————————— **Nervous Nellies** ————————————————
May 17

The ancient Greek concept of hubris
was invented for people such as the
                violent-worded Lyndon Johnson
who at a Democratic fundraising repast in Chicago said

    "There will be some Nervous Nellies and some who will become
    frustrated and bothered and break ranks under the strain.
    And some will turn on their leaders and on their country
    and on our own fighting men. There will be times of trial
    and tensions in the days ahead that will exact the best that is
    in all of us."

        This was just before he increased the bombing.

———————————————— **Napalm Synapse** ————————————————
May 28

        Some sense of the napalm/evilness synapse
        was vocalized at last
        outside of Dow Chemical headquarters
        as demonstrators chanted

                "Nazi ovens in '44
                US napalm in '66"

June 2
>   the first American spacecraft, *Surveyor I*
>>   to soft land on the Moon

————————————— **The Miranda Decision** —————————————
June 6

>   in a big blow against goony interrogations & forced confessions
>   the Supreme Court ruled, 5-4
>   in the case of Ernesto Miranda
>>   that a suspect must be informed of his or her rights
>>   before a confession can be valid
>
>>   This became codified as the great American practice
>>   known as the
>>   Reading of Rights

June 8
>   130 students plus faculty
>>   walked out of the NYU graduation exercises
>>>   as warmongering Robert McNamara
>>   Secretary of Defense
>>>   travailed the air with his warmind

————————————— **CIA Moves Against *Ramparts*** —————————————
Spring–Summer '66

>   *Ramparts* was THE magazine to read
>>   on the liberal-left during those years
>   It took on the American military empire
>>   with pizzazz & accuracy
>   thanks to its editors and its founder Warren Hinckle

The CIA learned that *Ramparts* was going to run in its June '66 issue
a story by Stanley Scheinbaum (and Robert Scheer)
on the CIA's use of Michigan State University
>>   to train the Saigon police

On April 18, CIA head William Raborn
ordered a "run down" on *Ramparts* "on a high-priority basis"

This was a violation of the Agency's '47 charter
>   to keep its fingers from the throat of the domestic States

174

The CIA began to research the finances of *Ramparts*
—the excuse, as always, was to ascertain whether there
were gunny sacks of gold coming in from the Russkies
                    (There weren't)

The CIA was also looking for a legal way
                    to shut down *Ramparts*

especially since the magazine seemed determined to run
                    additional articles on the CIA's domestic activities

———————— **China Out of Reach of American Attack** ————————
                    June 17

        China bragged quietly about its first h-bomb explosion
        joining the 5-gov't club
                    of cancer-spreaders

            & then on October 27
            it exploded its first guided missile
                            tipped with a nuke

        There was no way now
                    that any nation, including the USA
                                could invade it

June 17
        the once far-sighted Tennessee Valley Authority
                    formed in the '30s to be the vanguard of
                    a gentle, planned economy
                    now waxed nuke-batty as General Electric
        was granted a contract to build the "world's largest nuclear plant"

June 25
        James Meredith, who'd integrated Ole Miss back in '62
        was shot in the back June 6
                on Highway 51
                        marching for civil rights in Mississippi

June 29
        LBJ increased the bombing of North Vietnam
        This time it was the acronymic POL
        for Petroleum, Oil & Lubrication facilities
                            in Hanoi & Haiphong

It was supposed to retard the ability of the North to
infiltrate the South

It didn't
but surly Johnson frothed forward
locked in a death-dance
with death-heads

─────────── **Helms Takes Over the CIA** ───────────
June 30, 1966

It had been a rule since the CIA's founding in '47 that the 2 top CIA
jobs be divided between the civilian and the military

Admiral William Raborn had been chosen as head of CIA in 1965
with Richard Helms second in command

The Admiral reportedly was not that swift in the noggin
& so Richard Helms
moved up the ladder
& the Admiral off

Helms was a "protector of unfettered behavorial research,"
wrote John Marks
in his very informative book, *The Search for the "Manchurian Candidate"*
—The CIA and Mind Control—The Secret History of the Behavorial Sciences.
During the Helms years, the CIA's Office of Research and
Development (ORD) worked steadily on human control techniques.
Creating amnesia was a priority. There was research into techniques of
brain surgery using electrode probes in order to sever
"past memory and present recall,"
to use Mr. Marks' words (p. 225).
The CIA seems to have developed a drug that helps program
new memories into the mind of an amnesiac subject.

The military-industrial-surrealists have not yet allowed
the accurate story of Helms and robo-research
to come out

176

National Organization for Women
June

In Washington there was the 3rd National Conference of
Commissions on the Status of Women
(established back in '61 by John Kennedy
        & chaired by Eleanor Roosevelt)

Title VII of the Civil Rights Act of 1964 had prohibited
     discrimination by unions or employers
          on the basis of sex

but conference leaders refused
to allow a resolution to the floor asking
the Equal Employment Opportunity
Commission (EEOC) to ensure that Title VII was enforced

to which in response the
National Organization for Women was founded that very month
with 300 charter members
     & Betty Friedan the organizing force

Black Power
July 4

Out of the River of Expectation came Black Power
to rile the cash-castes badly
& to cause photocopy fumes by the
        tens of millions of cubic feet
        to rise in the locked zones of the Secret Police.

Words that catch the drift of fate
such as "Dada" or "surreal"
—it's sometimes difficult to figure out
        who said them first.

I always thought I'd thought of "flower power" first
in a poem of '66
     but it turns out that Allen Ginsberg
          beat me to it

And so it was with "Black Power"

Rep. Adam Clayton Powell in a speech
at Howard U on May 29, 1966
                    mentioned Black Power

and then on July 4 of the same year
the Congress of Racial Equality
passed a resolution that cut to the issue—

"The only way to achieve meaningful change
                              is to take power,"
said CORE's national director Floyd McKissick.

It was Shudder Time for J. Edgar Hoover
                    as the concept gained strength
& the Black Panthers were founded in Oakland
                                    the coming fall.

            There was a reason for it:

        You can vote
        You can go to school
        You can use the restrooms
        and eat queasy food in dimestores

        but you're still poor
                    & why is that?

        Black Power traced why:

        a racist System that revels
        in the demoted Other

        & a greed-suffused Structure that builds a
        tssk-tssk'd class of powerless poor
                    in the classic Marxist analysis

    —a class with many blacks
    the knowledge of which began to forge
    a movement of anger, militancy, bitterness

    and the wall-rattling cry of "Black Power!"

—a cry to send
the cap-eyes awry!

July 7
    The Massachusetts Supreme Court
    thanks to the good work of Allen Ginsberg & attny Ed de Grazia
    ruled that William Burroughs' *Naked Lunch*
                      is not obscene

July 12
    24-year-old Richard Speck
        killed 8 student nurses
               in Chicago
       then quickly was seized
          to the fascination of the populace
              for the details of US murd-punks.

July 25
    Almost 11 years after Allen Ginsberg had chanted
    about the "taxicabs of absolute reality" in the great poem "Howl"

    the bard Frank O'Hara
        was struck on a Fire Island beach
             by a sand taxi
       and passed away in the hospital

———————— **The Freedom of Information Act** ————————
July, 1966

Though it's still often difficult to get files,
a marvel of America
       was passed this month called the
Freedom of Information Act

which requires that US gov't records
be made available to the public.

(The law exempted 9 classes of information
including some related to national security)

The FOIA was amended by the Privacy Act o' '74
which forces federal agencies to fork forth to
individuals
    any information in their files relating to them
    & to amend incorrect records.

Glory in the Time-Track to Representative John Moss
of California!
    who worked 10 years to get the FOIA passed!
& then worked another 8 years
    to get 17 strengthening amendments passed
    (helped by Edward Kennedy)!

Moments for America

August 1
    It was 98 degrees at the top of the
    27-story tower at the University of Texas at Austin
    as Eagle Scout & altar boy Charles Whitman
        brought a bunch of guns, food & water
        and went as bloodbatty as Richard Speck
        shooting 12 to death
        before he was killed

—the second chill-thrill that summer for Americans
        mulling their murd-punks

———————————————— **Lenny** ————————————————
August 3

They found Lenny Bruce face down on the bathroom floor
a needle sticking from his right arm
    & a blue bathrobe sash around his elbow

        he'd been sitting
        on the toilet

when the Scythe Man

came slashing down the hill
in Los Angeles

A few days later the Fugs took part in a memorial
for the great comedian
at the Judson Memorial Church
off Washington Square

August 7
Seven US planes down over Nam
the record so far

August 8
Dr. Michael DeBakey and team installed the first successful
artificial heart pump in Houston

August 16–19
Like Dracula
—dead at the end of one movie
alive at the beginning of another—
the House Un-American Activities Committee
refused to pass away
and subpoenaed anti-war activists in California

But it was not 1947
& the '60s generation was fully geared
to confront these authoritarian twerps
at hearings dubbed "disorderly"

(HUAC would cling to its grubby life
till dissolved in 1975
in the post-Watergate reforms)

The Beatles Stadium Tour

On August 23
    45,000 at Shea Stadium
        a big bowl of shrieks for
            the young men the tabloids tabbed
                the Fab Four

& then on August 29
    their final gig in the USA at Candlestick Park in San Francisco

        just a few days after the release of *Revolver*
        with excellent songs such as
            "Good Day Sunshine," "Eleanor Rigby"
            "Got to Get You into My Life"
                and of course George Harrison's "Taxman"

New Left v. Old

        These things are somewhat dreary to parse
           decades after the fray

        but a good part of
        the fragmented, redbaited/redbaiting remnants
        of the once-strong socialist movement
        (such as the Socialist Party)

           trotted rightward
           to support the Vietnam War
        and against what they understood as Black Power

Bayard Rustin, for instance, broke with Martin Luther King
over opposition to the Vietnam War.

(The most conservative socialist faction
would form the Social Democrats, USA in '72

A second group, led by Michael Harrington,
created the Democratic Socialist Organizing Committee in '72

which around 1982 merged with the New American Movement
to form the Democratic Socialists of America
        with a minuscule membership of 5,000)

Can 5,000 influence 250 million?
They can, but just about every moment in every day
                has to be spent
                making leaflets, phone-flaming,
                giving speeches, twisting arms,
                begging for nuance, threatening authority,
                risking a bullet, hovering in pov
                & studying in between meetings
                in anxious lonerness

As Margaret Mead once wrote,
        "Never doubt that a small group of thoughtful,
        committed citizens can change the world.
        Indeed, it's the only thing that ever has—"

                but get ready for eyes
                that look like bruised apples in October

September 9
        saw the first episode of "Star Trek" on NBC
        produced by Gene Roddenberry
                formerly chief writer for "Have Gun, Will Travel"

There was not much public passion at first
as it began a flow of 79 episodes
                that became classics of
                        Americana Spaciana

September 23
The US announced its use of defoliation
                in the demilitarized zone of Nam

                Thanks, Dow
                Thanks, Monsanto
                Thanks, evil

September 28
        André Breton passed at 70

October 11
        Johnson signed the Child Nutrition Act
                        no more thin limbs & staring eyes
                        from needless hunger
                                in the world's richest nation

October '66
New Orleans District Attorney Jim Garrison
began his investigation of the assassination
of John Kennedy

October 15
the US Dept of Transportation was created by Congress

———————————— **The Black Panthers** ————————————
October

Huey Newton and Bobby Seale were college friends in Oakland
Together they founded the
Black Panther Party for Self-Defense
which soon sent shudders
with their black leather jackets and berets
& a call for blacks to arm themselves

That October they wrote the
Black Panther Party Platform and Program

too lengthy to reproduce in full
but it had some notable points such as #'s 2, 3 & 4

2.*WE WANT full employment for our people.*
WE BELIEVE that the federal government is responsible and obligated
to give every man employment or a guaranteed income. We believe that if the
white American businessmen will not give full employment, then the means
of production should be taken from the businessmen and placed in the com-
munity so that the people of the community can organize and employ all of
its people and give a high standard of living.
3.*WE WANT an end to the robbery by the CAPITALIST of our Black*
Community.
WE BELIEVE that this racist government has robbed us and now we
are demanding the overdue debt of forty acres and two mules. Forty acres
and two mules was promised 100 years ago as restitution for slave labor and
mass murder of black people. We will accept the payment in currency which
will be distributed to our many communities. The Germans are now aiding
the Jews in Israel for the genocide of the Jewish people. The Germans murdered
six million Jews. The American racist has taken part in the slaughter of over
fifty million black people; therefore,
4.*WE WANT decent housing, fit for the shelter of human beings.*
WE BELIEVE that if the white landlords will not give decent housing to

184

our black community, then the housing and the land should be made into
cooperatives so that our community, with government aid, can build and
make decent housing for its people.

> They were inspired by works such as
> Frantz Fanon's recent *The Wretched of the Earth*

> Initially they were involved in "patrolling the pigs"—
> that is, monitoring police behavior in black areas—
> but they also created well-received Free-Breakfast programs
> > as well as schools & medical clinics.

> Just as it was a mistake when the Futurists taunted the
> > gendarmes of Austria
> > > as "walking pissoirs"
> it was a long-term error to call police "pigs."

> > The War Caste didn't dig the Panth's
> > & sent its secret police to destroy them
> > with relentless group-breaking pressures

October 24
> Cardinal Spellman at a US base near Saigon
> announced the war to be a
> > battle for civilization
> > > and cudgeled for total victory

———————————— **The Manila Meeting** ————————————
October 25–26

> Johnson flew to Manila
> for a conference of Nam-fighting nations

> New Zealand, Australia, Thailand,
> the Philippines, South Korea, South Vietnam
> > & of course the USA dioxin-droppers

> Pages of High Flown Words fluttered forth
> > on the noble purpose of the fray

> > but the Napalm, Fragmentation Bombs,
> > Agent Orange & Land Mines
> > > eviled onward

October 28
    President de Gaulle called for the US to leave Vietnam

———————————————— **Model Cities Act** ————————————
                        November 3

        It had the ponderous, tongue-thickening name of
        The Demonstration Cities and Metropolitan Area
                                    Redevelopment Act
        but was known in public as the Model Cities Act

        with a billion dollars for "urban renewal"

                    Its vision was good
                    but in America crooks flock
                            so often to people-helping projects!

                    —lots of parking lots
                    & the decimation of fine old buildings
                            in 60 inner cities

That same day
    Johnson signed the Clean Waters Restoration Act

    & also the Fair Packaging and Labeling Act
        which covered around 8,000 food products, cosmetics & drugs
        It forced businesses to print net weight on packaging
        It banned "slack filling" and deceptively big containers
        & made them list the precise names and amounts of ingredients

& then November 4
    hideous rains in central and northern Italy
    especially in Florence
                where the Arno overflowed
                        to ruin great works of art

    & rubber rafts plied the flooded streets
    —the bronze door of the Duomo
                was torn off and borne away

    90-mph winds and rainy days
                sloshed upon the Ponte Vecchio
                        where Dante met Beatrice
                                but did not fracture and destroy it

186

The Uffizi galleries
        whose beauties bound
            like Venus from Botticelli's shell
                were on an upper floor & undestroyed

                It was a hint how every million years or so
                the chalkboard gets erased

November 8
Ronald Reagan was elected Governor of California
                        over Edmund Brown

    while in Massachusetts, the first black in the US Senate
                        Republican Edward Brooke

November 18
US Roman Catholics
        no longer had to hold their Fridays meatless
                    except during Lent

            Grr, eat that flesh!

December 5
Dick Gregory went to North Vietnam
        a trip arranged by Bertrand Russell

        the State Dept warned Gregory his passport might
        be revoked.

December 5
the Supreme Court ruled unanimously
that the Georgia State Legislature had
        crackerishly & un-Constitutionally
twice excluded the duly elected Julian Bond
                because he was opposed to the war
                (not to mention his skin color)

December 30
England invited South and North Vietnam and the USA
        to arrange a ceasefire
            at a meeting on British Territory

      Sorry, snarled the War Caste

Go to hell, snipped the Mil-Ind Complex
Eat it, gasped the Gore-Heads

Novum Sub Sole '66:
 the Office of Inquisitor
  which brought us the rack, torture, fake charges & witchroasting
   was finally, centuries too late, abolished by the Vatican

 Marcel Breuer and Hamilton Smith's Whitney Museum in NYC
 fiber-optic telephone lines
 but, to the shudder of preservationists,
   Pennsylvania Station was torn down
     to make something squatsome

 The US Dept of Health, Education & Welfare
 issued guidelines to force desegregation
   under the '64 Civil Rights Act

 (Schools in the South that were slow to integrate
  faced loss of federal education money under the
   Primary and Secondary Education Act of 1965)

 Anne Sexton, the Pulitzer Prize in verse for her *Live or Die*

———————————————— **Legacy** ————————

  Hank Williams' widow Audrey
    won $220,000 in '66
     song royalties for "Cheatin' Heart," "Kalaijah"
      & the other tunes of the Hillbilly Shakespeare

Libri of '66:
 Robert Ardrey's *The Territorial Imperative*—uh oh—
 that humans, as other animals, "are driven by territoriality."

 Konrad Lorenz *On Aggression*

 Hunter Thompson's *Hell's Angels*
 Masters and Johnson *Human Sexual Response*
     just in time for a sex-crazed era, &
 Truman Capote's *In Cold Blood*
 Valley of the Dolls by Jacqueline Susann

Joe Orton   *Loot*
Anaïs Nin   Vol 1 of her *Diary*
Thomas Pynchon   *The Crying of Lot 49*
Bernard Malamud   *The Fixer*
John Fowles   *The Magus*
Graham Greene   *The Comedians*

MacBird by Barbara Garson
& Mark Lane's *Rush to Judgment*
                    from Holt, Rinehart & Winston—
            history will come to accord Mr. Lane
                            his proper due

───────────────── **Marcuse** ─────────────────

It was the year that
Herbert Marcuse's *Eros and Civilization* was republished

Marcuse was a big influence on the American New Left

He'd fled the Nazis for NYC
where he taught at Columbia, Harvard, then Brandeis
                        which fired him in '64
and then he went to UC San Diego
where he came beneath the hateful grrrs of the
                            California right

Also Novum:
    Hal Prince's *Cabaret* at the Broadhurst Theater, NYC Nov 20
    The first year of The Poetry Project
            at St. Mark's Church on 10th Street & 2nd Avenue
    Arvo Pärt's *Symphony #2*
    the Beach Boys' "Good Vibrations"
                    with its thrilling Thérémin fills
    Simon & Garfunkel's *Parsley, Sage, Rosemary & Thyme*

        "Strangers in the Night"   Sinatra
        Mothers of Invention   *Freak-Out*
        The Fugs   *Second Album*

    Steve Reich   *Come Out*
    Samuel Barber   *Antony and Cleopatra*
    Stripsody   Cathy Berberian

The Beatles' fine "Yellow Submarine"
Bob Dylan's *Blonde on Blonde*

'66, the Flames of Ra devoured the Boats of
Alberto Giacometti on January 11 at 65
Buster Keaton on Feb 1 at 70
Anna Akhmatova Mar 5 at 77
Margaret Sanger at 82 on Sept 6
Walt Disney at 65 on Dec 15

and some films:
Alfie with Michael Caine
Truffaut's *Fahrenheit 451*
Georgy Girl with James Mason, Lynn Redgrave

& on the tube: "Hollywood Squares"   "Mission: Impossible"
"Batman"   "The Monkees"

They say our solar system
is second generation star dust
& now Lenny Bruce & Frank O'Hara
were placed aground till Stardust 3

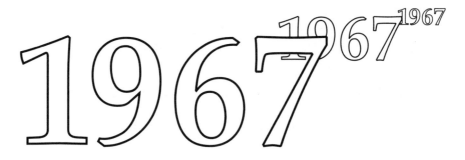

On January 3
Jack Ruby passed away in Dallas
of cancer, with his "mind filled with violent hallucinations"
as one chronicle termed it.

One of Ruby's "delusions"
was that the ultraright was behind JFK's demise.

Some delusion.

January 6
> US and SV troops
>> forged a big shove into the Mekong Delta

January 8
> Next it was the Iron Triangle northwest of Saigon
>> where the US began a "scorched earth" ruination
>>> including baby-killing "free fire zones"
>>>> to make the place uninhabitable to the VC

>> Civilians were forcibly removed
>> tropical forests were burned
>>> a vast system of tunnels
>>> was cleared by pumping in nausea gas
>>>> then wrecked with blasting

—— **A Napalm & Defoliation Tax on All Americans** ——
early '67

>> Something had to pay for all that nausea gas
>> so Johnson proposed a 6% war tax
>> in his State of the Union Speech for
>>>> all Americans

>> which was increased to 10% by year's end

>> Thank you, Lyndon

January 12
> Cassius Clay's request for a draft exemption as a
>> Black Muslim clergyman
>>> was turned down by a draft board in Louisville

> Clay had been upped to a 1-A draft status
> and said "I ain't got no quarrel with them Viet Congs."

————————— **The Great Human Be-In** —————————
January 14

The posters called it a "Gathering of the Tribes for a Human Be-In"
as 20,000 came to San Francisco's Golden Gate Park polo field

for a celebration of Flower Power, communality,

191

long hair, psychedelics, peace pipes, sharing,
    the gathering of spirit-mammals
                in nonrectilinear blob-formations,
observations of Galaxy in stared-at patterns of this and that
    the singing of American Open Space, communal touching,
              balling & electric rock.

The name had its origins in the Sit-Ins at lunch counters
                           in 1960,
the popular Teach-Ins against the war in Vietnam
& earlier than that
        in the sit-down strikes in the auto industry

The bard Gary Snyder began it with a riff on a conch shell
after which the Grateful Dead, Jefferson Airplane, Quicksilver
    Messenger Service, Jerry Rubin, Timothy Leary,
    Lenore Kandel, Allen Ginsberg & others
            made words and music.

All across America that spring
there were Be-Ins, Smoke-Ins, Love-Ins
    to raise a cultural banner for the year

——— The Great Beatnik-to-Hippie Name Change ———

It gave me a thrill when racists in the South
called Civil Rights activists
    "beatnik race-mixers"

But a mysterious nomenclature switch-over occurred
    not long after the Great Human Be-In

The word "beatnik" seemed to disappear
    and the word "hippie"
        displaced it almost entirely
        at least for a few years

    And then after the Be-In a new exclamation
    full of wonder & expectation
    spurted out of the Anarcho-Karmic Flow:

    "Far fucking out!"

January 27

nuclear weapons were banned from outer space
in a treaty
            signed by 60 nations
                        including the USSR and the USA

(not banned were dangerous plutonium power supplies
                        on US or Soviet satellites)

That same day January 27
    3 military officers
    Virgil Grissom, Edward White and Roger Chaffee

    were in the Command Module
    at the top of a 36-story Saturn Rocket
                        on launch pad 34

    practicing for their trip into orbit on Feb 21
    aboard *Apollo 1*

    when an arc of electricity
                stabbed into plastic
                        catching it aflame

    in the pure oxygen of the cabin
    but the choking astronauts could not use the escape system

    because it was blocked by the structure that held
                                the rocket in place

    to the horror of the nation
                as all 3 passed away

Early this year
    Martin King advisor Stanley Levison
                    was heard on FBI wiretaps
                    urging King to consider running for president
                    as a peace candidate
                        in 1968
                    with Dr. Benjamin Spock as vp

February 1
> the USA abandoned its plot to build dams in the Grand Canyon

> whew

February 2
> General Anastasio Somoza Debayle
> whose family had run Nicaragua
> > for U.S. interests
> > > since 1933
> became president
> > & ruled with a bomb-his-own-country mentality
> > > till the Sandinistas would rout him
> > > > in 1979

———————————— **The 25th Amendment** ————————————
February 10

> The 25th Amendment went into effect today
> to clear up the transfer of power
> > in an era of h-bombs & political murder
> It allows the VP to act as Pres
> when the Pres becomes physically or mentally unable

> & that the President can nominate a VP
> if the #2 spot becomes vacant
> > by death or resignation
> to be approved by a majority vote
> of the House & Senate

———————————— **CIA Scandal** ————————————
February 14

> The center-left magazine *Ramparts*
> just about the most influential American magazine of its era
> > in its vehement & ethical advocacy
> > ran large ads
> > in the *Washington Post & N. Y. Times* on 2-14
> > to announce an article in its March issue:

> "The CIA has infiltrated and subverted the country's student
> leadership. It has used students to spy. It has used students to
> pressure international student organizations into Cold War

positions, and it has interfered in a most shocking manner in
the internal workings of the nation's oldest and largest student
organization."

The CIA went tweedily bonkers
They naturally wanted to know how much *Ramparts*
        had learned of the inner workings of the Agency

They created some detailed files on *Ramparts* backers
        and sicced the IRS on as many as they could

as when on February 15, 1967
when requested by the CIA, the IRS forked over copies of
Ramparts' tax returns to Richard Ober
        the CIA counterintelligence officer
        looking to harm *Ramparts* as much as possible

Not long later, a right-wing break-in man
(hired by right-wing California grape-growers
        also to steal César Chávez's supporter list
        to try to break the national grape boycott)
stole the *Ramparts* CIA files in California
        and they were brought to DC
        where 2 CIA officers
            took a look at them.

——————— **Robert Kennedy's Take on the CIA** ———————

During the scandal over the CIA money-flow
        to the National Student Association
        Johnson putatively ordered the CIA
to end all secret programs assisting student groups

Around this time the writer Jack Newfield
had a chat with Robert Kennedy about the CIA
and later published Kennedy's positive views:

"What you're not aware of is what role the CIA plays
within the government. During the 1950s, for example, many
of the liberals who were forced out of other departments
found a sanctuary, an enclave, in the CIA. So some of the
best people in Washington, and around the country,
began to collect there. They were very sympathetic, for

example, to nationalist, and even Socialist governments and movements. And I think now the CIA is becoming much more realistic, and critical, about the war, than other departments, or even the people in the White House. So it is not so black and white as you make it."

———————————————— **Crucifixion** ————————————————
March 2

Robert Kennedy arose in the Senate to speak on the war
that had sent 400,000 men to its widening
                                                  slaughter

He raised his voice against the escalation
& urged the Nation to "dare take initiatives for peace."

The singer Phil Ochs had flown down from NYC
                                                  for the speech
Afterwards Jack Newfield brought Phil
to Kennedy's office where Phil sang an
a cappella version of his song "Crucifixion"

with lines especially meaningful to RFK such as

"The stars settle slow, in loneliness they lie.
Till the universe explodes as a falling star is raised.
The planets are paralyzed; the mountains are amazed;
But they all glow brighter from the brilliance of the blaze.
With the speed of insanity, then he dies!"

Jack Newfield later recalled the response:

            "Kennedy quickly grasped
            that it was half about his brother—
            and it was a very heavy scene
                —he was wiped out by it."

March 1–2
    at the Abbey Road studio in London
    The Beatles recorded John Lennon's
                era-stirring tune, "Lucy in the Sky with Diamonds"
                for *Sgt. Pepper's Lonely Hearts Club Band*

March 1
   In New Orleans District Attorney Jim Garrison
      announced the arrest of 54-year-old Clay Shaw
      formerly the head of the International Trade Mart
      on charges of conspiring to kill John Kennedy.

      On March 17, a 3-judge panel ordered
      Shaw to stand trial.

      Shaw would be acquitted in early '69
            though it was pretty much successfully argued
            in books such as *Deadly Secrets* by Warren Hinckle
            & William Turner
                  that Shaw had connections with Oswald

      (And, at the time of Shaw's trial, CIA director Richard Helms
      had ordered his top assistants to "do all we can to
      help Shaw")

            and that Shaw was associated with the CIA

March 6
   Johnson put forth a plan to set up a draft lottery
   because the middle & upper classes
                  in classless America
                  were keeping their children from slaughter
                  at the expense of working families

March 26
   There were Be-Ins in many parts of America
   as when 10,000 gathered at the Central Park Sheep Meadow
                                          to glow and flow
                  light incense sticks
                  hold hands & twirl in huge circles
                  convinced that bright colors
                        were going to help move the age
                                          toward Peace-Share

———————————— **King Against the War** ————————————
April 4

At Riverside Church in New York City
the great Martin Luther King arose to face
                  the maddening glut of evil:

"Somehow this madness must cease. We must stop now.
I speak as a child of God and brother to the suffering poor of Vietnam.
I speak for those whose land is being laid waste,
whose homes are being destroyed, whose culture is being subverted.
    I speak for the poor of America who are paying the double price
    of smashed hopes at home and death and corruption in Vietnam.
    I speak as a citizen of the world, for the world as it stands aghast
    at the path we have taken.
    I speak as an American to the leaders of my own nation.
    The great initiative in this war is ours. The initiative to stop it
                            must be ours."

He urged young men to boycott the war by becoming
                            conscientious objectors.
The speech caused the napalm liberals in the White House
                        to burn with anger

    & there were hostile responses in places like *Life*
    and the *Washington Post*.

    Get ready to die, MLK

───────────── **First Mass Draft Card Burning** ─────────────
April 15

    The War Resisters' League Peace Calendar
    points out that the
    first mass burning of draft cards
            occurred this Palm Sunday as
        200,000 marched in NYC and 80,000 in SF

& on the same day
    462 faculty members at Yale
        called for a end to the bombing of North Vietnam.

        "A Call to Resist Illegitimate Authority"
        written by Raskin and Waskow
            of the Institute for Policy Studies
                in the spring of '67

        was spread widely through the anti-war movement
        & inspired the anti-draft campaigns

& helped, ultimately,
                    to bring about the demise of the
                                        military draft
              (but not till 1973)

—You can find "A Call to Resist Illegitimate Authority"
in the appendix of Jessica Mitford's 1969 book
                            The Trial of Dr. Spock

National Mobilization Committee
———————— to End the War in Vietnam ————————
(The MOBE)

After the big demonstrations on Palm Sunday
David Dellinger (w/ guys like Rennie Davis & Tom Hayden)
                organized the MOBE
        to demonstrate on October 21 in DC

Showing the good side of America

———————— CIA Helps Overthrow Greek Gov't ————————
                April 21

to the shame of time the CIA
abetted a right-wing takeover of Greece
                by a "conspiracy of colonels"

to keep the center-left coalition of Georgios Papandreou
                            from coming to power

after which, for 7 hurtful years,
                violative of Greece's ancient traditions
                right-wing sleaze ruled Greece

                jailing 45,000 putative "subversives"
                while banning beards, long hair,
                            miniskirts and protest songs
                with all young ordered to go to church

        during which time the US power structure quietly
        abetted the curse of the colonels

April 30
> the 25-year-old Muhammad Ali
>> had his heavyweight boxing championship
>>> taken away
>> when he refused to be inducted into the army

> & on May 8 he was indicted in Houston

May 1
> Elvis Presley, then 32 & the co-author of
>> "Heartbreak Hotel,""All Shook Up" and "Love Me Tender"
>> was wearing a tuxedo in Las Vegas
>> when he married 21-year-old Priscilla Beaulieu
>>> resplendent in a pearléd gown

> They'd met in '59 in Germany
> She was the daughter of a Lt Colonel in the Air Force

───────────── **Tribunal Rules Against the USA** ─────────────
May 2–10

Bertrand Russell's International War Crimes Tribunal in Stockholm
ruled that the US was guilty of aggression in Nam
> & systematic bombing of civilians

a ruling that has stood firm in the time-track

May 12
> at the Cannes Film Festival
>> the Gold Palm to Antonioni's *Blow-Up*

───────────── **Rights of Children Decision** ─────────────
May 15

> The Supreme Court voted 8–1 that
> children in Juvenile Courts
> were to be given
>> the Constitutional protections

> of adults
> including the right to an attorney
> the right to cross examine
> & the right

200

to be told it
was okay to be silent
            "to avoid self-incrimination"

──────── **Too Much Anger & Hatred in the Mid-East** ────────
May

In the swirling cultural illness of war-swoon
UN emergency troops on May 17
were pulled from the Egypt/Israel border
at the request of President Gamal Abdel Nasser of Egypt

who then banned Israeli ships from the narrow Gulf of Aqaba
            leading from the Red Sea to the southern tip of Israel

On May 30 Mr. Nasser formed an "unexpected" military alliance
                        with King Hussein of Jordan

& true to its tradition of razory word-strings
the vice president of Iraq
            said it was time to "get rid of the Zionist cancer"

May 27
Biafra in the southeast seceded from Nigeria
& a civil war was provoked
                and later a giant famine began
                when Nigeria
                        cut off food supplies

            to Ibo-led Biafra

──────── **King's Economic Philosophy Getting Bolder** ────────
late May

He began to mark out the great change needed
                        to make America lastingly just
as in a conference when he said

"For the last twelve years we have been in a reform movement. . . .
But after Selma and the voting rights bill we moved
into a new era, which must be an era of revolution. I think
we must see the great distinction here between a reform
movement and a revolutionary movement."

The latter, he said, would "raise certain basic questions about
the whole society. . . . The whole structure of American life
must be changed."

June 1
    Sgt. Pepper's Lonely Hearts Club Band came to market
        a perfect record for the Summer of Love

        & a consolation in the Summer of Napalm,
            Riots & Carpet Bombing.

    The record reached just about the summit
            of popular art
        (and all of it recorded on a 4-track machine!)

    The bribe-taking governor of Maryland
    a fluff-in-the-timetrack named Spiro Agnew
        led a drive to ban
        "With a Little Help from My Friends"

& moon-crooners from the John Birch Society
suggested that the Beatles practiced "the principles of brainwash"

        —Well, they did—

& were of the "International Communist Conspiracy"

        Of course

———————————— **Headphones at Dawn** ————————————

Just as young people studied City Lights pocket poets
        or mimeographed magazines
            for news that was Really News

    by the mid and late 1960s they studied stereo albums
    as if they were religious texts
        or as an anodyne to the crimson chaos
            or even to help them build courage to
                stand up for change

    Raptured at dawn with headphones listening to Cecil Taylor
    Jim Morrison & the Doors

Joni Mitchell
the wild wail of Janis

Dylan & other mind-mending mind-bending
mixes from the revolution in multi-track over-dubbed recording

—gifts from what Charles Olson called the Electromagnetic Aeon

—————————————— **The Six-Day War** ——————————————
June 5–10

After the war of 1956
the United Nations Emergency Force stayed in place
to keep a sore peace between Egypt & Israel

The Suez Canal, nationalized by Egypt,
was closed to Israel
& there was a boycott of Israel by Arab nations

In May of '67 Egypt forced the removal of the UN troops
and made a deal with Jordan for Egypt
to command Jordan's military.

(Egypt during those years called itself
the United Arab Republic)

An invasion seemed imminent
& so on June 5 Israel attacked the airfields of
Egypt, Syria, Jordan & Iraq
& moved into the Sinai Peninsula
as far as the Canal

By June 8 the Jordanian West Bank, all of Arab Jerusalem
(Jerusalem had been divided 'tween Israel & Jordan
since the war of '56)
was controlled by Israel.

In the north, in 2 days, Israel drove Syria from the
Golan Heights

The Six-Day War concluded on June 11
when the UN was able to negotiate a ceasefire.

There were UN resolutions that year
"requiring" Israel to pull back to the pre-Six Day War borders
& calling for a resolution of the issue of
		the hundreds of thousands of Palestinian refugees
but they were never enforced.

It was a big victory for Israel
which began moving settlers into the conquered territories

& the decades thereafter were deciduous
		with blood & bombs & cyclical aggression

Loving v. Virginia
June 12, 1967

The Supreme Court tossed out
Virginia's laughable "racial integrity law"

Mr. Loving
		a white
& Ms. Loving
		part black
were married in DC in '58
then returned to Virginia

where they were prosecuted under the '24
Bl/Wh Wedding No! law

China Out of Reach of American Attack
June 17

China bragged quietly about its first h-bomb explosion
joining a five-gov't club

& then on October 27
it exploded its first guided missile
				tipped with a nuke

There was no way now
		that any nation, including the USA
				could invade it

The Burning Stratocaster of Ra
June 18

There was a music festival in Monterey, California
                    which attracted 50,000
                    for a celebration of peace, love & flowers

w/ the Byrds, Jefferson Airplane, Otis Redding,
Janis Joplin, the Mamas and the Papas
        Ravi Shankar and the Who

                D. A. Pennebaker made a famous film about it
                Especially brilliant was Jimi Hendrix
                who knelt on stage
                        in the flash of hope
                        & set his guitar on fire
                                as if Ra on High could be
                                        summoned to a burning Strat

Deconstruction Occurreth!
1967

It was the year of Jacques Derrida's
                De la Grammatologie
        on, heh heh, the "deconstructing" of texts
                                heh heh heh

to prove the imprecision of language
        & the, heh heh, "variability of meaning."

Thus the interpretation of everything from the Bible
                to a box of banana flakes
                        was up for grabs

since the reality of a text comes about
        from the reader's assumptions
        as much as from the writer's intentions

                so that any statement of absolute value
                wails away in a place of rustling curtains

        Grrr away, o Fundamentalists!

A brilliant generation of underground comic artists flourished

which featured Robert Crumb
> whose comics, such as *Zap   Snatch   Mr. Natural*
> set high standards for the era
& let us also praise Gilbert Shelton for his
> *Fabulous Furry Freak Brothers* and *Feds 'n' Heads*
> with their well-drawn, interesting story lines

And there were artists such as Art Spiegelman, Skip Williamson &
Spain Rodriguez, who brought a taste of Marx to his
> *Trashman: Agent of the Sixth International*

> & Trina Robbins, Rick Griffin & Greg Irons

& then a bright flow of rock concert posters from the artists
Wes Wilson, Stanley Mouse, Gary Grimshaw, Alton Kelley
> Victor Moscoso and others

> Speaking of underground, of course there was

─────── **The Underground Press Movement** ───────
'64–'73

The CIA & the Military-Industrial Surrealists
> hankered to stomp the Underground Press
> > into the dust of Iran, Guatemala & Camelot
> because the press was having an impact
> & stood in the way of
> > unregulated slaughter.

There were some wonderful underground newspapers
paid for by ads from the zones of psychedelic commerce
(plus movies, concerts, head shops, record co's & "personals")

which the national security grouch apparatus
> disliked intensely
to the point of breaking them up

206

Some of them were the

Los Angeles Free Press   East Village Other   Chicago Seed
San Francisco Oracle   Milwaukee Kaleidoscope   Detroit's Fifth Estate
Berkeley Barb   Georgia Straight   Great Speckled Bird
                         & many others

         part of the glory of the '60s
         brought to us by the unused portions
                 of the great Bill of Rights

         The nation's Red Squads were ever busy
                 scheming to stomp the undergrounds to death
      & the CIA itself, as we shall see,
                 chomped its tweedy fangs
                       into the movement later in '67

June 23 & 25 1967
     Aleksei Kosygin
     & Lyndon Johnson
     met at the home of the president
     of Glassboro State College
             in New Jersey

     China had just detonated an h-bomb
     & Kosygin reportedly was suffering shudders of Chicom-noia

     as he and Johnson talked about the Middle East,
             the search for peace,
             Anti-Ballistic Missile systems, & Vietnam

                     now that there was a new
                     triangle of nuke-dread

                  USA

         China   USSR

June 25
     The Beatles sang "All You Need Is Love"
         to 400,000,000 earthlings
         in a live broadcast over the BBC

thanks to the Early Bird, Lana Bird & ATS/B satellites

It was just in time for
        what was called. . . .

───────────── **The Summer of Love** ─────────────

which grew out of the Great Be-In back in January
and drew power from the new rock & roll,
ecstatic singing and dancing, the underground press,
light shows and things like Tim Leary's lectures on
turning on, tuning in and dropping out

Part of it was a lifestyle protest
against excessively acquisitive capitalism
       & part of it was a surge of love for the Out-of-Doors
       and Rock Music
       and Love and Eros
       and Communal Living
       and Primary Colors
       and Freedom of Psychedelics

       against the Culture of Death & Napalmed Children
       the Stifling Conformity of the Creeping Meatball
       the Worship of Robot War
          & the Looting of America by the War Caste

so that by late June it was in Full Swirl!
Some rushed to the cities
where there were urban crashpads
        & opposition from the police.
Community bulletin boards
& telephone switchboards
       were set up in places like Taos & Mendocino
       to serve the roaming

Sgt. Pepper was on the turntable
hookahs were in the head shops
there was lots of balling and pot
& guys in Afghan vests & Berber necklaces
sold acid on the Haight
while children in Primary Colors
were walking toward Tompkins Park

with lit incense from the Psychedelicatessen
                                    on Avenue A

Others sat reading or strumming in yurts
or splashed in the hot springs of a mountain pass

or danced around Rittenhouse Square and Dupont Circle

to savor the Goof Rose

Feeding its anxiety was a dislike of the war
& a kind of mid-19th-century search
                        for a communal style of living

with a few actual explorations of Allen Ginsberg's great line
                from his poem "America":

When can I go into a supermarket and buy what I need
with my good looks?

It made great copy for mass culture sources such as
the 6 o'clock news or *Life* magazine

but nothing is easy
& the long-time all-level fierceness
required to forge such social change
was not quite there in the Zone of Fun

so it was a sweet-sour yes-no win-lose up-down
hurt-heal swirl-feel live-die laugh-cry
                            trail of months

such as when I turned my Peace Eye Bookstore over
to the "community" during the Summer of Love

and it became a temporary crash pad
looked after by a youth named Groovy

who just a few days before the Exorcism of the Pentagon
was murdered in a basement on Avenue B
with his girlfriend Linda Fitzpatrick

        a famous crime of the Fall of Dread

when the incense stick stuck in the curb
had long burned dead

──────────── **Here Come the Buttons** ────────────

Sometime in the year or so before the
Summer of Love
the buttons began to alight on lapels

to enlighten the Aeon
—a few here arrayed
from the magnificent
counterculture collection
of Tuli Kupferberg

──── **The Summer of Love/AEC Summer of Nuke Blasts** ────

During the Summer of Love
the Atomic Energy Commission started defiling the earth
with a Summer of Cancer-Leaks

through its ghastly Plowshare Program
which experimented with underground nuclear explosions
to enrich the oil & gas tycoons

There was Operation Gasbuggy
in which the government helped the El Paso Natural Gas Company
      place a nuclear weapon
      in a drilled hole 4,240 feet deep
      near Farmington, New Mexico
            (finally detonated December 10)

Other cancer-blasts occurred near the Rocky Mountains
for a few years
      which were finally stopped by
      Americans raising health & environmental issues

July 7
    Nigerian gov't soldiers
          snarled into Biafra to try to end the secession

          starve starve starve

The same day William "Give us more Kill Power" Westmoreland
    asked for more troops in Nam from Robert McNamara & LBJ

July 27
    John Coltrane
      genius of the tenor sax
      died on Long Island of liver cancer
      He was 40

      & left behind much evidence of greatness
      on miles of oxide-dappled tape

————————————— **The Riots of July** —————————————

The history & causes of the inner-city riots of the late '60s
are given little space in most chronologies

but beginning in late June in Buffalo
and then in Newark July 13–16
      where 26 died, 1,500 were injured, & 1,000 arrested
      in the dry statistics of printed insurrections

      the armored scenery of a long hot summer
          clanked into place.

Then Detroit caught fire on July 23
in a surge of destruction which killed 43 & left many blocks
                    destroyed for the rest of the century
                                                    & beyond

On July 24, LBJ ordered 4,700 troops to Detroit
and for 2 days soldiers & uprisers
                    traded gunfire.

The battle had the taste of Vietnam, with headlines such as

**TANK CREWS BLAST AWAY AT ENTRENCHED SNIPERS
WITH 50-CALIBER MACHINE GUNS**

till the riots were quelled by the 26th

On July 27 Johnson spoke to the nation
        & announced a National Advisory Commission
        on Urban Disorders to be headed by
        Governor Otto Kerner of Illinois
                    and Mayor John Lindsay of NY City

(Its 1,400-page report, issued a few months later,
attributed the uprising of blacks to white racism

The USA, it said, was at risk of becoming "two societies,
one black, one white—separate but inequal—"

and proposed around 150 steps
                which could be undertaken to
                    bring about economic & social justice.

It seemed clear what was causing it—
poor housing, hostility from surrounding white communities,
inferior schools, unemployment, lack of money. . . .

Boom!)

——— **The FBI & Army Intelligence Not Buying It** ———

The US military viewed the situation with alarm
Army Intelligence tallied riots & looting in 100 cities
                                        that summer

The FBI thought that Commies & other "subversives"
were helping to create the riots
                    and so did the US Army

The head of Army Intelligence in '67 and much of '68
was a human named Maj. Gen. William P. Yarborough

who was a counterintellligence and psychological warfare
specialist. Yarborough thought that rioters
were "insurgents" manipulated by the
                                    Communist Party.
When Detroit began to boil that summer
General Yarborough announced to his staff,
"Men, get out your counterinsurgency manuals.
We have an insurgency on our hands."

— Army Psyops Agents Question Black Men in Detroit —
after the July riots

Agents of the Army's Psychological Operations Group, in civilian attire
(in conjunction with the Behavior Research Institute of Detroit)

brought 496 black males arrested for firing weapons
                                    during the Detroit riot
to a warehouse to the north of Detroit
and asked each black man dozens of questions

Of the 496, 363 gave astounding answers to the question
                    "Who is your favorite Negro leader?"

Was it Stokely Carmichael? No.
            Was it Huey Newton? No.
                        Was it H. Rap Brown? No.

It was Martin Luther King Jr.!!!

July

Detroit and Grand Rapids weren't the only places feeling
strange energy gone to destruction
as radioastronomers Jocelyn Bell Burnell and Anthony Hewish
discovered the first "Pulsar"

a collapsed neutron star emitting spew-outs of radio energy

August 1
    Stokely Carmichael
            called for Black Revolution in the US
                    at a conference in Havana:

                    "We have no alternative," he said, "but to use
                    aggressive armed violence
                    in order to own the land, houses & stores
                                    inside our communities
                    & to control the politics of those communities"

    and in Virginia around the same time
    H. Rap Brown, current head of the
                    Student Nonviolent Coordinating Committee
    said "we stand on the eve of a black revolution"

                    then August 3 Lyndon Baines Johnson
                            said 45,000 more would be sent to Nam
                            adding to the 464,000 already there

                    a mere 4 days after General Westmoreland
                    begged for more kill-power

                            ai yi yi Part I

August 4

Meanwhile, the underground press was thriving
                across the nation
                and supporting the drive for massive social change
                    the use of psychedelics
                        the legalization of grass
                            plus giving aid & comfort

214

to the Panthers &
Anti-War Groups

The insolence of it! the energy! the treason!
It was riling the minds of the
                    Military Industrial Surrealists

and so in the early August of '67, the CIA began its enormous
and mostly still-secret program called Operation Chaos
               for spying on and
                    looking for ways to
                         stymie the anti-war left

A telegram was sent out to a slew of CIA field stations
setting up a "Special Operations Group"
to be run by counterintelligence head James Jesus Angleton.

Angleton selected a human named Richard Ober
                    to lead what would not long ahead be called
                    CHAOS or MHCHAOS.

It was illegal for the CIA to try to
                    destroy domestic newspapers
                    such as the underground press

CHAOS was one of the most secret of all secret programs.

LBJ knew full well about CHAOS
     because it is known that Ober's reports
                         were sent to his desk
                                   (and later to Nixon's)

Ober was given a staff of ten, at first,
                    and set out to "disrupt the enemy"

The CIA fed the National Security Agency a "watch list"
of 1,700 dissident Americans in 1967
so that the NSA could
          monitor phone calls
                    & other communications
          —a monitoring that went on till 1973

                    Thank You, o Twerps of Chaos

The CIA in 1968 spent our tax money
        to index some 50,000 members of the
        California Peace and Freedom Party
        One of hundreds of anti-war
            groups
            the CIA surveilled.

            Thank you, o twerps.

        At least the CIA wasn't slitting the throats of
        anti-war editors at *The Los Angeles Free Press*
                or *The Berkeley Barb*

        as might have happened in South Vietnam where
        its Operation Phoenix, operating in vile secrecy,
        without any trials,
        murdered at least 20,000 civilians
        "who were suspected of being members of the Communist
        underground"
            as Howard Zinn notes in his book
                The Twentieth Century (p. 224)

—— **Johnson Shrieks the C-word at Johnny Apple** ——
              August 7

New York Times reporter R. W. Apple published
a front-page story which stated the war "is not going well. . ."
and that victory "may be beyond reach"

In one of his phone rages Johnson called
an embassy official in Saigon
& screamed that Apple was a "communist"
& demanded that the embassy get Apple out of Nam
            & force other journalists to
                "get on the team."

Fortunately America is not Nazi Germany
& the blustery phantom from the Pedernales
              could only rave

August 25
    a human named John Patler,
        editor of something called *The Stormtrooper*

killed George Lincoln Rockwell, head of the
                        American Nazi Party
                        in Arlington, Va.

Patler was apparently irate over being banned from the party
for "creating dissension between dark-haired and blond Nazis"

August 30
        an overwhelming majority in the Senate voted to approve
        Thurgood Marshall to the Supreme Court

        Marshall had been chief legal officer for the NAACP

        His most famous case was *Brown v. Board of Education*

─────── **Sham-a-Scam Election in South Vietnam** ───────
                        September 3

Johnson's administration fretted that US journalists in Nam
were not swallowing the assertion that undemocratic elections
                        were good for the glory of the West.

The poet Allen Ginsberg pointed out
                        that fall in an anti-war essay that
"Elections in South Vietnam. . . excluded all candidates who
proposed reconciliation with the Viet Cong or Neutralism."

And so elections in South Vietnam
                sham-a-scammed forth
        electing General Nguyen Van Thieu as president

                with less than 1/2 of the eligible voters voting

September 12
        California Governor
                Ronald Reagan
                        suggested "leaking to the VC" that America
                        was ready to use nuclear weapons

                        ai yi yi Part II

early fall '67

The CIA plane
        searched at night
                above the Bolivian forests

with a new-fangled ultrasensitive infrared night camera
        in its belly
        to locate the heat trail
                of Che Guevara's band

Che noted in his diary
                that planes were overhead

A big map was developed
                from heat signal film

The CIA wanted it to appear to be a Bolivian hit
so US officers were brought from the Canal Zone
                to train Bolivian Rangers

Two Cubans from the odious Operation 40 were brought
in to work on the project
                including a human named Felix Rodriguez
                who would soon steal Che's wristwatch

October 3
    Woody Guthrie was only 55
    when he passed away after 13 years
                afflicted with Huntington's chorea

        the author of brilliant Americana such as
                "So Long, It's Been Good to Know You"

──────── **The Murder of Che Guevara** ────────
October 8–9

In a canyon near La Higuera, Bolivia
the Rangers ambushed Che's group
                and Che was wounded in the leg

Felix Rodriguez was there.
The CIA killer who was in charge of hunting down Che
        stole Che's Rolex watch
                as if it were a mugging in a NYC alley

        & wrapped the tobacco
                    from Che's final pipe
                to steal that also.

They took Che to a schoolhouse
then the next day a Bolivian Ranger shot him to death

        They lashed him to the right skid
        of a helicopter

and flew him away from La Higuera
to show his body like a hunting trophy
                at a news conference in Valle Grande, Bolivia

            where photos were taken which
            gave him the look of a
                    revolutionary deity
                    —to the chagrin of the CIA—
            for the revolutionary masses

A Trial for the Killers of
──────── Schwerner, Chaney & Goodman ────────

    Back in December o' '64
    19 men were indicted for the Freedom Summer slayings

    They were charged not with murder
    but for conspiring to violate the constitutional rights
                of the 3 murdered heroes
                        under an 1870 statute.

    After many twists & injustices in the time-track
    to fling dirt on the

the trial of the 19 charged with conspiracy occurred
7 of whom were found guilty on October 20, 1967
9 were acquitted & the jury was hung on 3

The 7 fought jail on appeal
                but finally entered Federal prison in 1970

────────────── **Draft-Card Turn-Ins** ──────────────
October 20

The Military & the CIA did not dig the well-planned
                turn-ins of draft cards
                around the States that October

The day before the Exorcism of the Pentagon, for instance
                there was a demonstration outside the Justice Department
                and then 4 Americans took inside what their
                later indictment called a "fabricoid briefcase"
                                packed with draft cards

The 4, not long thereafter indicted, were
William Sloan Coffin, Mitchell Goodman, Dr. Benjamin Spock
& Marcus Raskin

heroes in the struggle against evil

────────────── **Out, Demons, Out!** ──────────────
October 21

There were at least 200,000 demonstrators who
marched across the Memorial Bridge
                                from the Lincoln Memorial
including a flat-bed truck containing the Fugs &
a group of San Francisco Diggers
                plus filmmakers Shirley Clark & Barbara Rubin
                (magician/filmmaker Kenneth Anger also was there)
                to exorcise the Pentagon.

We parked our truck in a Pentagon parking lot
& stood on the bed
in front of microphones chanting
        "Out, Demons, out! Out, Demons, out!"
                over and over and over

praying to the Universe for the strength of seed syllables
chanted in purity
        to chant Evil thence

Up near the Pentagon itself the 200,000 assembled
   & 250 were arrested
        including Norman Mailer and Dave Dellinger

        It was at this demonstration it seems
        that an upset Lyndon Johnson
        first heard the kids chant

        "Hey, hey LBJ
        How many kids did you kill today?"

─────────────── **Missed Exorcism Target** ───────────────
(as the CIA began its ghastly Operation Phoenix)

    In addition to the Pentagon
    we should have also exorcised
        the CIA at Langley that day

    because it was not long after
    the chant of "Out, Demons, out!"

    the CIA began its ultra-evil Phoenix program
    in South Vietnam
        which was responsible
        for 20,000+ Vietnamese murdered
        (by US count)
        or 41,000 (by Saigon's)

    The CIA set up Provincial Interrogation Centers
    in Vietnam's 44 provinces

    & recruited CT (counter-terror) teams
    who used terror-horror, assassinations, kidnappings
    & imposition of Fear against the VC leadership

Of course, VC leadership
meant anyone a snitch chose to snitch
for whatever reasons of snitch

A time of disgrace for America

────────────── **A Multi-Species Protest** ──────────────
October 27

Father Philip Berrigan and 2 others
asked to see their Selective Service draft files in Baltimore

They opened briefcases then
tossed a blood-mix, their own with a duck's
into some open file drawers

for which they were arrested by the FBI

October 29
Hair opened at the Public Theater on LaFayette Street in NYC
w/book & lyrics by James Rado & Gerome Ragni
and music by Galt MacDermot

November 3
the new Greek gov't stomped out trials by jury
(for "common" and political "crimes")

Thank you, o CIA

November 7
Ronald Reagan was elected governor of California
eyeballing the Rose Garden
all the while

November 14
The war-hearted Secretary of State named Dean Rusk
spoke to the Foreign Policy Association
at the NY Hilton

that the US must continue its escalation in Vietnam

Several thousand protesters were outside
some tossing eggs

The war-dinged Mr. Rusk could have used some
"Out, Demons, out!"
rather than the ovoids of derision

―――――――――――――― **McNamara Splits** ――――――――――――
November 27

It was not known till decades later that Robert McNamara
had grave doubts about the Vietnam War

Instead he fled from office
& Johnson named him the
president of the World Bank

Before Mac headed back to moneyland he
ordered the creation of
what came to be called the Pentagon Papers

Its official name was the malphonic
"History of the U.S. Decision-Making Process on Vietnam Policy"

which kudzooed to 47 volumes
& was written by about 40 scholars

before it was stealthed to *The New York Times*
in 1971.

―――――――――― **The First Human Heart Transplant** ――――――――
December 3

A team of five surgeons in Cape Town, South Africa
with Dr. Christiaan Barnard at the lead
inserted the heart of a 25-year-old woman
into the chest of a grocer named Louis Washkansky
who lived for 18 days
but passed away on the 21st
from pneumonia

―――――――――――――― **Stop the Draft Week** ―――――――――――
December 6–7

In a week to make the CIA tweedies bite dents
in their pipe stems
activists intervened at draft induction centers

in major American cities
Edward Sanders was among those arrested
downtown near Wall Street

Then late in the month more than 546 were arrested
trying to shut down a NYC draft induction center
Dr. Benjamin Spock & Allen Ginsberg among them

& there were pickets in Iowa against evil Dow's
manufacture of napalm

bite your stems, o tweedies!

A Time of Confluence

The fall of 1967 saw a police-state confluence
of alarm
from the FBI, the Army, the CIA over
1. anti-draft activities
2. the anti-war movement (the big numbers at
March on the Pentagon)
3. King and the Poor People's Campaign
4. Blacks rising up

The CIA began Project Resistance
to move against the anti-draft activists

The Poor People's Campaign
December 5

Military Intelligence became alarmed
at an early December speech wherein

Martin Luther King Jr. put
his epoch-making leadership
behind a huge Poor People's March
to occur in Washington the coming spring.

It was an action which
had Martin King lived to see it in play
might have changed America profoundly

as the war continued

to suck out cash
                once headed for the Great Society.

The Southern Christian Leadership Conference
started work on the
                Poor People's Campaign

to demand from the economy
an amount equal to the $70 billion
                spent on arms (in 1967)
                FOR JOBS, FOOD, HOUSING

Army Intelligence wasn't the only group alarmed.
J. Edgar Hoover, after King's speech,
ordered the FBI's Division Five
(responsible for Domestic Intelligence)
to tap all 10 phone lines at the
                Southern Christian Leadership Conference

                Ping!

———————————— **Briefing the Tweedies** ————————————
                late 1967

Meanwhile Operation Chaos chaos'd forward as
an Army Counter-Intelligence agent named Ralph Stein
briefed some tweedies from the CIA
                on "radical" activities inside the US
                apparently including such dangers
                as *The Berkeley Barb* and SDS manuals

December 7
    the right-wing Cardinal Spellman
    was buried at St. Patrick's cathedral
                having lived to 78

December 8
    Senator William Fulbright
                spoke to his colleagues of

    "an immoral and unnecessary war"
    where the United States was "using its B-52s, its napalm
    & all those other ingenious weapons of counter-insurgency
    to turn a small country into a charnel house."

The Army Goes After Civilians
—————— in the US After March on Pentagon ——————
fall 1967 & thereafter

The Defense Department had underestimated the
"strength" of the March on the Pentagon

so a committee was formed to
examine the role of Federal troops in civil unrest

which came up with a plan.

A directorate for Civil Disturbance Planning and Operations
was created and operated in what was known as
the "Domestic War Room"
        located under the Pentagon mall parking lot.

The US Army's chief intelligence Officer, Maj. Gen William Yarborough,
thought that the Russkies and the Chicoms
        were behind the protests

Yarborough established a communications network known as
Operation IV, with a nationwide teletype network to supply it
information. Over 1,000 army agents in civilian attire
worked out of 300 posts across the USA
        to slurp up political/personal data on civilians

The Army Intelligence center became known as
Continental United States Intelligence (CONUS Intel)
and operated out of the
Army Intelligence school & headquarters
        at Fort Holabird, Maryland.

————————— **Military King-Noia** —————————
December 12, 1967

An "intelligence analysis" was distributed during a Pentagon
conference which described the upcoming
        King-led March on Washington
as "a devastating civil disturbance whose sole purpose
is to shut down the United States government."

The analysis raved on about King as "a

Negro who repeatedly has preached
the message of Hanoi and Peking."

They were eager, ahh eager, to deal with King.
But how?

Ping!

———— **Agents Fanning Out in the Counterculture** ————

And so, for the next few years
        the Army sent its agents
                upon the counterculture.

Some did it stiffly
but some Army agents, mostly young men, liked it
—it was a chance to
hang out in bars & coffee houses
spiffle through membership lists
smoke some pot
listen to the Doors & lock limbs w/
loose-tressed damsels
        in paste-up rooms lit by sticks of incense

        all in the name of
                protecting America

———————————— **The Wah-Wah Pedal** ————————————
1967

Not everything that year was Out, Demons, Out!
as when the electric wah-wah pedal was invented
by Bradley Plunkett & Lester Kushner
        who were working on a switch
                for a Vox amp
when somehow the wah concept grew, a circuit was built
and then wired into a volume pedal
& wow! I mean wah! the wah-wah pedal,
named after the "wah-wah" sound of the
                        muted jazz trumpet
& put to beauteous use almost at once
by groups such as the Fugs
        & Jimi Hendrix

Novum '67:
    and new too in the Year of Love:
        breathalyzer tests, the microwave oven,
            quartz watches
                the first Super Bowl
                    th' Public Broadcasting Service

        dots of belief
          on the time-lace

Colorado became the first state to allow abortion
Denmark and the Netherlands stopped busting people
              for possession of grass

the American surgeon René Favaloro
    developed the coronary artery bypass operation
      —grafting additional blood vessels in the heart
          to bypass narrow or obstructed arteries

        All right!

US scientist Charles Caskey and friends
showed that identical forms of messenger RNA produce the
    same amino acids in a variety of living beings
      informing us that the genetic code is common to all life forms
    & confirming the poetic insight that the human form divine
          is not that different from a May Fly's

Two scientists, S. Manabe and R. T. Wetherald
      warned about the greenhouse effect
         —that rising temperatures
           would cause sea levels to lift

      —but not much attention paid to Glo Wa in '67

Dolby noise reduction for tape recording
   Rosencrantz and Guildenstern Are Dead   Tom Stoppard

    Louise Nevelson's retrospective at the Whitney
         & the rise of thunder-throated Aretha Franklin!

The political film collective called Newsreel was formed that fall
    after the demonstrations at the Pentagon

& began to make films such as
Boston Draft Resistance, Columbia 1968,
The Haight, Miss America & The Panthers

It soon had offices in 11 cities
in a bid to create a counter-media

Ahh that Newsreel had thrived till it now
comprised a Huge Free Third Voice
on the national screens!

Finalities in '67:
J. Robert Oppenheimer on Feb 18 at 62
Muhammad Mossadegh on March 5 at 97
Jean Toomer on March 30 at 72
May 15 Edward Hopper at 84
Langston Hughes May 22 at 65
June 7 the underrated Dorothy Parker at 73
Spencer Tracy June 10 at 67
June 29 Jayne Mansfield at 34
Vivien Leigh at 53 of tb on July 8
Basil Rathbone on July 21 at age 75
July 22 Carl Sandburg at 89
August 24 Henry Kaiser at 85
Ad Reinhardt on August 30 at 53
Carson McCullers at 50 on Sept 29
André Maurois at 80 on Oct 9
December 10
into the brrr-ful waters of Lake Monona
on his first tour in his own private plane
the singer Otis Redding born in '41

Libri: *The Confessions of Nat Turner*   William Styron
One Hundred Years of Solitude   Gabriel García Márquez
Giles Goat-Boy   John Barth

Jimi Hendrix   *Are You Experienced?* and soon: *Axis: Bold as Love*
"(I Want) Somebody to Love" & "White Rabbit"   Jefferson Airplane
The Doors' "Light My Fire"

"A Whiter Shade of Pale" from Procol Harum
The Monkees "I'm a Believer" & "Last Train to Clarksville"

"Ruby Tuesday" from the Rolling Stones
"Groovin'" from the Rascals
"All You Need Is Love" & "Penny Lane" from the Beatles

—a good year for tunes

Films '67:

The Graduate   *Bonnie and Clyde*
Magical Mystery Tour   *Belle de Jour*

The Countess from Hong Kong   Chaplin
Warhol's *Chelsea Girls*

In the Heat of the Night (winning the Oscar)
Cool Hand Luke
Guess Who's Coming to Dinner
Far from the Madding Crowd
The Dirty Dozen

and in potatoland: "Rowan and Martin's Laugh-In"
"The Flying Nun"
"Morley Safer's Vietnam" on CBS

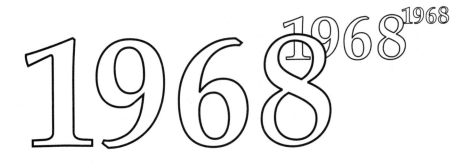

<hr>

Evil

Evil came slashing and burning—

a soldier using a Zippo lighter
set fire to a thatched hut

babies were shot in a ditch

the naked girl of Vietnam
ran down a street in napalm flames
from the US military

& gunfire cracked the history of the USA

They can snicker
They can say war is hell
They can grin complacently
They can sneer
but it was evil

It was the year
the nuclear elite
declared Bikini Island
site of bomb tests
to be safe

& its tossed-off inhabitants were allowed to return
—a bit prematurely

since 10 years later, in 1978,
the health hazards of nuclear fallout were
reappraised & Bikini's residents
were once again removed

Thank you, c-spreaders

January 2
LBJ appointed an 18-man commission
under William Lockhart, dean
of the U of Minnesota law school
to look into ways of dealing with
porn in films, sex toys & porn books

(their report would not be released till 9-30-70)

January 4
troops were increased to 486,000
in the slaughter zone

while in Newark the same day the poet Amiri Baraka
—surveilled & hounded for his politics—

was sentenced to 3 years in prison
(later overturned on an appeal)
for weapons in a van during the '67 Newark riots

while out in Los Angeles a beaknosed guy named James Earl Ray
went to a hypnotist on January 4
(He'd been seeing hypnos
now and then

since coming to California
the fall of '67)

He sped up his phone installation
by claiming he was working
to get George Wallace on the
presidential ballot

On January 19 James Earl Ray enrolled
in a 6-week bartending course in LA
perhaps already being worked up as a patsy

January 5
    The Anti-Draft movement
        threatened the youth-grabbing cogs of the killing machine
    & so today the government indicted
    Dr. Benjamin Spock, Rev. William Sloane Coffin of Yale
        Harvard grad student Michael Ferber
        novelist Mitchell Goodwin, and
        Marcus Raskin of the Institute for Policy Studies
            for counseling young people to resist the draft

(They had helped gather the satchel of draft cards
                that was turned over to the warmongers in DC
        just before the Exorcism)

January 5
    Alexander Dubcek became first Secretary
    of the Communist Party of Czechoslovakia.

        It was expected that he would allow more freedom of the press
            & take Czechoslovakia on a path more independent
                of the

January 18
>   the singer Eartha Kitt
>> was invited to a luncheon at the White House
>>> whose topic was "urban crime"

>> & then in front of a miffed Lady Bird Johnson
>> Kitt spoke out against the war
>> linking the escalation of the Nam scam
>>> to the luncheon's theme
>> "You send the best of this country off to be shot and maimed
>>> No wonder the kids rebel and take pot"

January 21
>   a B-52 smashed into a bay near Greenland
>>   releasing radiation from four h-bombs

>>   Thank you, Mr. Teller

January 23
>   the US intelligence ship *Pueblo*
>   calling itself an "environmental research ship"
>>   was seized by North Korea

>   (with its crew finally set loose on December 23)

>>   It has been speculated that the seizure was planned
>>   to divert attention to Korea
>>>   during the rev-up to the Tet Offensive

———————————— **The Tet Offensive** ————————————
January 30

The National Liberation Front attacked the new 6-story white-hued
>   US embassy in Saigon

>   They blammed a hole through the 9-foot-tall wall
>   then 19 of them surged into the compound
>>   running toward the main building

>>>   but a marine slammed and clamped shut the
>>>   huge teak doors before the NLF
>>>>   could shoot inside
>>>>   and fly the

                    Viet Cong flag
                    upon the parapets

Thus began the Tet Offensive
described as the great turning point of the Vietnam debacle
as the NLF attacked 90 towns & cities in South Vietnam

The idea was to snuff out the regime
o' General Nguyen Cao Ky and General Nguyen Van Thieu.

        The much belovéd CBS newsman Walter Cronkite said
        "What the hell is going on?
                I thought we were winning the war!"

January 31
        the Island of Mauritius in the Indian Ocean
                shook free at last from the British Empire

February 1
        It was brutal image time
        as a violent chump named Nguyen Ngoc Loan
                chief of the South Vietnam police

                executed a captive
                being walked along a Saigon street

                his arm outstretched to the victim's head
                then blam!

                an image shown the world
                by AP photographer Eddie Adams
                & NBC TV

The same day
        in New Hampshire
                Richard Nixon began his
                        search for the White House
                        (though he never really found the place
                                        where Lincoln lived)

February 6
        Charles de Gaulle opened the Winter Olympics in Grenoble, France
        Peggy Fleming won the women's figure-skating title

& Jean-Claude Killy
>> a customs officer in France
>> won all 3 Alpine ski events

February 8
>> the Orangeburg Massacre in South Carolina
>>> with 3 black students murdered
>> trying to desegregate a bowling alley

while, on the same day,
> George Corley Wallace
>> from the sleazesome side of Populism
>>> entered the race for President

─── Seeger Finally Sings for the Smothers Brothers ───
February 27

In its tradition of demi-semi-hemi liberalism
CBS television aired "The Smothers Brothers Comedy Hour"
featuring Tom and Dick Smothers
whose topical humor
> satiric skits & songs
>> were something to watch during '67 & '68

till it was censored from the air,
>> though very popular, in June of '69

One great moment was when the Smothers Brothers
brought back the black-listed Pete Seeger to national TV!

Seeger sang "Waist Deep in the Big Muddy"

It hadn't been easy
The previous September Seeger had sung it
>> but CBS had censored it out.

"Waist Deep in the Big Muddy"
> is set in World War 2 where
> a platoon of soldiers is ordered to ford a river

They tell the captain it's way too deep
but he orders them onward
deeper deeper

till he drowns
 w/ its famous lines

 "Waist deep in the Big Muddy
 And the Big Fool says to push on."

Though it's really a universal tune about
justice & following stupid orders

 in '68
 it meant just one thing:
   Vietnam

February 29
 the Kerner Report on the summer of '67 riots
 warned of the US becoming "two societies, one black, one
   white, separate and unequal."
 Sometime around then, Johnson decreed the
   "affirmative action" program
   —that gov't contractors would have to give preferential
   treatment to African-Americans
      & other minorities

———————— **More MLK Smut-Ink from Hoover** ————————
late February/early March 1968

There was a sleaze-flood of FBI reports on Martin King
   to Johnson's White House
    in the months leading up to his death

One went out to Hoover's wide para-net of civil & military
agencies on February 20, with long sections on the
Poor People's Campaign plans, King's anti-war stance,
the finances of the SCLC & the putative Communist influence
on King and SCLC
   plus, most thrilling, yet tsk-tsky to the
   national security grouch apparatus

   plenty of ink on sex sex sex sex sex
      sex sex sex
      sex sex
       sex

236

There was ink on a putative "all-night sex orgy" in Miami at an SCLC
workshop; plus some ink on the Willard Hotel '64, and then
some ink on "King's Mistress" which averred
he was having an affair with
a California dentist's wife.

February 29
both NY senators Robert K
and Jacob Javits
spoke out against the war

RFK noted that more than a million US and Vietnam troops could
not protect "one major city in the Tet offensive"

———————————————— **Gold Crisis '68** ————————————
March–April

There was what the chronologies call a
"speculative flight" from the US dollar into gold
which destabilized the "international monetary system"

The London Gold Market was shut down March 15–April 1
at the request of the President
to stop the heavy selling of gold
On 3-17 the central banks agreed to a two tier set-up for gold:
with official dealings at $35 an ounce &
"commercial dealings" at a "free" price

and then on March 19 the President signed a law
eliminating the requirement
that 25% of US currency be backed by gold

The gold crisis was a murky thing
I've never really understood—
It may have had to do with
France hoarding gold

to punish the USA for Vietnam
(They were apparently upset with France
for having oodles of gold
while at the same time
spending oodles for labor peace
—as we shall see when we trace
the May Uprising)

It may take the US another century
to learn that Social Democracy
is the price Capital pays
for peace in the streets

On March 2
the human named James Earl Ray
got his diploma
from the International Bartending School
and on the 5th
had the sharp tip of his nose
removed by a plastic surgeon
in LA

I wonder if he was then already
in the clutches of the Artichokers
fixing him up to be one of those "three month patsies?"

Hoover Determined to Prevent a Black "Messiah"
────────── (i.e., Martin Luther King Jr.) ──────────
March 4

Hoover issued his famous proclamation updating the Cointelpro
"Black Nationalists" program. Here's the fullest version
I've been able to put together. The names were initially
obliterated when the Bureau finally released it:

"For maximum effectiveness of the Counterintelligence Program,
and to prevent wasted effort, long-range goals are being set.
1. Prevent the coalition of militant black nationalist groups. In unity
there is strength; a truism that is not less valid for all its triteness. An
effective coalition of black nationalist groups might be the first step
toward a real 'Mau Mau' in America, the beginning of a true black rev-
olution.
2. Prevent the rise of a 'Messiah' who could unify and electrify the
militant black nationalist movement. Malcolm X might have been such

a 'messiah'; he is the martyr of the movement today. Martin Luther King, Stokely Carmichael and Elijah Muhammad all aspire to this position. Elijah Muhammad is less of a threat because of his age. King could be a very real contender for this position should he abandon his supposed 'obedience' to 'white, liberal doctrines' —nonviolence— and embrace black nationalism. Carmichael has the necessary charisma to be a real threat in this way.

3. Prevent violence on the part of black nationalist groups.... Through counterintelligence it should be possible to pinpoint potential troublemakers and neutralize them before they exercise their potential for violence.

4. Prevent militant black nationalist groups and leaders from gaining respectability by discrediting them to three separate segments of the community.... the responsible Negro community; ....the white community and to 'liberals';.... (and) in the eyes of Negro radicals, the followers of the movement...

5. A final goal should be to prevent the long-range growth of militant black nationalist organizations, especially among youth. Specific tactics to prevent these groups from converting young people must be developed."

A memo of disgrace in a sizzling time

───────── An Actual Earth of Value ─────────
March 6

The very influential television newsman named
Walter Cronkite denounced the Vietnam War
                    —it made a mark on the time

It was also the day in Gloucester, Massachusetts, the bard
                                        Charles Olson
wrote a poem as he was "reading about my world":

> an actual earth of value to
> construct one, from rhythm to
> image, and image is knowing, and
> knowing, Confucius says, brings one
> to the goal: nothing is possible without
> doing it. It is where the test lies, malgré
> all the thought and all the pell-mell of
> proposing it. Or thinking it out or living it
> ahead of time.

March 9
   General William Westmoreland
      requested 206,000 more soldiers for Vietnam

   but Johnson foisted forth only 35–50,000 in reply

         There's never enough troops
         to satisfy war's whoops

March 11
   Robert Kennedy knelt in prayer with
                  César Chávez
      as Chávez was ending a 25-day fast
      in the midst of his historic search
         for fair pay & safe conditions for farm workers

March 12
   Eugene McCarthy
      running on the ☮ peace-in-Vietnam plank
         almost slid ahead of Johnson in the New Hampshire primary

      McC got 42.2 percent to Johnson's 49.4 for war

   & Nixon beat write-in candidate Nelson Rockefeller

That same day March 12
   Hoov'-sleaze sent a "new" 21-page report titled
      "Martin Luther King, Jr.: A Current Analysis"
         to LBJ, AG Ramsey Clark, the CIA,
            the State Department, and a bunch of military offices

            Ping!

———————————————— **My Lai** ————————————————
                  March 16

   In a tiny fishing village called My Lai 4
   Americans landed in helicopters
            and began four hours of the most hideous slaughter
            known to humanity

      There were rapes, disembowelments,
      the burning of innocent thatched huts,

women forced to do blowjobs then slaughtered
mothers facing death protecting babies
        & people desperate
                to slide beneath the already dead

all in the name of American glory

The 105 American troops were called Charlie Company
they'd been in Vietnam for 3 months
Finally, after the hours of evil
400 old men, women, children lay killed

and then a heroic helicopter pilot named
Hugh Thompson
     with crewmen Lawrence Colburn & Glenn Andreotta
     by chance in the air above
     landed while soldiers were still killing civilians
                    in a ditch
     and ordered the troops of Charlie Company
                   to stand away

     Thompson had his support crew put guns on
     the Americans, said he'd shoot them
                if they killed more Vietnamese

     then had his staff, in his own words,
          "wade in the ditch in gore up to their hips"

     while he and his crew rescued about 11 Vietnamese
          from the butcher-batty young men

     Thompson, now seen to be an American hero,
     was, back then, ostracized, threatened with a
     court martial,
         and risked assassination from the
         Phoenix-wrecked climate of murder
            in the long thin land of hell

March 16
   Robert Francis Kennedy announced for President
                   on My Lai morn
  in the Senate Caucus Room
        where his brother once declared

Ethel was there with 9 of their kids
Robert stood in a blue suit
             and a gold PT-109 tieclasp
reading his speech
             from a black notebook typed in overlarge letters

and then he headed for
      NYC
             to march in the St. Patrick's Day parade.

―――――――――――― **LeMay on Robert Kennedy** ―――――――――――

General Curtis LeMay
had retired from the Air Force
             and was living in Bel Air, in Los Angeles.
The singer Eddie Fisher
             wrote in his autobiography (p. 340)
about visiting LeMay
      not long before Bobby announced his run:

      "Toward the end of our visit
      I happened to mention that I was going to
      Bobby Kennedy's for his wife's telethon.
             'Bobby Kennedy?' LeMay said without expression.
             'He's going to be assassinated.'"

―――――――― **Skull Valley Nerve Gas Sheep Kill** ――――――――
March 13–17

At the Dugway Proving Grounds
             about 60 miles southwest of Salt Lake City
the Army was experimenting with the outdoor release of
the superpotent VX nerve gas (one drop on the
             skin can
                   kill you
                         in 15 minutes)

On March 13, they exploded a VX artillery shell
& burned about 160 pounds of "nerve agent"
                         in an open pit
and also sprayed VX from a plane
             (maybe down on some test animals)

It has been claimed that a valve stayed open, perhaps stuck

on a spray tank
    as the airplane went up to a higher altitude

  so that the drifting death-mist killed 5,000 sheep
    at Skull Valley, about 27 miles away
        by the next day

  The US Army utilized Lenny Bruce's Rule # 16
    (deny deny deny)
      for the next 30 years

  till it finally admitted in 1998
    it had caused the ovinocides.

  Utah of course was well used to drifting death
  as in the radioactive cancer clouds
    that drifted into the state from Nevada
    in the open-air tests of the '50s & early '60s

  (It occurred to me 33 years later that
  the Army might have been experimenting with gas
  for use in search and rescue missions in Cambodia or
  Laos—
    see the Tailwind controversy of September '70)

      deny deny deny
      let victims sue or cry

March 17
  Martin King was in California
  to speak to the Democratic State Council
    in Anaheim

  & James Earl Ray that day
  filed a change-of-address card
    to general delivery Atlanta
      King's home city

—————————— **The Youth International Party** ——————————
March 19

A bunch of us, including myself, Abbie Hoffman, Jerry Rubin,
Paul Krassner, Phil Ochs, the producer Jacques Levy,
Allen Ginsberg (who unhooked his harmonium

and sang "Hare Krishna"), Allen Katzman of the *East Village Other*,
and others
                held a press conference at the Americana Hotel in NYC
                            to announce a Festival of Life
                            in Chicago
                at the time of the Democratic Convention in August.

                The plan was to hold a big-time rock fest
                commixed with radical proposals.

                With not nearly as strong a plan as, say,
                        the Wobblies had
                                early in the century
                                        for "One Big Union,"
                the Yippies, as they were called,
                strutted forward in the time-track
                                to rile the cash-caste & the militarists
                                for the next few years

                "We demand the Politics of Ecstasy!"
                                        our leaflets thundered—
                though in the glare of 35 years' hindsight
                it seems a tactical error to have announced that
                500,000 people
                                were going to make love
                                        in Chicago parks

March 22
        The President named General William Westmoreland
                                        as Army Chief of Staff

It was the month
        The Movement for a Democratic Society
        was formed in NYC
                        for the Radicals Conference in Boston that month

        with a working paper by Bob Gottlieb and poet Marge Piercy
        both formerly active with SDS

                —where is the Movement for a Democratic Society
                                        now when we need it?

A young man named Sirhan Bishara Sirhan
had been employed as an exercise boy
         on a thoroughbred horse ranch
in Corona outside LA
         and hungered to be a jockey.
In September of '66 he fell from a horse
and though his injuries were not serious
he had blurred vision and pain,
         and gave up his passion to race.

He lived with his mom in Pasadena
& dropped out of sight
         'tween January and March '68

It may have been then
they made him into a patsy,
         or a programmed assassin.

In his *The Search for the Manchurian Candidate*
John Marks quoted an unidentified CIA researcher,
from the old days, who alleged it would be much easier
to make a "patsy" programmed to "make authorities think the patsy
committed a particular crime," than to program a robot assassin.
Hypnosis expert Milton Kline, unpaid consultant to CIA researchers,
guessed to Marks he could
         fashion a patsy
           in a mere 3 months.

Sirhan was very, very easily hypnotized

The Great Martin King Interrupts
—————— **Preparations for the Poor People's Campaign** ——————
to Help a Union in Memphis
March 18

He was working full-frenzy on
        another great March on Washington for April 22
        which, had it been allowed to happen,
        might have
           changed America
              for the permanent better
      (which is perhaps why it wasn't allowed)

or it might at least have trembled America
        with its simple yet powerful demand for
                "jobs, income and a decent life"

The plan was for 3,000 poor people
—blacks, Puerto Ricans, whites, Indians, Mexicans—
to go by caravan to DC, pitch tents and sleep in them
& then each day delegations
        would go to government departments

The numbers, it was planned, wd increase
                                to great size
& the ever-increasing Campaign wd stay camped out
        till there were results from the gov't

                It had enormous implications
                should it have grown & threatened
                        the military-industrial-surrealists.

It was truly a day of fate
when Martin King broke into the March plans
(at the request of a close friend, a minister, in Memphis)
& flew to Memphis
        where there'd been a strike for over a month
        by the 1,300 trash collectors (mostly black)
                & their union (AFSCME) the
                American Federation of State County
                        and Municipal Employees

(Memphis had treated the trashmen trashily
        the mayor had replaced them with scabs
                police had maced some ministers
                during a rally in support of the strike

                & then there was a boycott of
                        downtown business

                & the great Social Democrat
                        felt bound to help them)

        There was a big crowd on hand
        to hear King on the 18th
        He told them he'd return
                in a few days to lead a General Strike

246

"I want a tremendous work stoppage,"
                                    he said
"All of you, your families and children,
will join me and I will lead you on a march
                              through the center of Memphis"

        Ping!

March 27
    James Earl Ray purchased a rifle in Birmingham
                then exchanged it the next day for a Remington 30.06
                            a pump-action weapon
                                        with a telescopic sight

    It was a rifle similar to those w/ which
    the Memphis Fire and Police Commissioner Frank C. Holloman
    a former FBI agent
    was outfitting a group of 5 new anti-sniper squads
                            for duty in Memphis

March 28
    King flew back to Memphis from New York
    (where he'd been on a fundraising tour with Harry Belafonte)
                to lead a march on City Hall
                from the Clayborn Temple A.M.E. church

                His plane was an hour late
                & by the time he arrived
                the large crowd was already marching

            King noted the disarray
            with people crowding the sidewalks
            more of an irritated swell than a march

            but nevertheless got out of his car
            linked arms with ministers
            & began to walk
                    singing "We Shall Overcome"

Then there was the sound of breaking glass
                        and the grabbing of American largess
                        from store windows

whether urged on by provocateurs or not
                is not clearly known

though what is totally clear is that the whole
             Civil Rights/Black Power kettle
             was being double double toil & troubled
             by Cointelpro & the secret police

In any case the difference between boycott & window bashing
             was not that clear to a few youth

after which there was violence as the police donned gas masks
and crushed the march with tear gas, mace and clubs

King was rushed away to a hotel   (not the Lorraine)

Other young people, many of them high-school kids,
fought back
           the police becoming hysterical
                  beating bystanders & marchers
                          —a 17-year old youth was killed.

King was very despondent
               over the breakdown of nonviolent discipline
while the FBI's Division 5 in DC
             did everything but jack off in exultance
             at the violence
                 hoping it would discredit the great King

March 30
        there was an acrimonious meeting at the Ebenezer Baptist Church
                              in Atlanta

Some felt King should keep a total focus on
               the Poor People's March

just 23 days ahead on April 22
but King was determined to return to Memphis
& lead a successful, nonviolent march
            to counter the bad ink the violence had spawned.

               The fact-fonting Fates were pulling flax
                    twisting thread
                         snipping

late March

Meanwhile the great troubles
at Columbia University began

On March 27th a member of SDS named Mark Rudd led
about a hundred fellow students to Low Library
(the administration building)
with a petition against the Institute for Defense Analysis
       one of those kill-'em or control-'em better
           intellectual war tanks
           funded by the government
               which had a close relationship with Columbia
               and did research, for example,
                    on something called "riot control"

    Rudd and SDS demanded that Columbia
    break relations with the IDA
               (which was operating on 12 US campuses)

————————————— **Johnson Says Goodbye** —————————————
March 31

Lyndon Johnson announced tonight, on April Fool's Eve,
                 that he would not run for re-election
& he decreed a cessation of bombing north of the 20th parallel.

A Gallup poll released that day had said that a mere 26% of Americans
                liked his handling of the war

There's still a big "why?"
       on the reason or reasons
          that crabby, grabby Johnson ceased to crab-grab

     One theory is that he was afraid the next term
     would give him a fatal heart attack

         Mars was murdering
         the Great Society
         while Venus was
           listening to the Doors

days leading to the bullet

It appears that Martin King was under total
                    visual, photographic & electronic surveillance
by the FBI & the US Army & perhaps too by the CIA
                    & the National Security Agency
in the days drumming toward his demise.

――――――― The 111th Intelligence Group in Memphis ―――――――

According to a lengthy & excellent study
        by reporter Stephen Tompkins
        (which he still stands behind)
        in the 3-21-93 *Memphis Commercial Appeal*

    when King returned to Memphis on April 3
    "Army agents from the 111th Military Intelligence Group
    shadowed his movements and monitored radio traffic
            from a sedan crammed with electronic equipment."

    Tompkins, who if it were just a slightly better world,
    would have been given a Pulitzer for his reporting,
    also wrote that during King's final day & a half
    "Eight Green Beret Soldiers from an
            'Operations Detachment Alpha 84 Team'
            were also in Memphis
            carrying out an unknown mission.
            Such A-Teams usually contained 12 members."

In his book *The Phoenix Program* (p. 338) Douglas Valentine
describes Operation Shamrock, a counterintelligence operation
against the antiwar movement by the "Defense Intelligence Agency,
servicing the Joint Chiefs and working with the Army chief of staff
for intelligence, General William Yarborough."
Operation Shamrock was headquartered at Fort Holabird, MD.

Valentine says this about mil-int in Memphis:
"Allegedly as part of Shamrock, the 111th Military Intelligence Group
(MIG) in Memphis kept Martin Luther King, Jr., under twenty-four-
hour-a-day surveillance and reportedly watched and took photos while
King's assassin moved into position, took aim, fired, and walked away.
As a result, some VVAW [Vietnam Veterans Against the War] members

contend that the murders of King, and other less notable victims,
were the work of a domestic-variety Phoenix hit team."

(The Justice Department, during the Bill Clinton era,
issued a report denying that mil-int was
in Memphis shadowing King)

────────────────── **Frank Holloman** ──────────────────

A 25-year-veteran of the FBI named Frank Holloman
had been Memphis Police and Fire Commissioner
$\qquad\qquad\qquad\qquad\qquad$ since the fall of '67

He was reputed to have taken part in the FBI's
$\qquad\qquad\qquad\qquad\qquad$ hate-forged campaign
$\qquad\qquad\qquad\qquad\qquad\qquad$ against King
& he was on duty those fateful days in early April
$\qquad\qquad\qquad\qquad\qquad$ at police headquarters

Memphis Police Spy on King from a Firehouse
────── **as the Fates Begin to Spin and Measure** ──────
$\qquad\qquad$ April 3

King flew to Memphis from Atlanta
and checked into the black-owned Lorraine Motel
$\qquad\qquad\qquad\qquad\qquad$ where he often stayed

(It appears that King had been scheduled to sleep
$\qquad\qquad$ in a room downstairs
$\qquad\qquad\qquad\qquad$ out of sight of snipers
$\qquad\qquad\qquad\qquad\qquad$ but had been moved to
$\qquad\qquad\qquad\qquad\qquad\qquad$ an easy target location
$\qquad\qquad$ based on a phone call the motel owner had received
$\qquad\qquad$ urging that he be moved)

Around noon a black detective named Redditt
went to a back room at a nearby fire station
and taped a newspaper to a window
$\qquad\qquad\qquad$ that looked out upon the 3rd-floor balcony
$\qquad\qquad\qquad$ of the Lorraine (King's room)

He cut out holes in the newspaper
$\qquad\qquad\qquad$ then put his binoculars up against them

in order to jot down the license plates
                        and names of visitors
and, as much as possible,
                        to note who did what.

The detective was joined by another black patrolman
                        & between them they could identify
                                virtually all the
                                        black activists in Memphis

In the early evening of 4-3, not long after 7
            James Earl Ray
                    in role as Eric S. Galt
                            checked into the New Rebel Motel
                                                in Memphis

———————————————— **A Thrum of Rain** ————————————————
                        Evening April 3

A spring rain thrummed the metal roof
                            of the Masonic Temple
            as 2,000 supporters wildly applauded
            when Martin King came up the steps
                            for a glorious speech

at the end of which he spoke with the same tone of
acceptance
            as Malcolm X had
                    just before the Audubon Ballroom.

"And some began to talk about the threats that were out," said King
"of what would happen to me
                    from some of our sick white brothers. . . .
Well, I don't know what will happen now.
We've got some difficult days ahead.
But it really doesn't matter with me now.
                            Because I've been to the mountaintop!"

There was great applause, with thunder and lightning outside

"And I don't mind. Like anybody I would like to live. . . a long life.
Longevity has its place. But I'm not concerned about that now. . . .
I just want to do God's will! And He's allowed me to go up to
                                        the mountain. . . .

And I've looked over, and I've seen the Promised land.
I may not get there with you, but I want you to know, tonight,
that we as a people will get to the Promised land!
So, I'm happy tonight. I'm not worried about anything.
I'm not fearing any man!
      Mine eyes have seen the glory of the coming of the Lord!"

*—a speech everyone should
view & hear*

———— The Dire Day of Dream-Doom ————
April 4, 1968

The dire day of Dream-Doom
      whirls with hidden fury
            35 years later
for an evil that Evil wants kept in the cauldron
      evil'd forth that bright spring Southern day

and just as Akhenaten's name
      was chiseled out of
          ancient Egypt's memory
so too modern power
      has sought to erase what power
          did to the great King.

After many years of studying the King case
I have come to think that the books of William Pepper
have come the closest so far to tracing the truth
of what the military allowed to happen
      & a racist power structure
      despicably committed

Army Officers Go to the Roof
———— of the Fire House the Day King Was Shot ————
Morning, April 4

It was exactly a year since King spoke against the
      war at Riverside Church
      "Somehow this madness must cease...."

A man named Carthel Weeden was captain of the Fire Station #2
located across the street from King's room 306
      at the Lorraine Motel

253

(The Fire Station was just down the same street as the rooming house
    where James Earl Ray rented a room)
    Captain Weeden was on duty the previous morning
    when two United States Army officers approached.
    They said they needed a lookout for the Lorraine Motel.
    They had briefcases, and indicated they had cameras.
    Weeden escorted the military men to the fire-station roof
    Where, behind a parapet wall, they had a bird's-eye
                    view of the open balcony in front
                    of Martin King's room

(as well as a clear view of a brushy area where the actual
                                firing might have taken place)

    Weeden left them there and returned to his duties

On April 4
    the 2 camera men returned
                and were in place
                    throughout the afternoon

                including the fatal moment
                            at 6:01

Army Security Agency Bugging the
───── King Party at the Lorraine that Afternoon ─────

    Though Lenny Bruce's rule # 16 (deny deny deny)
                    always is utilized
                    in order to scissor the past
        it is fairly certain that the ASA bugged 3 rooms
    at the Lorraine that day
                including Room 306
                    King's room

    & another room where a meeting with King went on
            during the afternoon

Pulling a Black Police Surveillor
───────────────── from Fire Station #2 ─────────

    Black Memphis Police Detective Edward Redditt
    (in the 1990s a school teacher in Somerville, Tenn)

at the time of April 4, '68
>	had been assigned to the intelligence bureau
>	and reported to a Lt. E. H. Arkin

>	Redditt was sent with black patrolman
>	Willie Richmond of the intelligence bureau
>	to the locker room at the rear of Fire Station #2
>>	on April 3–4

>	where they could view the Lorraine Motel
>	from a window in a rear door

>	As we have noted they cut holes
>	in paper placed over the window glass
>	in order to place binoculars up against them
>	to monitor the comings and goings
>>	at the motel

>	On dream-doom day Officer Richmond arrived
>	between 2 and 3—Redditt was already on duty.

>	Sometime after 4 pm
>	Lt. Arkin appeared and asked Redditt
>	to follow him to police headquarters.

>	He did, entering a conference room "where he said
>	he saw assembled twenty or more people, many of
>	whom he didn't recognize. Some were in
>	military uniforms,"
>>	as William Pepper describes on p. 250
>>	of his book called *Orders to Kill*

>	Chief Holloman told Redditt that a Secret Service
>	agent had flown in from Washington to tell
>	Holloman that a contract had been put out on
>	Redditt's life and therefore security would be provided
>	for Redditt and family.

>	Redditt protested, but Holloman ordered him home.
>	& just as Redditt came to his house
>	word came over the radio of the killing.

James Earl Ray, using the name of Willard
              checked into a second-floor rooming house
                     above Jim's Bar & Grill
                     with a bathroom window view
                                 down the hall
            (somewhat obstructed
                  by trees and foliage)
   of Martin King's room at the Lorraine Motel

(I wonder if the use of the name Willard
was not a twerpish mote of secret police satire
since Willard was the name of the hotel in DC
in which the FBI had acquired those
erotic tapes from early '64 they compulsively passed around.)

And then at 4 pm, Ray drove to a gun shop
             in his white Mustang with Alabama plates
             to purchase some binoculars
                     (or somebody did)

Law enforcement
alleged that Ray
   crouched
    & leaned
  his 30.06
on the sill
 till King
paused on
th' balcony

but a later judge (who was an expert at rifles)
pointed out that
Ray's rifle was a pump-action
and would have kicked back
if he had leaned the pump on the sill
as he fired
making it almost impossible
to hit his target as he
stood, maybe with one foot in the bathtub
one foot on the floor
waiting for his brief moment
in history

Pulling the Firemen

There were only 2 black firemen
at Fire Station #2.

That day they were pulled from duty there
and sent to another station

Filming from the Fire-House Roof

From the roof of Fire House #2
as Douglas Valentine wrote in
his book *The Phoenix Program* (p. 338)
the military intelligence officers, perhaps
the very ones that Captain Carthel Weeden
conducted to the roof the previous day
and who had returned that dream-doom afternoon
"reportedly watched and took photos
while King's assassin moved into position,
took aim, fired, and walked away."

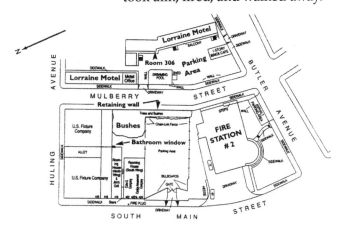

257

King and Reverend Ralph Abernathy
were in a meeting in Room 201
& then, at 5:40, went up the steps
       to Room 306.

Then, just before 6
King came out onto the balcony

His associates were arrayed down below
& there was a limousine on loan from a
        local black funeral home
   to take them to dinner

He stood on the balcony
    for a minute or two
then went back into his room

Abernathy wanted to put on aftershave lotion
King said he'd wait for him on the balcony
where he chatted with people
     including young Jesse Jackson of Chicago

It was just at the moment
he was ready to walk down
     the iron-edged steps

    there was a single shot
    and King fell down
      blood spurting from his jaw

According to Ralph Abernathy's biography
And the Walls Came Tumbling Down (p. 441)

"the black woman operating the motel switchboard
at the time of the shot
    . . . .suffered a heart attack and died,
   thereby making outgoing calls impossible."

—perhaps one should not rule out saxitoxin

In William Pepper's book, *Orders to Kill,*
he writes (p. 434) about interviewing one
of the two army photographers on the roof of
                                        Fire House #2
across the street from the Lorraine.

At the moment of death
one photographer on the fire-house roof had
his camera trained on King on the balcony

& the other was filming and viewing arriving autos

                    Bang!

The photographer filming King "said he was surprised
and in rapid succession quickly snapped four or five
photos following Dr. King as he fell to the balcony floor."

The other photographer, filming arriving autos previously,
"almost instinctively swung his camera from its parking
lot focus to the left and, focusing on the brush area,
caught the assassin (a white man) on film as he
was lowering his rifle. He then took several shots of him
as he was leaving the scene."

The two military photographers hand-delivered the pictures
to a Military Intelligence officer
but the one who had filmed the shooter
kept the negatives and made another set of prints.

The sniper, Mr. Pepper was told, was not James Earl Ray.

──────────── **The Thicket of Mulberry Bushes Cut** ────────────

You know how young mulberry trees can grow
                                in bushlike profusion.
Photos taken at the hour of the murder show
there was a profusion of mulberry

by the edge of an 8-foot-tall retaining wall
       in back of
            the rooming house

    where a shooter might have hidden himself

    (The rooming house's backyard
    was higher in elevation than the
    street in front of the Lorraine Motel

    & the retaining wall dropped down from
    the back yard's higher elevation
            to the street)

By the next day the scrub brush that stood
    between the bathroom window
          at the back of the rooming house
          & the retaining wall

    presenting clear sight difficulties
          for someone leaning a pump-action 30.06
          on the sill of the window
          to focus on King on the balcony

              had been cut away

———— **Branch in Front of the Bathroom Window** ————

    Pepper interviewed an assistant to
    Fire and Police Commissioner Frank Holloman
    named Ed Atkinson

    who recalled being at police headquarters
    after the assassination

    with 2 other officers

    one of whom said that he had been at the
    bathroom window in the boarding house's rear
    with 2 FBI agents

    One of the FBI guys said that a tree branch
    would have to be cut

lest no one would believe that
        an assassin could
            make the shot

(Many more details of this government murder
are to be found in William Pepper's excellent book of 2003
An Act of State—The Execution of Martin Luther King)

———————————— **Anger, Grief, Riots** ————————————

Anger and grief
    and a solid plutonian wall of injustice
            from the earth to the moon

        caused big riots in over 125 cities
            nationwide

    —Chicago, Baltimore, D.C., Detroit, Boston—

    55,000 troops were sent to quell them

April 9
    Gen. Creighton Abrams
        became U.S. Commander in Nam
            & the napalm, defoliation,
        fragmentation bombs
            evil'd onward.

———————————— **Civil Rights Act of 1968** ————————————
April 11

Unearned suffering garnered a law as Lyndon Johnson
signed the Civil Rights Act of 1968
        which made housing discrimination illegal
  & added to the penalties against those
        who take away or deprive people of their civil rights

    Agents of the police, however, were exempt from this law:
"The provisions of this law shall not apply to acts or omissions
on the part of law enforcement officers,
        members of the National Guard. . . or members
    of the Armed Forces of the United States, who are engaged
    in suppressing a riot or civil disturbance. . ."

In order to get conservative and right-wing support for the bill
certain "Love me, I'm a Liberal" members of Congress
added a section providing up to 5 years in the slams to anyone
crossing state lines or using interstate facilities
                    (including phone and mail)
"to organize, promote, encourage, participate in, or carry on
                                                            a riot."

        A riot was defined as an action by 3 or more people
                            "involving acts of violence."

            Authoritarians next year would use the law
            to indict the Chicago 8.

────────────────── **Tastelessness in Chicago** ──────────────────
                        April 15

Mayor Richard Daley announced that from now on
police would "shoot to kill" arsonists and "shoot to maim" looters.

It was tactless, tasteless, and out of sync
                with the soul of what was needed

but it was meanly real
        rhyming as it did with a streak of meanness
                        in some of the American fabric

────────────── **The Columbia Take-Over Begins** ──────────────
                        April 23

The president of Columbia University, one Grayson Kirk
was so out of touch with the era that he
                could not bring himself
                to join hands with students
                        at a memorial for Martin Luther King
                        & sing "We Shall Overcome"

For years Students for a Democratic Society had
                demanded the end of CIA recruiting on campus
and the closing of Institute for Defense Analysis war work.

In addition Columbia was seeking to build a gymnasium
on city-owned land in Morningside Heights Park in Harlem

262

with separate entrances for
students and the "community"

The Time-Track flared like a book of matches on April 23
when there was a rally
    in front of Grayson Kirk's office
                to protest the placing of 6 SDS leaders
                on probation for demonstrations

which turned into a sit-in against the gym

and then protesting blacks plus members of SDS
took over 5 university buildings
including Hamilton Hall
            Columbia's administration building

        & the nation entire started paying attention.

An "emergency faculty" committee convened and
                recommended stopping the gym plans

On campus people wore colors like ancient Byzantium
                Red armband for strikers
                Blue for jocks and conservatives
                White for faculty
                Green for amnesty supporters

Just before dawn on April 30 1,000 police were called in
and strikers were brutally removed
                from the five buildings
Those arrested were clubbed
            and made to run whacking gauntlets
                        on their way to the arrest wagons

so that of the 712 arrested
148 had head injuries

after which a general strike began
                that kept the university closed
                        for the rest of May

        President Kirk resigned
        de facto amnesty was granted

the university pulled out of the IDA
         & the gym was never built

The raw data of its chrono-flow
         do not trace its power
but the Columbia take-over
was part of an April-to-August
         swing of months
             so dizzying, so energizing
             so terrifying, so thrilling

         that the year became a Year

———— An Attempted Revolution in France ————
May 2 till mid-June

In early May the spirit of 1789
         with its ever-thrilling motto
             Liberté Égalité Fraternité
         danced to life again
         with a new uprising in France

where due to its multi-century tradition of
disparate elements of French society joining forces

the students were actually able to forge an alliance
             with the workers.

Demonstrations at the University of Nanterre on 5–2 spread
to the Sorbonne in Paris
and then through the May month
         there were riots
         and just about every university
             in the nation
               was closed.

Students wanted more money spent on education
the "modernization of curricula"
& "reduced spending on nuclear arms"
plus the war in Vietnam & US facilities in Paris
         were targets of student derision

In Paris there was street fighting, barricades, overturned autos
            (some of them burning)

and "industrial action" by French workers which, at its peak,
      came close to a general strike
      so that the economy was halted
      in an action that lasted till late June

Farmers on their tractors wheeled to the cities
to join the students
demanding: full employment
             fair taxation
             higher income
             a larger voice in government

In the end de Gaulle promised university reform
and the French industrialists
         a 10% increase in wages that very year
(plus 1 to 2 hours of work reduction per week)
and a 33% rise in the minimum national wage

        Great victories for workers!

(yet in the June National Assembly elections
      the Gaullists improved their position in the gov't)

May 3–June 23
    Not such a great victory for the poor in America as
    the Poor People's March went forward, Memphis to DC
      led by the Reverend Ralph Abernathy Jr.
         but without the overwhelming power
            it would have had under King

They were able to muster about 50,000 in DC
         but not the 500,000 the great King

      with his call for the reform
         of the capitalist structure
            could have attracted

Yet on May 7
    Robert Francis Kennedy won the Indiana primary
      & seemed on his way to bring about
         some of the proposals of the great King

Smut-maddened FBI honchos
set up a new branch
of its Counterintelligence Program
                    this one targeting the New Left

One of its first goals was to smear what they called
                                    Key Activists—
as a Bureau Memorandum of 5-9-68 stark-inked it:

"The New Left has on many occasions viciously and scurrilously
attacked the Director and the Bureau in an attempt to
hamper our investigation of it and to drive us off the college
campuses. With this in mind, it is our recommendation
that a new Counterintelligence Program
be designed to neutralize the New Left and the Key Activists. . . .

"The purpose of this program is
                    to expose,
                            disrupt and
                                    otherwise neutralize
the activities of this group and persons connected with it. . . ."

            All FBI offices
                    were required to "submit an analysis of possible
                    counterintelligence operations on the New Left and
                    on the Key Activists on or before 6-1-68."

            Cull that smut, o secret police!

──────────────── **The Catonsville Nine** ────────────────
May 11

In Catonsville, MD
        9 demonstrators took 400 individual draft files
                            and burned them in a parking lot

        They were Reverend Phil Berrigan and Thomas Lewis,
        Father Dan Berrigan, Brother David Darst, John Hogan,
        Thomas Melville, Mrs. Marjorie Melville, George Mische
        and Mary Moylan

all taken to jail & ultimately to 2 to 3 & 1/2 year terms

American heroes

──────────────── A Sleazesome Robo-Diary ────────────────
May 18

The 9:45 am entry in Sirhan Sirhan's diary
shuddered the era:

"My determination to eliminate R.F.K. is becoming more the more of an
unshakable obsession port wine   port wine   port wine   R.F.K. must die—
RFK must be killed Robert F. Kennedy must be assassinated R.F.K. must be
assassinated R. F. K must be assassinated R.F.K. must be assassinated. . ."
    —and repeated nine more times before the grim words:

"Robert F. Kennedy must be assassinated before 5 June '68. . . ."

Although it appears to me that the words 5 June '68
were written in a different handwriting
and that the pages of this diary
                might have been written during robo-mumble

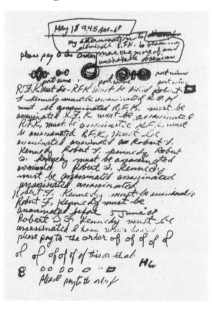

Speaking of sleazesome robo-mumbles
the record of history is clear
that the CIA worked long & hard
to develop techniques of mind control
& even to create what could be termed
                    hypno-robotic killers
                        w/ very bad memories

(see pp. 264 & 283
of *America, A History in Verse, Volume 2*
for info on the CIA's successful research
                    at getting people to do things
                    for which they have no memory
            particularly the technique known as Artichoke)

The record is also quite clear
that a good amount of mind-control research
                    was conducted in California—

Take the case of the one-time supermodel Candy Jones
who, as believably traced in the 1976 book
                    The Control of Candy Jones
worked twelve years ('60–'72) as an
                    unwitting
                        courier for the CIA

Her programmer was a doctor in California
who created within her an alternative personality
which was summoned forth by means of
            the good Doctor speaking
                        hypno-phrases
            sometimes by telephone

The courier work was done by the alternate personality.

The book reveals that on June 3, 1968
Candy Jones was brought to a CIA-funded institute
in California for a seminar
                    conducted by another CIA robo-official.

One question that awaits further releases
of CIA/California robo-research history

is whether Sirhan Sirhan
came into their clutches
& maybe even James Earl Ray himself
(when he was in Los Angeles
in early '68)

Too weird?
Nothing is too weird for 1968

──────────── **Spank Spank for Burning Draft Cards** ────────────
1968

the Supreme Court in *US v. O'Brien* ruled against
a Draft Card Burner named David O'Brien
who'd been sent to prison for burning his in '66

Young men had to carry their draft cards at all times
it was the law
(though many of us didn't.   I burned mine
at a rally the spring o' '68)

but the Supreme Court upheld his conviction
siding with the "smooth and efficient function" of the draft system

May 24
There was a standing ovation for the defendants
as a judge sentenced
Father Philip Berrigan and Thomas Lewis
(from Artists Concerned about Vietnam)
for pouring human & duck blood
onto draft files the previous October

Berrigan had said at the pouring
that the USA would
"rather protect its empire of overseas profits than welcome
its black people, rebuild its slums and cleanse its air and water"

──────────────── **The Pulsars Pass-Over** ────────────────
1968

The work of an Irish grad student named Jocelyn Bell
detecting certain radio signals
from space
went unhonored in the rolls of glory

As a member of a research team at Cambridge U
        Jocelyn Bell was the one who detected strange signals
                that pulsed at 1.5-second intervals

It was thought at first that perhaps
        they were the pulses of
                extraterrestrial life

The research team concluded finally
that the blips came from a quickly spinning object
        around 4,000 miles in diameter

Now, decades later, it's believed pulsars are
neutron stars
        —the debris/remnants of exploding stars called supernovas

Jocelyn Bell was passed over when the '74 Nobel Prize went
to a couple o' members of the Cambridge team

May 28
    McCarthy won o'er Robert Kennedy
        in the Oregon Democratic primary

        Kennedy gulped, but then
        revved up his famous vim
            for the California primary
        a week ahead

May 29
    the Truth-in-Lending Act
        was signed by LBJ
    to require that interest data and lending terms
    be disclosed to potential borrowers BEFORE the signing
        of any loan agreement

    + the act "standardized" methods of disclosing interest rates
        by credit card companies and banks

May 30
    The Beatles began the White Double Album
        at the Abbey Road studios in London
        Yoko Ono was on hand for the first time
        as the young men

did take 1 through 18
                of "Revolution 1"

        —the last 6 minutes of the final take
                were used as "Revolution 9"

June 3
    The artist named Andy Warhol
    had a fancy new studio
            on the north side of Union Square
                    with its long park sacred to
                    the history of unions & workers' rights

    A writer & actress named Valerie Solanas
    that afternoon entered the studio
                and shot Mr. Warhol with a .32 automatic
                Warhol survived, barely

June 4
    John Lennon re-recorded the lead vocal
    for "Revolution"
                lying flat on his back
                        at the studio on Abbey Road

That afternoon
    Sirhan Sirhan went target practicing
                    in the company of a pretty young woman
            quick-firing 300 to 400 rounds with a .22
            at the San Gabriel Valley Gun Club
                        in Duarte, outside LA

The same day Soviet tanks and troops
                    bullied their way into Czechoslovakia
                                ostensibly for maneuvers

June 6
    Just after midnight
            Robert Kennedy was shot
                    and slid to the floor in front
                        of the ice cabinet
                            in the Ambassador kitchen

                in his hour of victory

(see *1968, A History in Verse*, for a more complete account
of his assassination)

June 10
General William Westmoreland
forked over command in Vietnam to Creighton Abrams

& no end in sight to kill-philia

June 20
US combat deaths now numbered over 25,000

June 26
Earl Warren quit as head of the Supreme Court
Warren sensed ah too well that
his opponent Nixon might be icumen in
so he wanted to give LBJ a chance to appoint a
new Chief Justice

Within days the President chose Associate Justice Abe Fortas
after which there was a filibuster of rage
from Southern senators
& a sequence of stories about
Fortas's financial affairs
such as the fees he received for lectures
so that, alas in the sands of time,
that coming October
Fortas wd ask his name to be withdrawn

July 1
The US, the Soviet Union and 59 others signed the
Nuclear Nonproliferation Treaty

July 3
The Beatles began work
on the theme song of '68
"Ob-la-di, Ob-la-da"

& the next day Paul McCartney
laid down the lead vocals
in the amazingly fast way
their Muses allowed

July 4
>The starvation in Biafra became a issue
>>among many Americans

>England kept selling arms to Nigeria
>>—money from pain keeps an empire crisp—
>while it at the same time offered famine-easing food to Biafra

>Biafra said no thanks on July 4,
>>not while you're selling weapons to N

>>& then on August 18 1,000
>>gathered to pray
>>in front of the UN building
>>to urge the UN nations
>>>to run the blockade with food

>>—as the gaunt eyes of starvation
>>on television & newspaper photos
>>were stirring opinion
>>>in favor of Biafra

————————— **Right-Wing Cuban Terror** —————————
the summer after MLK

For all my adult life
>no real colloquy on Castro and Cuba
could be conducted safely in the United States
because of the threats of right-wing Cubans
like a sleaze-slash of CIA-funded metal-winged
>>>>hornets

>>as when in early July right-wing Cubans
>>began a campaign of bombing and terror in NYC:

July 5 they bombed the Canadian and Australian tourist offices
& July 8 another bomb hurting two at the Japanese tourist bureau
>>(the goal was to stop them
>>>from helping travelers
>>>>go to Cuba)

and then, the same month, they fired a grenade
>>into the Grove Press offices on University Place,

invaded a NYC radio station,
& bombed the Cuban and Yugoslav missions.

The 20th-century curse on free discourse from
right-wing Cuban-Americans
fell like caustic spittle on the Bill of Rights
but it was successful

———————— **Four Tracks to Eight Tracks** ————————
July 31

Having made some of the best music of the era
on 4 track recorders
the Beatles for the first time
used an 8-track!

as they added overdubs to
the great meandering tune "Hey Jude"

———————— **Erie Is Dead** ————————

Lake Erie was declared a "dead" lake—it was so polluted—
by the House of Representatives

———————— **Nixon Is Here** ————————
August 8

at the Republican Convention in Miami Beach
Nixon promised "to bring an honorable end to the
Vietnam War"

Sure, Tricky, sure

The Convention selected Spiro Agnew
to be his "running mate"
over Gov George Romney of Michigan

———————— **The Soviets Invade Czechoslovakia** ————————
August 20–22

200,000 troops from th' Sov U, Poland, Hungary, Bulgaria and E Germany
crossed into Czechoslovakia
to crush any evolving

"Socialism with a human face"
as Alexander Dubcek had termed it

Dubcek was arrested and hauled to Moscow
while the occupying army went to 650,000

I didn't like the image of Soviet tanks
in the ancient city of Prague
to enforce censorship of rock lyrics
the banning of political clubs
& many other excesses

as when the night of the 22nd
the Soviets seized the national radio station in Prague

It was just before the police riots
in Chicago

—— Garden Plot & the Agents-to-Demonstrators Ratio ——

Arriving in Chicago were between 5 and 6,000 demonstrators
of which, as Military Intelligence told CBS
1 out of 6 were undercover agents.

Also on hand were 6,500 National Guard troops on the streets
and 5,000 Army personnel nearby.

As we have seen, Army Intelligence, a branch of the
Defense Intelligence Agency

had set its agents into action against the anti-war counterculture.
Earlier in '68 the 113th Military Intelligence Group, at
Ft. Sheridan outside Chi,
began supplying the right-wing Legion of Justice terrorist group with
Mace, surv equipment, money, and tear gas to go after the anti-wars

& the Legion of Justice used wiretapping equipment supplied

by Army Intelligence to bug and to break into the
                                        offices of the anti-wars

It was all part of the huge government scheme known as
                                        Garden Plot

set up in 1968 to bring the military into close coordination
with domestic police
                        to deal with the anti-wars

It seems that part of the Garden Plot apparatus
was set into motion in Chicago

The operation was code-named Rancher III
and was directed out of the Army Security Agency
                        (an arm of the National Security Agency)
                                        headquartered in Arlington, VA.
Rancher III utilized Army and Air Force intelligence units from
                                        Texas, VA & Illinois

All these agents did nothing to stop
                the Chicago police from bloodying those who
                stood chanting "The Whole World Is Watching"
                                outside the Chicago Hilton

──────── **The Democratic National Convention** ────────
August 24–28

Meanwhile, glowering like a war-crazed deity in a
                                William Blake poem
Lyndon Johnson I think expected the Convention
to rise up out of its chaos
                & call him forth
                        as a Savior Candidate.

Johnson threatened Hubert Humphrey if he dared to
                wobble even a microwobble
                from the fury of the war

And then, no doubt to the jubilation of the war caste
Hubert Humphrey was nominated August 29
                while the streets raged with protest &
                                head-bashing police

276

Humphrey lacked the savvy & fortitude
to tell the vengeful Johnson to go to hell
napalm hell   Phoenix hell   fragmentation bomb hell
carpet-bomb hell   Agent Orange hell   Body Bag hell

     but the peppy former mayor of Minneapolis
     from the unified Democratic & Farmer-Labor Party
          trembled like
          a sick bird in a bush.

The Convention was conducted
like a casting call for a movie about
          incipient fascism

with goons shoving & jostling

& so while Hubert Horatio Humphrey was being nominated
(and the violence raged in the streets of Chicago)

CBS-TV's Dan Rather gave a live report
from the convention floor:
"A security man just slugged me in the stomach,"
to which Walter Cronkite replied,
        "I think
        we've got a
        bunch of thugs
        here, Dan."

Meanwhile Senator George McGovern
put himself forth as a last-minute peace candidate
after McCarthy refused to lead a floor fight
          against Humphrey

Senator Abraham Ribicoff was giving his nominating speech:
   "With George McGovern," said Ribicoff,
   "we wouldn't have Gestapo tactics on the streets of Chicago."

Mayor Richard Daley, his face reddened with malevolence,
shouted from the front row, "Fuck you, you Jew son of a bitch!
          You lousy motherfucker, go home!"

Ribicoff looked down at the red-faced mayor and said
          "How hard it is to hear the truth."

September 8
A few days later, in an interview in *The New York Times*
the racist police-statist J. Edgar Hoover
(who after all had lost his biggest money-makers
    since the death of Martin King & the
    shrinking of the Communist Party down to a few thousand
    many if not most of whom were FBI informers)
announced that the Black Panther Party
was "the greatest threat to the security of the country"

Sure, Edgar, sure

'68 was the year Mr. Hoover outsleazed himself
when he allowed a totally innocent man, not a mobster,
named Joseph Salvati
    to be given a life sentence in Boston
    for a mob hit he did not commit

    It wasn't just that the FBI turned its eyes away
    but the FBI deliberately framed Mr. Salvati
    whose wife visited him every week for 32 years
    while he languished in prison

    until the Bureau memos to Hoover
            on the frame
                came to light

Take that name off that building!

———————————— Miss America Protest ————————————
September 9

Protestors hooted at the Miss America contest that year
                           for its portrayal of women

A group called Radical Women threw bras, girdles, curlers, wigs
                           into a Freedom Trash Can

A sheep was crowned Miss America
and more & more were beginning to agitate for Women's Liberation

Not long thereafter, an activist ensemble called WITCH
for Women's International Terrorist Conspiracy from Hell
came to the Stock Exchange floor
to confound the cap-eyes

──────────────── **Nixon's Strategy** ────────────────

Since the stammery, cruel-crusted rightist campaign of '64
had been so easily mush-gushed to defeat
Nixon looked to a combination of ploys
to carry the fall

1. He said he had "a plan to end the war" (he didn't mention
all those upcoming years of bombing & deceit)
2. There was the first overt use of the "Southern Strategy"
which was to seek votes among those in the South
who hated the Civil Rights movement

(or Northerners who hated public housing in
non-ghetto areas)

Much of it was implied, as when
he made sure the Republican platform had an
anti-schoolbusing
plank
3. There would be safe streets, he promised
4. & tougher law enforcement
5. He blamed the Supreme Court for "permissiveness"
6. He would do something about an issue that was
displeasing a good portion of the public:
campus agitation
7. & finally he spoke to "the forgotten Americans. . . .
those who do not break the law,
people who pay taxes and go to work, who
send their children to school, who go to their
churches, people who love this country."

With Humphrey weak & confused
it was a strategy that would
squeak Nixon into the house of Lincoln

The American Independent Party
    met in Dallas on September 17 & nominated George Wallace

    and then Wallace announced on October 3
    that Curtis "When in doubt, bomb" LeMay would be his running
    mate.

A right-wing Texan named Nelson Bunker Hunt
(who had paid for the creepy ad in a Dallas newspaper
        the morning of John Kennedy's fatal trip to Dallas)
        set up a million-dollar trust fund
                    to lure the general aboard the ticket

————— **Pre-Olympic Slaughter in Tlatelolco Plaza** —————
October 2

    3,000 workers, students, teachers & parents in Mexico City
        came to the Plaza of the Three Cultures
        for a march to protest
                the ongoing gov't take-over
                of the Polytechnic Institute
                and several vocational schools

        It was a peaceful rally
        but the military thirsted for slaughter

        In the evening the uniformed army
        and what's often called "Paramilitary Forces"
            —i.e., right-wing slaughter-spores—

    surrounded the unarmed innocent students
    & "fired from every angle"
            as a book by Claudia Campuzano
            later revealed

        & as in Jackson State two years later,
        shot also into the surrounding buildings

        They murdered 300 innocent victims
        (though the Mexican gov't lied it was 28)
        and 200 more were wounded
                with 1,500+ arrested

They fire-hosed the blood from the plaza
for evil soaps evil
and then told lies about the victims
right up to the day I type this
on a laptop in Woodstock, NY

October 3
an emergency meeting of the International Olympic Committee
where by a single vote
it was decided the Olympics would continue

October 2
The right wing finally had its fangy way
as it often does in America

when a vote failed to cut off
a rightist filibuster in the Senate
against the selection of Abe Fortas
as Supreme Court Chief Justice

(14 shy of the 2/3 needed for cut-off)

and with the Senate just about to
go home for the year
the nomination was doomed

Johnson, wounded and weak of soul
said he'd let the next president place a potential
Chief J before the Senate

October 3
the silly, repressionist House Un-American Activities Committee
had subpoena'd the Yippie known as Jerry Rubin
who arrived to give his insights
into the Chicago police riots
bearing a toy M-16, face paint & Viet Cong trousers

—one of Rubin's best moments

——————— **A Trace of Treason in the Fall, I** ———————
October

Anna Chennault, a DC conservative activist &
widow of General Claire Chennault, as reported by columnist

Jack Anderson, "was picked up on tape as she allegedly lobbied
with the South Vietnamese Ambassador to sabotage a peace
conference on the eve of the 1968 US Presidential election."

Anderson wrote that his "excellent sources" told him
she was secretly taped warning the South Vietnamese Ambassador
Biu Diem that Humphrey was going to pull US troops
from Vietnam right away when elected
then the commies wd take over
& gov't officials would be executed

Mrs. Chennault was acting as an agent of Nixon
when she issued her warning
which was forwarded to Saigon

where it had the effect of disrupting a planned peace conference.
The Saigon's gov't denounced the peace conference
& President Nguyen Van Thieu
(elected in a sham in '67)
said he'd not participate

──────────── **A Trace of Treason in the Fall, II** ────────────

After a faulty start, Hubert Humphrey
closed the gap with Nixon
He'd broken with LBJ on the issue
of escalation of the war
was about a single percentage point behind
& seemed likely to squeak to victory

but Henry Kissinger stopped it. How?
Through a trace of treason.

During '67 Kissinger had won the
trust of the US secretary of defense
by offering to do secret shuttle diplomacy
to Paris to see if the NV were
ready to negotiate

He tried, but no dice.
Then, after the '68 Conventions
Kissinger again came to Paris to the Talks
pretending he was pro Humphrey.

He picked up inside information that Johnson
was going to call a bombing halt by October 15
without NV agreeing first to stop the war

Negotiators Averill Harriman and Cyrus Vance believed
they'd gotten SV approval for the Conference
    and then Kissinger leaked it to Nixon's campaign
    who tipped off Anna Chennault.

The war would gore onward for 6 more years
during which time 25,000 Americans
and how many hundreds of thousands of Vietnamese
                                        would die

    Only a few dared call it treason
    and Kissinger, old but still harumphing
                as I write this

    will soon be just a headstone & harsh memories
    & never punished
    except by the invisible spatters of
                needless blood from his heedless ego

    & if it wasn't treason
    it was a kind of mass murder
                —all for a few years of power

October 11–22
    Apollo 7
        with a crew went up to orbit, testing the moon system

October 20
    Jacqueline Kennedy wed Aristotle Onassis

        It was announced that the couple would divide
        their moments of breathing
        'tween NY, Athens, Paris, Montevideo, Monte Carlo &
                    the Greek Islands.

The ghosts of the gunned-down students seemed nowhere there
as the USA won 45 gold medals
the USSR 30, Japan 11
in the contest of the nations

but the highlight for those
opposing American racism
was the stunning tableau of October 17

when Tommie Smith and John Carlos
won 1st & 3rd in the 200-meter run
& then each raised a fist in a black glove
during the National Anthem
on the victors' platforms

It was a moment for America

but hated at the time as
they were tossed from the Olympics the next day

On October 28
after serving as a CIA officer working on
the Olympics

Philip Agee was even more troubled than ever
as he wrote in his *CIA Diary*

on the final day of the Olympics:
"The CIA, after all, is nothing more than the secret
police of American capitalism, plugging up leaks in the
political dam night and day
so that shareholders of US companies
operating in poor countries
can continue enjoying the rip-off.
The key to CIA success is
the 2 or 3 percent of the population
in poor countries that get most of
the cream. . . ."

Nixon's Image

Gone in '68
was the the Lazy Shave look of 1960

In its place was the New Nixon:
statesmanlike, mature, secure

He said he had a plan to end the nightmare of Nam
and then on October 22, '68 a Nixon staffman saw
a "Bring Us Together" poster
at a campaign rally in Deshler, Ohio

It was brought to N's attention
and he began using it as a hook line

William Safire recalled it when writing N's
post-victory statement

"We want to bring America together again."

November 1, 1968
On television Lyndon Johnson
announced a halt to the bombing of North Vietnam

and that North Vietnam in exchange
would allow the South Vietnamese gov't
to participate in the Paris talks

—a bit too late to help Humphrey

November 5
   Nixon 31,770,237 over Hubert Humphrey at 31,270,533
   and Wallace/LeMay at 9,906,141.

The Democrats kept its majority in Congress

Nixon won by only .7 of one percent
He won the entire West, the Upper South, and the
Border states, and some of the Midwest industrial states

(Pre-election surveys had predicted a bigger turnout
      for Wallace than actually occurred. He won 45 electoral votes
         and 13% of the popular vote)

            Some blamed the streets of Chicago
                              for Humphrey's defeat
            but the truth is that
                     Humphrey defeated Humphrey
                              &
                     Johnson defeated Humphrey
                              &
                     Nixon defeated Humphrey
                              &
                     & maybe a little nudge from the
                     Military-Industrial-Surrealists
                              defeated Humphrey
                              &
            the thirst for Domestic Tranquility
                     defeated the War Party

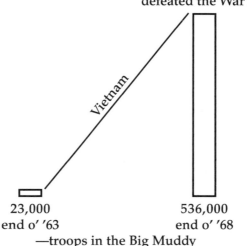

            23,000   536,000
         end o' '63   end o' '68
            —troops in the Big Muddy

November 12
    Arr Harr!
    the US Supreme Court
        tossed away
        a law in Arkansas
        which banned the teaching of evolution in public schools
                                                            Arr Harr!

———————————————— **The Walker Report** ————————————————
                            December 1

            It was officially known as *Rights in Conflict*
            and ran for 233 pages

            after a 212-member team
            run by Daniel Walker
            president of the Chicago Crime Commission

            started hearings on September 27
                    heard 1,410 witnesses
                            & read thousands of FBI reports

            watched oodles of newsreels & photos

            The Walker Report confirmed that "at times"
            the fuzz sank Chi
                    to a "police riot"

            in the malevolent spirit of Mayor Daley's
            "Shoot to kill" blurble
                    after the MLK murder

December 9
    a group called Zero Population Growth was founded
            by Paul Ehrlich, Charles Remington, Richard Bowen
                to push the population increase
                        down to zero

            in a human equation
                    where the thirst for replication
                            seems the final calculus

287

December 15
    a new Greek Constitution was inaugurated
        but thanks to CIA repression-assisters
            the "articles on personal freedom"
                    were suspended

December 16
    476 years too late
        Spain "voided" its 1492
            decree from Ferdinand and Isabella
                tossing out Jews

December 21
    the first astronauts
    took off from Cape Kennedy
    James Lovell, William Anders, Frank Borman
        & reached an orbit of the moon on Christmas Eve
        Ten times they circled it, with
        direct TV transmissions to earth

    (back in September the Russian *Zond 5* spacecraft
        had successfully orbited Selena also)

        On Christmas Eve
            the 3 astronauts
                broadcast live to earthlings

            some of whom were stringing
                tinsel on Christmas trees.

By '68's close
    warlike America had over a million soldiers
        stationed here and there around the world

    It had almost 2,000 bases on the globe
    It had its CIA in around 60 countries
    It armed an additional 2 million troops here and there
    many under the control of military dictatorships

    The Mil–Ind–Surrs seemed to cherish
                military gov'ts

        which was one of the reasons I was beginning

to question the benignity of the
US space hunger

Would it ultimately be used
for space guns, arrogant colonies
and wars on Mars?

1968 losses to the dust:
February 4 Neal Cassady just before his 42nd birthday
April 16 Edna Ferber at 80
the great socialist Helen Keller on June 1 at 87
June 14 Salvatore Quasimodo at 67
Ruth St. Denis on July 21 at 90
Oct 2 Marcel Duchamp at 81
Upton Sinclair brilliant socialist at 90 on Nov 26
Norman Thomas of the Socialist Party
            on December 19 at 84
Dec 20 John Steinbeck at 66

————— Advice from Warhol: "Don't Blink" —————
1968

Andy Warhol
was having his 1st Euro-retrospective
at the Modern Museum in Stockholm
& in the catalog essay he scribed
his famous
        "In the future everyone
        will be famous
            for 15 minutes"

Mad Science—Measles for the Yanomami
————— & Neutrons for the Testicles of Prisoners —————
1968

In his book *Darkness in El Dorado—How
Scientists and Journalists Devastated the Amazon*

Patrick Tierney traces some ghastly
activities of well-known geneticist James Neel
in 1968
        accusing Neel & a colleague of deliberately injecting
        Yanomami tribespeople
                in southern Venezuela

with a virulent measles vaccine
in order to trigger a measles epidemic
which killed hundreds & maybe thousands

while refusing to provide any medical assistance
to the ill & dying Yanomami

apparently to test Mr. Neel's theory
            that the survival-of-the-fittest
            Yanomami ethos
            should have selected certain ones
                for greater survival due to
                stronger immune systems

There was plenty of mad science in the 1960's
For example, in 1968, as traced by Eileen Welsome
            in her finely written *The Plutonium Files*

a doctor at the University of Washington
who had conducted experiments at the
            Washington State Penitentiary
                x-raying the testicles of inmates
                    to see what happened
            (see pp. 375–380 of *The Plutonium Files*)

proposed that he be allowed to bombard testicles
                        at the same prison
                                with neutrons.

The doctor was turned down
            then appealed the turn-down

but was ultimately stopped by the brave resistance
of a woman named Audrey Holliday
who headed the research division
            of the Washington Department of Institutions

Good for you, Audrey Holliday.

The often highly armored and ultrasmug psyches
of death researchers and macho scientists
snarl starkly
            in defense of
                their "research"

Welsome is particularly good at depicting
the macho post-Nazi God-on-my-side mentality of those
who relished injecting plutonium
into the unsuspecting

Novum Sub Sole '68:
state-financed nursery schools were set up in Italy—yes!
the first 911 emergency phone system, in NYC
waterbeds, the Jacuzzi
huge amounts of oil were discovered in Alaska
under land by the Arctic Ocean

Libri '68:
Eldridge Cleaver's *Soul on Ice*
Allen Ginsberg   *Airplane Dreams*
John Updike   *Couples*
a ghastly look at early '60s Republican suburbanites
Gore Vidal   *Myra Breckinridge*
Gary Snyder   *The Back Country*
Richard Brautigan   *Trout Fishing in America*
Gunslinger, Book I   Edward Dorn
Philip Dick   *Do Androids Dream of Electric Sheep?*
(made into the film *Blade Runner* in '82)
Tom Wolfe's *Electric Kool-Aid Acid Test*
Herbert Marcuse   *Psychoanalysis and Politics*
Noam Chomsky's *American Power and the New Mandarins*
The Joys of Yiddish by Leo Rosten

the first issue of the *Whole Earth Catalogue*

Paul Ehrlich's *Population Bomb*
with the dire prediction that the world's population
increasing more quickly than the food supply
would cause water rationing in the USA by '74
& food rationing by 1980
—so much for prophets

Music from Big Pink by the Band
"Mrs. Robinson"   Simon and Garfunkel
Joni Mitchell   *Song to a Seagull*
Marvin Gaye   "I Heard It Through the Grapevine"
Beggars' Banquet from the Rolling Stones
& from the Fugs   *It Crawled into My Hand, Honest*
& Tenderness Junction

Not always, but sometimes
those with skill at apothegms & condensations
                        can sway a culture

& so it was with a group of women writers those years
such as the activist Kathie Sarachild
who fashioned the phrase "consciousness-raising"
            and the power-sentence "Sisterhood is Powerful"

Upcoming in '70 was *Notes from the Second Year*
in which Carol Hanisch brought to a larger audience
            the concept that "the personal is political"

& that the personal-political synapse
resided in all rooms: the bedroom, the boardroom, the kitchen sink
full of dirty dishes, the washroom, the warroom, the doomroom,
                        the dourroom, the doughroom.

And then there were a number of influential publications

>   *Voice of Women's Liberation*   in Chicago
>   *It Ain't Me Babe*   in Berkeley
>
>   *off our backs*   in DC
>   *No More Fun and Games*   in Boston
>
>   Women's liberation groups those years
>   set up the first battered women's shelters,
>   rape crisis centers, abortion counseling centers,
>   feminist book stores
>
>   & between '68 & '70
>   there were women-forged lawsuits in over 20 states
>   to remove laws against abortion

Movies '68:
    The Producers   a great film from Mel Brooks
    Stanley Kubrick's *2001: A Space Odyssey*
    Night of the Living Dead
                Rosemary's Baby   *The Odd Couple*

Zeffirelli's *Romeo and Juliet*
        Planet of the Apes

Potato: "Laugh-In"   "Hawaii Five-O"
          & on September 24, 1968
          the first broadcast of the News Magazine
          "60 Minutes," which while never really straining
              the strict big-corporate leash of CBS
              nevertheless
                  delivered some truth & reality
                  to Americans
                      during the next few decades

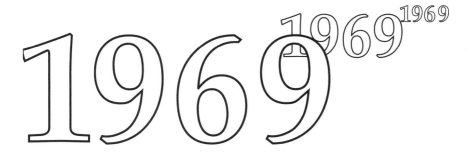

40% of American workers were women

January 4
    Students from Queens University in Belfast
    held a 4-day protest walk from Belfast to Londonderry
    for one person/one vote rights for Catholics
           & for abolition of the requirement that
           you had to own property to vote.

        200 Protestants in Londonderry
        with sticks and stones
        bashed into the 100 marchers
              chasing them & wounding many with
                            head-cudgel

January 7
    smooth-mouthed Ronald Reagan
    asked the California Legislature to
        "drive criminal anarchists and latter-day Fascists" off campuses

January 14–15
    The Russian *Soyuz 4 & Soyuz 5* were the first manned vehicles
                                        to dock together in space

---------------------------------- **Nixon** ----------------------------------

brought in Henry Kissinger, Nelson Rockefeller's associate
                      to be his National Security Advisor
Kissinger had offered to work for Humphrey,
          but secretly worked for Nixon's election
                    as we have seen

Kissinger was what they called a power freak
He was vindictive, quick to anger
and he had a Cosmic Ego, as if he'd taken too much acid
                without actually taking any
He was a secrecy-batty would-be Metternich
               who, the time-track will reveal,
               cared not many whits
                    for napalmed civilians
                    & glazed eyes in the world's ditches

       Nixon selected humans named H. R. Haldeman
       & John Ehrlichman
            as his "personal aides."

       They were living labs of "power corrupts"
           & served as his political knife-men

       All three were classic examples of what the historians
       Charles & Mary Beard once called
           "advisers swollen with infallibility"

------------ **Nixon Begins Sneak-Bombing Cambodia** ------------
                 early 1969

       They didn't call him Tricky Dick for nothing
       as Nixon now began 14 months of secret bombings
                       from B-52s
       on neutral Cambodia
       which he hid by falsification of Air Force records.

       The CIA trained Cambodian "units" in
           CIA-compliant Greece

leading to a Khomeini-style karma
                              for Kampuchea
            —the bone bins of Pol Pot

January 26
    cashing in on his angry imperfections
    Lyndon Johnson sold his memoirs for $1.5 million
                              in '69 money

January
    10 hijackings of airliners to Cuba this month

January 28
    a nightmare of pollution
                    off Santa Barbara
        when an oil driller ruptured an "underground fault"
        spewing an otter-murdering
        underwater torrent of red-brown crude oil
                              up and out to the shores

        Environmentalists demanded the end of oil drilling
        in Santa Barbara Channel
                    & Feb 3 all drilling was halted

February 3
    The Palestine Liberation Organization
                    selected Yasir Arafat as its chair

    Arafat had founded the Al Fatah guerrilla group in '63
    which now made up the most powerful component
                    in the loose array of groups in the PLO

February 6
    Peru seized the International Petroleum Company
                              and all its holdings

        Nationalize   Nationalize   Nationalize

        & roll those eyes

────────── **Cable Splicer/Garden Plot** ──────────
February 10

Cable Splicer was the name of Garden Plot exercises
    held in California
            to train for confronting domestic dissent

At a Cable Splicer planning meeting on February 10
Governor Reagan of California told 500 military men,
police officials and various corporate executives that if
his political enemies could see him
heading up such a meeting
            then they would know for sure he
                "was planning a military takeover"

────────── **Supreme Court Okays Anti-war Armband** ──────────
February 24

Mary Beth Tinker wore a black armband
against the war
            to her 8th-grade classes
            in Des Moines

She was suspended in December o' '65

& thereafter the case wended slowly to DC
till 1969 Ms. Tinker won! &
Justice Fortas wrote that "state-operated schools
may not be the enclaves of totalitarianism"

A Quiet Moment for America

March 6
    Sirhan Sirhan testified he didn't recall killing Robert Kennedy

March 9
    there was a sleep-in at Columbia U
            of almost 100 women from Barnard College
            wanting co-ed dorms

March 3–13
    Apollo 9
        tested the moon vehicle in Earth orbit

then on May 22 *Apollo 10*—
　　another test in which the "lunar module"
　　　　went down to within 50,000 feet of the Moon

　　　　　Kennedy's promise almost fulfilled

March 11
　　James Earl Ray
　　　　(in a move that made him chew his knuckles
　　　　in shdn't-have-done-it-hood
　　　　　　for the next three decades)
　　　　　　　pleaded guilty to killing Martin King

　　　　and today arrived at the Tennessee State Prison
　　　　　　　　　　to serve a 99-year jail term

　　　　He had tried to speak of a conspiracy when he entered his plea:

　　　　"Your honor," he said,
　　　　"the only thing I have to say is that I can't agree with Mr. Clark."

　　　　The Attorney General Ramsey Clark
　　　　　　　& Hoover of the FBI
　　　　　　　had concluded that Ray acted alone.

March 20
　　Edward Kennedy suggested the US close its bases on Taiwan

　　　　grrr　　grrr　　grrr
　　　from the mil-ind-surr's

March 25–31
　　John Lennon and new wife Yoko Ono
　　　　　held their famous "Bed-In for Peace"
　　　　　on their honeymoon
　　　　　　　at the Amsterdam Hilton

　　"We're lying in bed for a week," said Lennon,
　　"to register our protest against all the suffering & violence
　　　　　　　　　　　　　　　　　in the world"

March 28
   Dwight David Eisenhower
      World War 2 hero & former president
      died in DC
         of heart disease

— Hoover Sabotages the Panther Free-Breakfast Program —

      On orders from bloat-faced Eddie Hoover
      who certainly never missed his breakfast
      the FBI
         disrupted the Panther
                  Free-Breakfast programs
                  around the nation

      such as in San Diego
      where the FBI made anonymous phone calls
      to a Catholic Church official
      complaining about a certain priest's involvement
      in the Free-Breakfast Program

      Why? Did they like the idea
                  of hungry children?

—————— Nixon Plays the "I Am a Madman" Card ——————

Nixon wanted the communists to believe
he was crazy, a "madman"
         so he plunked down the
         right-wing Tarot card known as
                  Hooded Bonk-Bonk

"I want the North Vietnamese to believe I've reached the point
where I might do anything to stop the war,"
         he told his key assistant H. R. Haldeman
         just as Ike had threatened China and NK with nukes
                                             in secret

      Nixon thought the "I am a madman" persona
      with bonk-stressed fingers on red nuke buttons

      would bring Ho Chi Minh to Paris
                  "in two days begging for peace."

America was burning with anger in the streets
and Nixon had to announce a de-escalation—

so during the upcoming summer
        he announced SV forces would
take over some of the fighting then being done by Americans

It was called the "Nixon Doctrine"
a Vietnamization
and slow de-escalation of snuffing by US troops
accompanied by
            warcrimes-level bombing.

It was an old policy,
            going back to 1951
what the French had called *jaunissement*—
a "yellowing" of the battle.

    Didn't work back then
    Wouldn't work for Lazy Shave

──────────────── **The ABM** ────────────────

The military kept shoving an anti-ballistic missile system
                    at the taxpayers

With Nixon, they probably thought they could
it was something they might quickly foist
                upon an innocent Continent.

Early in '69 Senator Albert Gore Sr. of Tennessee
held hearings in which "leading scientists took positions against" ABM

Then in March
Nixon endorsed a system of missile sites called "Safeguard"
        but only a few were built
            and there was big opposition in Congress.

(The 1972 Strategic Arms Limitation Talks
had its Treaty on the Limitations of Anti-ballistic Missile Systems,
        which limited ABM bases in the USA & USSR)

    And so, dry-heaving in the time-track

the ABM was a bit like Dracula
dead at the end of one movie
alive in the next one's opening credits

1957 heave
1960 heave
1964 heave
    1969 heave

(1982 heave
2002 ho)

──────────── **Ridenhour Sends Letter on My Lai** ────────────
end of March '69

A soldier named Ron Ridenhour
           sometime during the first half of '68
was drinking a beer with someone in a tent
& heard the soul-tearing story of My Lai.
"I started to act on it, and I spent the remainder of my time
in Vietnam trying to locate people who had been there."

Ridenhour returned home where most of his relatives and mentors
told him to leave it alone, drop it, wall it off

At the end of March 1969, Ridenhour sent a letter to 30 congressmen
& senators. Congressman Morris Udall did something about it.

"He called on the House Armed Services Committee,"
                Ridenhour later recalled
"to call on the Pentagon to conduct an investigation, and they did so."

Ridenhour had the passion to keep pressing.
He telephoned the Pentagon's chief investigator
Colonel William V. Wilson, several times a week
        to bring forth the Feather of Justice

Ron Ridenhour, American Hero

──────────── **Daniel Ellsberg & the Pentagon Papers** ────────────

Ellsberg worked for the Rand Corporation
      "the brain trust" of the Air Force
          in Santa Monica

He joined the Defense Dept in '64
where he specialized in Vietnam
& became a gung-ho assistant
                in '66 to General Edward Lansdale

By '67 Ellsberg however was discouraged with the war—
Morton Halperin and Leslie Gelb then invited him to join the
supersecret Pentagon Papers Project
                late that summer

(The Papers whose official title was
"History of U.S. Decision Making Process on Vietnam Policy"
          were written & compiled 'tween June '67 and January '69.

              Upon its completion only 15 copies were made
              and those were classified "Top Secret")

Nixon won in '68
& Kissinger asked the president of Rand for a paper on
              options for Nam
              —Ellsberg was asked to write it.

Ellsberg, who thought Kiss/Nix might
              extricate America from the hemic mire

worked till March '69 on Vietnam for Kissinger
That same month he decided to read the entire Papers.
(Ellsberg had only worked on a section of it)

There was a copy stored at Rand.
& Ellsberg arranged to view it
then spent six months absorbing it, till the fall of '69

during which time he came to believe that Nixon
was not only not going to end the war
          but actually to increase the violence
            in order to force North Vietnam
              to accept a settlement
              on US terms

It appears that Ellsberg felt that Nixon
would mine Haiphong Harbor before
              the '72 elections

What to do?   what to do?
He started considering ways
how to release the Pentagon Papers to the public.

———— **CBS Kills "Smothers Brothers Comedy Hour"** ————
April 4

right-wing thud-a-duds
                    at the putatively liberal CBS
killed "The Smothers Brothers Comedy Hour"

accusing comedians Tom and Dick Smothers
of failing to submit tapes to network right wingers
                    for "previewing"
                    i.e. censorship
CBS right wingers
often cut out stuff that questioned the war
                    including Harry Belafonte

They replaced the Brothers with "Hee-Haw"

————————————— **Red Boots on Avenue A** —————————
early April

I left the Peace Eye Bookstore one early evening
and walked up Avenue A to our apartment
an old dental office with a marble fireplace
                    at 12th Street

I unlocked the door
and then I was rushed from behind
by 2 guys who tossed me to the floor
and pushed a knife against my throat

chanting "Where's the amphetamine,
                    Where's the amphetamine?"

I told them I never used amphetamine,
                    much less traded in it
and I swore to God
          I wasn't the one who'd burned them.

Finally, the one in the blue trenchcoat said,

"Hey man, the guy that burned us didn't have
                                    no red boots on."

And so my stylish red rock and roll boots
                    may have saved my life

— Pointing to an Underlurking Evil in Northern Ireland —
April 22

Bernadette Devlin, just 21 & newly elected to Parliament
from Belfast, Northern Ireland
gave her first speech
            in the House of Commons

                "There is no place for us, the ordinary peasant,
                in Northern Ireland.
                        It is a society of the landlords."

April 23
    Sirhan received a sentence of death in the cyanide chamber
                                                for RFK

May 9
    The secret bombing of Cambodia
                    was told to the public for the first time today
                    in *The New York Times*

            & the biasmophilic (violence-loving)
            would-be Metternich Henry Kissinger went bonkers.
            He called that day from Nix's pad in Key Biscayne
            three times to Hoover in DC
                    demanding to locate the "leaker"

    Wiretaps were ordered on two of the biasmophile's closest aides
    Morton Halperin and Helmut Sonnenfeld
                                and others

May 11
    Viet Cong rocket attacks and
                    ground surges
                        all over Vietnam

It was a situation that attracted the fierce national attention
                                                of the anti-war left

as 2,000 demonstrators fought National Guardsmen
            when UC Berkeley tried to evict street people
    from the vacant lot now known as People's Park.

They wanted to build some student housing on the 445′ x 275′ lot
when around 500 students, locals and faculty
        put down flowers, sod, statues and playground equipment

        Gov. Reagan then ordered in the National Guard
        & arrests continued for 3 days

        Then on May 15 James Rector, 25, a carpenter from San Jose
            was shot to death.

        500 mourners then went to Chancellor Roger Heyn's house
            chanting "murderer! murderer!"

    while as a guest gift from the
                        military-industrial-surrealist complex
        a National Guard helicopter
        hovered above those chanting "murderer!"
        and spew-sprayed them with a skin-stinging
        white powder alleged to have been used against the VC

                    Thanks, mil-ind-surr's

            (In the end, People's Park remained
            & the housing was not built)

May 15
    Abe Fortas quit the Supreme Court
                    under pressure

        a shame, because he was helping the Court
            to continue its freedom-expanding Warren pathway

        Right wingers were desperate to get him out of there
        and finally it came out he had received

$20,000 a year from the family foundation
of a financier in jail for selling unregistered securities.

      Warren Burger was chosen Chief Justice on May 21
      to succeed the great Earl Warren

Mr. Burger had been on th' District of Columbia Ct of Appeals
The Burger court was considered moderate
      supporting the right of women to have an abortion
      and also busing
         for racial balance
but the Nix-years began the Court's lurchy trek to the right
           through the '70s, '80s, '90s
      to the point where it could even
         steal an election

May 19
    The Supreme Court voted unanimously today
    to overturn two counts of Tim Leary's 1966 Federal pot bust

    declaring the federal laws unconstitutional that had
    required him to notify authorities and pay a tax
        when purchasing or importing the herb

      on grounds they violated the Fifth Amendment
      against self-incrimination

      It didn't stop the prosecution however
         because other state and federal
         anti-herb laws were kept in place.
    If you're very controversial
         & smoke pot in America
      they use it to get you

         —check what they did to
         Ken Kesey, for instance

——————— **The Climate of Sleaze Early in His Term** ———————
June 4

      Nixon's White House went tap-batty in 1969
      especially against newsmen
      & NSC & Defense Dept officials

It got the French secret fuzz even
to tap influential columnist Joseph Kraft
in Paris that spring

Mr. Biasmophile Henry Kissinger visited Hoover at the FBI on 6-4
to get a tap placed on Hedrick Smith
of *The New York Times*
after Smith wrote a column
that the first troop reductions would be announced
soon when Nixon and Vietnam's Nguyen Van Thieu
met at Midway Island

───────────── **Fiery Slime, Unlucky Ducks** ─────────────
June 22

Several miles of the Cuyahoga River in Cleveland
caught fire
on its slime of industrial waste

and just about the same moment it poofed to flame
2 ducks landed on the river
drifted
began choking
and died

───────── **Leftist Factions Fractiously Factioning** ─────────
June 23–24

There were group-rending oodles of squabbles
at the SDS National Convention in Chicago

'tween the Weatherman faction of national officers
and what one history book calls the
"disciplined subgroup from the neo-Maoist Progressive Labor Party."

Bernadine Dohrn led a walk-out of
around 700 delegates
who were partisans of the Weathermen faction
The Weatherman/PLP schism reduced SDS
to an historically typical biting, snarling
battle of sneery factions

while the Great Pain
that called for Solution
kept stacking skulls

──────────── **Bravery at the Stonewall Inn** ────────────
June 27

There comes a time when you stand up
in the slice-lines
no matter the end

and so on a day in late June on Christopher Street
an action for American freedom
as important
as the Berkeley Free Speech Movement

There was a police raid
at the Stonewall Inn
a gay bar on Christopher Street in the Village

The fuzz had a practice of lurching into gay bars
on blue-bash whim
to harass customers

Those at Stonewall finally had enough
of grrr-ing bullies
and there were 3 days of riots

Out of the Stonewall protests grew
a focused national network
of Gay and Lesbian organizations

Each year now on the last Sunday in June
big commemorations of Stonewall are held
with Gay Pride Marches in Chi, SF, NY, and
other places to say Never Again

July 9
the USDA banned DDT *pro tempore*
awaiting the results of studies

6 years after the history-trembling *Silent Spring*

July 14
Easy Rider opened starring Dennis Hopper,
Jack Nicholson, Peter Fonda as Captain America
& Steppenwolf's "Born to Be Wild."

July 16
Apollo 11 lifted aloft from Florida
with Edwin Aldrin, Neil Armstrong & Michael Collins aboard
on an 8-day trip to dusty Selena
and safely back

────────── **Friday on Chappaquiddick Island** ──────────
July 18

Edward Kennedy flew that afternoon from Boston
to Martha's Vineyard
and took a ferry to Chappaquiddick Island
a spit of sand
500 feet across from Edgartown, Mass

to a rented cottage where he took a swim
& then was driven back to the ferry &
across to Edgartown
where he raced JFK's boat Victura with a crew of 2
in the annual regatta

After the race he checked into the Shiretown Inn
and then returned to the cottage in Chappaquiddick
where he took a bath
heating his sore back

waiting for a party and cookout to begin
in honor of 6 women who had worked
on Robert Kennedy's campaign

Also at the party were 5 other men, including
Kennedy's driver, a Civil Defense official,
a former US attorney for Massachusetts, an attorney
and the president of a bank

Steaks were grilled outdoors
and the guests told campaign stories & sang

Around 11 pm Edward Kennedy asked his driver
for the keys to his Oldsmobile.
He said he was going to take Mary Jo Kopechne
who'd been one of Robert Kennedy's campaigners
to her hotel in Edgartown
                    before going to his own.

He turned onto School House Road
in the direction of the ferry
but instead of bearing left on Main Street
                            toward the ferry dock
he turned right onto Dike Road toward the beach

He drove about a half mile along Dike Road
till the Olds came upon a humpbacked unlit bridge
                                which angled to the left

Kennedy somehow steered to the right
                and the Oldsmobile crashed off the bridge
                and rolled over upside down
                into the pond below
where water rushed in through the windows

Kennedy apparently hit his head in the accident
He wasn't sure how he got out of the car
                but Mary Jo was trapped inside

He later testified he dived down repeatedly,
                            maybe 7 or 8 times
                            to no avail

Then he walked back to the cottage
a mile and a half away
& returned with 2 of the attorneys
who also tried to free Kopechne
                            but failed

Kennedy swam across the
water to Edgartown
                and to his hotel
                saying nothing
                    making no phone calls
                        to emergency crews

(there had been no phone at the Chappaquiddick cottage)

> Two bluefish anglers
> spotted the Olds in the water
> > in the morning

> They called the police
> & the car was traced to Kennedy

> That morning the Senator
> dictated a statement, which ended:

> "I was exhausted and in a state of shock. I recall walking
> back to where my friends were eating. There was a car
> parked in front of the cottage. I climbed into the back seat.
> I then asked for someone to bring me back
> > to Edgartown
> I remember walking around for a period of time
> and then going back to my hotel room.
> When I fully realized what had happened
> this morning I immediately contacted the police."

> "It marks the end of Teddy"
> > Nixon quipped to H. R. Haldeman
> > the next day
> while waiting to call the astronauts on the moon.

(An ex-cop named Anthony Ulasewicz had
been hired in the spring of '69 to do
> political investigation work for Nixon

John Ehrlichman, the very morning of Chappaquiddick,
wanted Ulasewicz to go to the Island
> and find out what was happening
He spent a week, then months,
> investigating the accident

He took pictures and drew diagrams
He posed as a reporter from various pubs
> including the *Philadelphia Inquirer*
and asked questions on the site

One of those he questioned was the writer Michael Crichton,
    who, a friend of Robert Kennedy,
            had gone to Chappaquiddick Island
    after the death

Immediately after Chappaquiddick, there's indication that
the forces of Nix began tapping
    Mary Jo Kopechne's house on Olive Street
    in Georgetown

    no doubt hoping to get eros-talk from
          her roommates
    about the cookout)

———————————— **The Sea of Tranquility** ————————————
July 20

Neil Armstrong
    piloted the 4-legged lunar landing module
       down upon the Sea of Tranquility
       dodging some boulders
          for a safe landing at 4:17 pm Eastern time

      "Houston, Tranquility Base here.
      The Eagle has landed."

    Six hours later, at 10:57, Mr. Armstrong descended
            to the poofy dust

      "That's one small step for a man," he said
      "one giant leap for mankind"

Something like 600 million were watching

Edwin "Buzz" Aldrin joined Armstrong within minutes
while the third crew member, Michael Collins
      orbited the moon on the command ship

Armstrong & Aldrin
hopped and bounded upon the dusty moon
    to the happiness of the nation
         for 2 hours & 21 minutes

They set up a tv camera   planted an outstretched American flag
collected rocks & set up scientific devices

> Then they re-entered the module
> for some sleep

> & a few hours later
> lifted away to the mother ship

Departing they left behind a gold olive branch
maybe as a gesture
                    to the scans of other civilizations

On a leg of the lunar module
was a plaque with the words
        "We Came in Peace for All Mankind"

It was a moment for America

──────────────── **Come Together** ────────────────
July 21

John Lennon & Yoko
had invited Tim Leary to come to Montreal
for one of their "Bed-Ins for Peace"
            to help in the recording of "Give Peace a Chance"

Leary had announced he was going to run
            against Reagan for California governor in '70
& Lennon asked what he could do for the campaign

> Leary suggested a song
> and Lennon began a tune based
> on Leary's campaign slogan, "Come together, join the party"

> which evolved into the Beatles hit "Come Together"
> It took the great group just 7 hours
> on July 21
>   to record the basic track at Abbey Road

Ten Years for Two Joints
July 28

2 1/2 years after poet John Sinclair's arrest
for rolling a couple of joints
             from a brown cookie crock
             to give to an undercover cop in Detroit

             who was pretending to be a volunteer
             for the Committee to Legalize Marijuana

the poet was sentenced to 10 years in prison
one of the most famous & unjust sentences
                          in the 1960s

The *Clearwater* Arrives at the Mouth of the Hudson
August 1

It was not quite as bad as the Cuyahoga in Cleveland
which actually caught fire back in June

but the Hudson River by '69
was oil-slicky, smelly with chem-waste
littered on its shores
             with the dreck of largess
& used as a toilet bowl
             by cities great & small.

The great song-writer & banjoist Pete Seeger
decided, with his wife Toshi and many friends
                          to begin the Healing of the Hudson

It took three years of reaching out to the public
(Seeger gave hundreds of benefits
and raised about a hundred thousand dollars himself

but the campaign also included
       —to the chagrin of a few of Seeger's leftist pals—
             reaching out to rich sailboat enthusiasts
                          & those with Hudson River estates)
to raise almost $200,000
to build a 106-foot sloop, the *Clearwater*
                          at a shipyard in Maine

with bunks for 15
and a tall main mast of Douglas fir.

At last the *Clearwater* made its maiden voyage from Maine
packed with Seeger & the Hudson River Sloop Singers
(raising $27,000 for the Great Healing
               with 25 concerts along the way)

till it passed through the Narrows
               & docked at the Statue of Liberty on August 1
where New York's impressive mayor, John Lindsay
               came aboard
               & took a turn at the tiller

               & then it sailed up the Hudson
          to begin its great work
               for the rest of the century
               & beyond

     It was a moment for America

─────────────── **Cielo Drive** ───────────────
August 8–9

His followers thought he was both Jesus & the Devil
& they lived in a peaceless frenzy of
sex, drugs, robbery, credit-card theft, music
          & their own fearful vision of
          a kind of racist Rapture
          & Final War

For reasons still not clearly revealed
the man named Charles Manson sent out his followers
to slaughter whoever was in the house
               on a hot night in early August
               at 10050 Cielo Drive
                    in Beverly Hills.

Slaughter they did
          till no more shrieks echoed faintly
               on the hillsides of Benedict Canyon

Dead were Abigail Folger, Voytek Frykowski, Jay Sebring,

Steven Parent, and the actress Sharon Tate
                    just about to give birth

They painted the word PIG in blood on the front door
& returned to the Spahn Movie Ranch
            where they were living
                    on the edge of the San Fernando Valley

Manson and a follower later that night went
            to the murder scene
                    to see what his spores had done.

The next night the horror team vom'd forth again
to the home of Leno and Rosemary LaBianca
who were tied up and slaughtered
                    a fork left jutting out of
                    Mr. LaBianca's stomach

August 11
    in Zambia
        President Kenneth Kaunda
                announced the nationalization of copper—

In the mid/late 20th-century US power structure
few things caused more flecks of rage-drool
than nationalization
                by a country
                smaller than France

———————— **Peace & Love at a Dairy Farm** ————————
                August 15–17

More than 400,000 came to Max Yasgur's farm
            in Bethel, Sullivan County, NY
                    for the Woodstock Festival

& heard some of the best popular music groups of the century
including Richie Havens, Joan Baez,
        Crosby, Stills, Nash & Young, the Who, Janis Joplin,
        Jefferson Airplane, Santana, Country Joe & the Fish,
        John Sebastian,
                & of course the great Jimi Hendrix
                with his heart-rending "National Anthem"
                        in the closing set

315

There was a drenching rain and oodles of LSD, pot,
nudity, fucking & communality

the birth of the freak-out tent
& Abbie Hoffman
            coming up with the concept of a
                        Woodstock Nation

with Free Food, Free Health Care, Free Fun, Free Music

            —a nation that still exists
            like a faintly burning coal
            in the stalk of Prometheus

            for Free has a power that awaits
                        its rightful centuries

August 20
        Black Panther Party Chair Bobby Seale
        was arrested for the murder of Alex Rackley
        whose body was found in Connecticut in May of 1969

        13 other Panthers, including Ericka Huggins,
                        were also arrested

        Rackley was a young Black Panther from NY
        suspected of being a police informant
        who was interrogated, tied to a bed, scalded,
                        then taken to a swamp and shot twice

        The actual executioner
        the one who had originally accused Rackley of being an informer
        was himself an FBI informant.

        (Charges against Seale & Huggins were dropped in '71)

─────────────────────── **The New Mobe** ───────────────────────
'69

        A new National Mobilization to End the War in Vietnam
        was formed after the Chicago riots
                        (excluding Yippies & SDS ers)

and began to work on 2 huge, upcoming
late-'69 Moratoriums

September 1
    27-yr-old Captain Muammar el-Khaddafi
    led a military coup on King Idris
        when the King was in Turkey tending to health problems

    and the Libyan Arab Republic was established
    whereafter Mr. Khaddafi set out to create a socialist/Islamic state

        Coming up soon: the nationalization of oil
        & many predictable years of
            military-industrial grrrs

Birth o' th' Nuke-Net
——————————— (Later the Internet) ———————————
September 2

    Two hefty computers
    were connected by a short gray cable

    & test-data were flowed between them
    in a lab at the University of California, Los Angeles

    —the birth of the computer network called Arpanet
        that would later become the Internet

    It was a Cold War project at first
    forged by the Defense Department
    for secret & secure communications
    able to survive in the aftermath
        of a nuclear war & its forestless
        melted eyeball nuclear winter
            with no telephone lines

September 2
    Ho Chi Minh
        passed away at age 79
        six years before Saigon would be renamed
            Ho Chi Minh City
    Ho had dedicated his life since 1919
    to the independence (& unification) of his nation

& since the 1920s to
         the creation of a Communist economy

———————— **Ridenhour Moves on My Lai** ————————
                    September

In early September 1969
        Lt. William Calley was charged for the My Lai massacre

Ron Ridenhour thought Calley would be the scapegoat
and no other officers charged. He said later
                            at a conference

he had felt "there were two massacres,
and Lt. Calley was one of many officers who,
            albeit too enthusiastically, followed orders"

so Ridenhour began his campaign to
            reach out to the press
            with his knowledge of My Lai

        It worked

"Suddenly, several weeks later, there was Sy Hersh. We connected,
and he took off from there."

        Seymour Hersh (then with a small press service)
        wrote a series of of dispatches on the case
        which helped change the course of the war

— **6-Year Secret US Bombardment in Laos Goes Public** —
                    September 7

We have traced how since 1964
US planes dropped gigantic amounts
            of napalm, defoliants, phosphor-bombs
            limb-shredding flechettes, and
                farmland wrecking explosives
        onto the successful *&* ancient farm area
        of the Plain of Jars in northeast Laos
During those years over 25,000 attack sorties were flown against
                the Plain of Jars

As the years went past
organized village life was impossible
            in the ever increasing sky-hell
so villagers moved deeper into the forests.
They farmed at night
            and lived in trenches, holes or caves

The multi-layer robotic bombing
                        was done in absolute secrecy
No American newspaper wrote about it
which changed in September '69
            when the US openly did its final
            evil to the Plain of Jars

            "The bombs fell like
                        a man mowing wheat"
            one villager told a reporter

    With the help of US soldiers
    the rightist gov't of Laos began a final offensive
    against the Plain of Jars
    to force the troops of the Pathet Lao away

In October of '69 any survivors were herded into refugee camps
        & nothing remained in the Plain of Jars
                    except for its ancient burial urns

    It was the model for layered robo-wars of the future

    Here's what Fred Branfman wrote
                in *Voices from the Plain of Jars*:

"The Plain of Jars, then, stands for far more than just a society of fifty
thousand that happened to be leveled. It is a very real symbol of
the fate awaiting Third World societies throughout the world unless
the capacity of the leaders of today's superstates to wage automated war
            unilaterally is checked."

    Branfman then asks "What does it mean when leaders
                of the richest and most technologically
                advanced nation in history use all their
                weaponry short of nuclear arms against rice

farmers who pose the most marginal of challenges
to their interests?"

It means that excessive worship of the Scythe
had captured the

Laos was also was the take-off point for
the CIA's Air America to ferry
heroin & opium into South Vietnam
for various drug lords.

The formula $D = QC$ (Dope = Quick Cash)
of course played a role in the century's history

& the formula $D + CIA = QC + A + V$ (arms & violence)
was a further crudescence of the equation

(See *The Politics of Heroin in Southeast Asia*,
by Alfred McCoy et al., for instance p. 155)

The Pathet Lao would ultimately prevail in Laos
but not till 1975

September 16
The Atomic Energy Commission
declared the Bikini Atoll in the Marshall Islands
safe for human occupation

From July '46 to '58
the cancer-spreaders had conducted some 23 nuclear tests
blowing up the atoll

(the original 167 residents had been resettled into
another island in the Marshalls)

——————————— **Chicago 8 Trial** ———————————
September 24

The Chicago 8 went to trial:
David Dellinger, Rennie Davis & Tom Hayden
of the National Mobilization to End the War in Vietnam

Abbie Hoffman & Jerry Rubin of the Yippies
John Froines, a chemistry teacher at the University of Oregon

Lee Weiner, a grad student at Northwestern University
& Bobby Seale, chair of the Black Panther Party

—all indicted for the rider placed on the 1968 Civil Rights Act
                    the so-called Rap Brown amendment

Bobby Seale demanded to represent himself
            and to cross-examine witnesses
                (his attorney Charles Garry had to have surgery
                        but the Judge wouldn't postpone the trial)

Seale kept interrupting the proceedings
            till finally Judge Julius Hoffman
                    ordered Seale bound and gagged
                        and there he was in court
                        like someone shackled in
                                a ship's hold

(November 5, 1969, Hoffman finally severed Seale from the trial)

Richard Nixon weighed in
            with his usual sour-souled analysis
                        on one of his secret tapes:

"Aren't the Chicago Seven all Jews? Davis is a Jew, you know."
    When someone told Nix that Davis wasn't Jewish, Nix
    noted that, well, Abbie Hoffman was Jewish

Army Intelligence and the CIA
———— Invade the Chicago 7 Defense Team ————

        The Defense Intelligence Agency
        had stepped on the Bill of Rights
                in seeking to retard the right
                of Americans to protest the war.

        As the Chicago 7 trial went into full sway
        an Army Intelligence officer named John O'Brien
        as he later testified
                was assigned to keep tabs on the defendants

and their attorneys
sometimes with the goal of "pure harassment," he said

O'Brien's military intelligence reports
were passed to the FBI, Secret Service, Chicago PD, et al.

In addition the 113th Military Intelligence Group
        received 3 or 4 cartons of documents stolen
        from the Chicago 7 defense office
        by the right-wing Legion of Justice
        a group which was being financially supported
        by military intelligence (as reported
                by Sanford Ungar in *The Washington Post*
                November 14, 1973)

For its Constitution-spattering part
the CIA sent one of its ace Chaos spores
                into the Chicago defense team

            Not a great moment for America

———— **After Ellsberg Absorbs the Pentagon Papers** ————
                September 1969

Daniel Ellsberg had studied the Pentagon Papers for
                        about 6 months
during which as he later wrote
"I became aware that a generation of presidents from
John Kennedy on had heard advice to negotiate out of
Indochina wars. And for some reason the presidents had
always chosen to stay in. Their determination not to suffer the
political consequences of losing a war outweighed,
                        for them,
        the human costs of continuing. . ."

That fall he learned from Morton Halperin
who had just resigned as Henry Kissinger's deputy
that Nixon had a secret plan which "included secret threats
of escalation unless there was a mutual withdrawal of
North Vietnamese as well as US forces."

            That was Straw 1
            which led to the Papers' release

Then, September 29, 1969
he learned that Army Sec Stanley Resor had decided
not to file charges against six Special Forces agents
accused of murdering
an alleged South Vietnamese double agent

(The CIA had barred its agents from testifying)

That was Straw 2. He telephoned Anthony Russo
    a Rand employee who'd also turned
    against the war
        and they arranged to photocopy the Papers

Ellsberg approached Senators Fullbright & McGovern
    but they wdn't release it.

He gave "a substantial portion" of the Papers to
Marcus Raskin and Richard Barnet at
                    the Institute for Policy Studies

Some, including McGovern, had suggested
giving it to *The New York Times*

                    tick tick
                    tick tick

────────────────── **Days of Rage** ──────────────
                October 9–11

The Weathermen actionists of SDS had hoped for 5,000
soldiers of pizza street
            but only 300 showed up
                    for the Days of Rage
            in Chicago
        at the start of the Chicago 8 trial

The pizza-streeters broke windows, smashed windshields
& fought with cops
            with 290 arrested.

Thus was born the Weather Underground
who were into bombings

There was a sequence of bombings the next few months

by Weathers
then in '70 they went underground.

It was what the Panthers used to call
                              "Custerism."

The Weathers were just a splintery few
whereas an ever-growing mass of Americans came to:

——————————————— **Moratorium Day in DC** ———————————————
October 15, 1969

There were two big demonstrations that fall
called Moratorium Days
                              across the nation

The first was on October 15

They had a kind of religious power
though Nixon pooh-poohed any thought that
                    the demonstrations would change his course

yet in his later Memoirs he wrote how the ☮ movement
made him stop scheming for a wider war:

"I knew, however, that after all the protests and the Moratorium,
American public opinion would be seriously divided
                    by any military escalation of the war."

——————————— **Effete Corps of Impudent Snobs** ———————————
October 19

Four days after the first Moratorium
a human being named William Safire
known for soaking the era with his clever bile

cobbled a speech for VP Spiro Agnew
to deliver at a Republican fund-raiser
that spoke of the Moratorium as
"encouraged by an effete corps of impudent snobs
                    who characterize themselves as intellectuals"

                    & as for the second Moratorium
                              scheduled for November

324

the bribe-taking Mr. Agnew
mouthed Safire's words that

"hardcore dissidents and professional anarchists"
were plotting "wilder, more violent" demos

—maybe a splintery few, but the vast most weren't

October 21
    that morning Jack Kerouac
        was watching the "Galloping Gourmet" TV show
        making notes in a pad
        & eating some tuna from a can
                when the blood from a burst
                vein bubbled from his throat

        & he passed from earth

─────────────── **March Orders for the Era** ───────────────

    "Well while I'm here I'll
           —do the work
  and what's the Work?

      To ease the pain of living
    Everything else—drunken
        dumbshow"

        —from "Memory Gardens"
        Allen Ginsberg's elegy for Kerouac

─────────── **Reaching Out to the "Silent Majority"** ───────────
November 3

It was a cunning & at times eloquent speech that Nixon gave
in a month when war protests were reaching the masses

In it he roused support for the so-called Nixon Doctrine
    (the gradual disengagement from Asia)

and then spoke directly to the people:

"If a vocal minority, however fervent its cause,
prevails over reason and the will of the majority,

the Nation has no future as a free society.
Let historians not record that when America was the
most powerful nation in the world we
passed on the other side of the road and allowed the
last hopes for peace and freedom of millions of
people to be suffocated by the forces of
                                totalitarianism.

And so tonight," he concluded, "to you, the great silent majority of
my fellow Americans—I ask for your support."

                The media nodded attentively
                —um, yeah, Silent Majority—

                a good hook w/ which to hook
                                the jittery masses

───────────────── **The Taking of Alcatraz** ─────────────
                    November 9

Before dawn
        an *ad hoc* group of Indians
                called Indians of All Tribes
                        grabbed the abandoned federal pen
                                        on Alcatraz Island
                                in San Francisco Bay

They claimed ownership under an 1882 law
providing that abandoned federal facilities
                        could be used for Indian schools

They offered to purchase it for $24 in glass beads
and red cloth
        to mimic the purchase of Manhattan

& proposed setting up a Center for Native American Studies
an American Indian Spiritual Center
                an Indian Center of Ecology
        a Great Indian Training School
                        & an American Indian Museum

        (too bad the power structure didn't allow it)

326

In December '69, the Congress passed a Joint Resolution
that "the President of the United States is directed
to initiate immediate negotiations with delegated
representatives of (Indians of All Tribes) and any other
appropriate representatives of the Indian Community
with the objective of transferring unencumbered title in fee
of Alcatraz to (Indians of All Tribes) or any other
designated organization of the American Indian Community"

It sounded good, but was not to be

The Indians held the island for 19 months
            till finally in June o' '71
                        the gov't tossed them off

It was a tremendously energizing set of months
for the Indian movement
            particularly the American Indian Movement
            which had been established in 1968

            by two charismatic Chippewas named
            Dennis Banks & Russell Means

November 11
    For the 20th time the UN turned down the admission
                        of the People's Republic of China

───────────────── **The Second Moratorium** ─────────────────
November 15

    The FBI strove with schism-batty glee
                to disrupt the Second Moratorium
    It typed a letter from
    a front group called the Black United Front

    to the Mobe which
    demanded a dollar for each
    protester who showed up in DC

and then a second letter came
announcing that if the Mobe didn't pay
the BUF would break kneecaps
                    coming out of arriving buses

(It wasn't till '72 that
ex-FBI agent Robert Wall
wrote in *The New York Review of Books*
that he and others in the Bureau had promoted
the confrontation between the BUF and the Mobe

Wall wrote: "The letter we composed was approved
by the Bureau's counterintelligence desk and was signed
with the forged signature of a leader of the black group.")

The FBI's hunger for a riven America
failed in the moral passion
                    felt by millions
          that the Nation was better than its war-caste

     and across the States there were rallies that day
     work stoppages, teach-ins, anti-war poetry readings
     with students and professors
                    wearing black arm bands
                              to defy the grrr-ing caste of shredded flesh

At least 250,000 demonstrators came to Washington
                    to instruct the Military-Industrial-Surrealists
                              it was time to halt the murder

I was there, and the memory is exquisite of
clanging the Justice Department doors
                    while chanting "Bring out your dead Bring out your dead"

                    & looking up to see wasp-eyed Nixonites
                              staring from the upper windows

Establishment figures such as Senators Charles Goodell,
George McGovern & Eugene McCarthy were on hand, and also
          Peter, Paul & Mary
                    Dick Gregory
                              Leonard Bernstein

(plus the thrill of standing there in war-stopping triumph while
          250,000 sang "Give Peace a Chance!")

     Nixon ignored the singing
     He was watching a football game
          while 40,000 walked back and forth

in front of the White House
each holding a card with the name of an American
                              dead in the war

But he knew
        even while scowl-gazing at kick, pass & tackle
        that the country might split
        into revolutionary chaos
        if the escalation continued

──────────────── **My Lai Emerges** ────────────────
November 19

The traces of My Lai's moaning ditch
began oozing to public knowledge

First there was a series of articles by young Seymour Hersh
sent out by Dispatch News Service

till finally, the "all the news that's fit to print" source
The New York Times
positioned an article on its front page under the heading:

G.I. Says He Saw Vietnam Massacre

November 19–20
    for the second time an American space ship
    this one the *Apollo 12*
        left Gaia for the dusty moon

    where Navy officers Alan Bean and Charles Conrad
    took two walks lasting more than 8 hours
    while Richard Gordon orbited overhead

    It wasn't as heavy a media trip
            as the TV camera malfunctioned

    They collected 50 lbs of moon rock
    set up some more experiments
    & walked into a crater to collect some parts
    from an un-personed craft, the *Surveyor*
    which had landed 3 years previous

                then they departed Selena

The Packing of the Supreme Court
with Right-Wingers Begins
November 21

Nixon's ghastly right-wing
nomination to the Supreme Court
Judge Clement Haynsworth of South Carolina
was rejected by a 55 to 45 vote in the Senate

thwarting, for a few years,
the ultimately successful efforts
of the American right
to spit the court back toward regimentation

November 22
Jonathan Beckwith and associates at Harvard Medical School
announced the isolation of the first single gene
—a tiny bit of bacterial DNA
which assists in the metabolism of sugar—

the same day that the S. Vietnamese gov't claimed
there was no massacre at My Lai
& only 20 civilians were killed

Nuclear Non-Proliferation Treaty
November 24

the Strategic Arms Limitation Talks (known as SALT)
opened in Helsinki in November
and then on November 24
a nuclear non-proliferation treaty was ratified

Bio-war Stockpiles Banned

The next day, November 25
Nixon ordered all methods of US biological warfare
be stopped
& ordered the destruction of
bio-war "stockpiles"

though the CIA kept a stock
of biologic toxins

in violation of the ban

(for more information, you might trace the six-year
non-stop work of Harvard geneticist Dr. Matthew Meselson
behind the scenes
            to help bring about the ban)

November 26
    Nixon signed a bill which established a lottery for the
                                conscription of war fodder

December 1
    LA police chief Edward Davis told a press conference
    that the Tate-LaBianca murders were solved

        Arrested were Charles Manson, Tex Watson, Linda Kasabian,
        Susan Atkins, Patricia Krenwinkel & Leslie Van Houten

                who had fled to the Death Valley area
                for a few weeks of roaming from
                camp to camp
                    in an assortment of dunebuggies
                                        & rail jobs

——————— **Search & Destroy Comes to Chicago** ———————
                    December 4

    We have traced how the FBI helped create violence
    among the Black Panthers & between the Panthers
            and groups such as the United Slaves in Los Angeles

            so that 28 Panthers had been killed
            many from the schemes of the secret police
            (provocateurs, false letters,
            snitch-jacketing the innocent, etc)
                            during the past 2 years.

    In Chicago on December 4
                the gov't campaign against the Panthers
                reached a frightening police-state low.

    It's a ghastly tale of murder
            which can be followed in greater detail, for instance, in
            Ward Churchill and Jim Vander Wall's

Fred Hampton had become the Illinois chair of
                    the BPP
He was young, well spoken and what the FBI
                    shuddered to contemplate:
            an effective black organizer
            & a Black Panther to boot!

You could move up fairly quickly
            in an organization under attack by Cointelpro
and so Fred Hampton streaked to power within the Panthers

He had traveled to California
to lecture before the UCLA Law Students Association
& was chosen by BPP hierarchy to
            become a "major spokesperson"

        The FBI went into a hostility-gasm
        against young Hampton
        as 4,000 pages of files were compiled on him
                    during the final 2 years of his life

In late '69
The FBI inserted a violent gun-nut provocateur
            into the Chicago Black Panther chapter

This guy tried to introduce the use of nerve gas
and a home-made electric chair
while he urged Panthers to commit robberies

In mid-November 1969
    FBI provocateur Wm O'Neal
    drew a floorplan of Hampton's Chicago apartment
    for his FBI control agent
    with special attention to the placement of beds

It's possible that at a late dinner at his apartment
the night of December 3–4, 1969
        that an FBI spore spiked
        some Kool-Aid with a knock-out substance

At 4 am the police gathered outside
and 30 minutes later stormtrooped the apartment

where Hampton and his pregnant girlfriend were sleeping
along with various other Panthers & supporters

One Panther, Mark Clark, fired off a single shotgun shell
    as he was falling dead
            from an M-1 police-state carbine

The police fired 42 shots
from an M-l and a Thompson submachine gun
                at Hampton's bed

        When it was apparent that Hampton
        was still alive, and one officer saying
            "He'll make it,"
        another officer then fired twice into Hampton's head

        There was a particularly disgusting photo
        of a bunch of leather-clad Chicago policemen
        laughing and smiling and smirking
            like stormtroopers
as they stretchered the lifeless Hampton out of the building

    It wasn't till 1973
    that FBI snuff-spore Wm O'Neal's
    role in the sketch, the stirring up of violence
               came to public knowledge.
        Murder is murder &

        too few cared
        when stormtroopers dared

December 6
    Mick Jagger of the Rolling Stones was just beginning the tune called
        "Sympathy for the Devil"
    at a big rock fest at the Altamont Speedway in Livermore, California

    when a young man named Meredith Hunter
        started toward the stage
            and Hell's Angels guards
                stabbed & stomped him to death

while the band played on

Earlier someone apparently bumped Angel king Sonny Barger's bike
& about 50 Hell's Angels raged into the crowd
hitting and beating

Lesson: don't hire stab-headed bikers
as your security

December 8
The first Venceremos Brigade, 216 Americans, arrives in Cuba
via Mexico to work on the sugar harvest
—there was a 10-million-ton harvest goal

Cuba paid their expenses so as not to violate US Treasury Dept regs

December 10
Samuel Beckett
once secretary to James Joyce
received the Nobel Prize for Literature

He did not give his acceptance speech
from inside an ash can
as might a character in one of his plays

American Murray Gell-Mann
won in physics for his "work on behavior of
elementary particles"

Americans Max Delbruck, Alfred Hershey and Salvador Luria the
Prize in Medicine for "findings on the genetic structure of viruses"

December 18
the Parliament in Britain
showing some pizzazz
voted to outlaw capital punishment

first the House of Commons on Dec 15
and then the House of Lords on Dec 18

another step back from cyclical cruelty and
multi-century vengeance

Right-Wing Version of
the Brookings Institute
December, 1969

A speech writer for Nixon named
Lyn Nofziger
sent around an idea for a "right-wing Brookings Institution"

Nixon counsel Charles Colson thought it might be called
the Silent Majority Institute

It never happened but the scheme
made the White House aware of
the right-wing CIA officer named E. Howard Hunt
(about to retire from the Agency)
who had been proposed to direct the
Silent Majority Institute

Some Wargasms in Custer Land
Christmas Week '69

The Weathermen held a final 4-day Wargasm conference
(formal name, National War Conference)
in Flint, Michigan
before going underground

400 people showed up in a room
which had a big cardboard machinegun
dangling from the ceiling

There was much talk about
forming a hidden guerrilla movement
and somehow a sympathy for the Manson group
crawled into the gathering

The beautiful Bernadine Dohrn, in a "Going Too Far" utterance
that will haunt her century, said
"Dig it, first they killed those pigs,
then they ate dinner in the same room with them,
then they even shoved a fork into the victim's stomach,
wild!"

Not wild, but going too far
with words.

At night there were group meetings billed as "wargasms"
They sang together from the Weatherman songbook.

One tune had the melody of "White Christmas":
        "I'm dreaming of a white riot
        Just like the one October 8. . . ."

& there was a glut of LSD, fucking & all-nighters
after which, on January 1, 1970
      the Red Army, 300 strong,
            went underground to
                  kill the Stockmarket

        The CIA & FBI must have been
        smiling with joy

──────────── **Murder of a Great Union Man** ────────────
New Year's Eve

The great John L. Lewis had led the United Mine Workers
                      for 40 years, till 1960

but his successor was a weaselly Company-kissing nothing
called Tony Boyle

Boyle finally faced a serious challenge from a fine union man
named Jock Yablonski
    head of a group called Miners for Democracy
    Jock had helped soft-coal miners
    afflicted with black lung
        get compensation

So, in 1969 Yablonski was running for president of the UMW
assisted by Ralph Nader and a Congressman named
                    Ken Hechler of WV
but lost the race in December
        though he was challenging the vote.

On New Year's Eve 3 spores of evil
hired by United Mine Workers president Tony Boyle
murdered Yablonski, his wife Margaret and daughter Charlotte
        as they slept in their farmhouse in Clarksville, PA.

Boyle had paid them $20,000 to do it
The triggermen were quickly caught because Yablonski
        had the habit of reporting to local police
            the license plates of vehicles
                    suspiciously lurking

but it took 4 years to nail Mr. Boyle
            who was finally sentenced to life imprisonment

Rise, o Unions, Rise!

───────────────── **The Gaia Theory** ─────────────────
1969

The Earth is a Living Organism

The Biosphere
        is a life Unto Itself
                said James Lovelock
                    a British biologist

It sounded ancient yet current
                & filled a hunger for the numinal
        to think that whatever
        angry men did to Gaia
                in the form of bombs *&* chemical scythes
        she lived

"The earth with a city in her hair
entangled of trees"
        as Charles Olson wrote in
        his *Maximus Poems*

───────────────── **Sexual Revolution** ─────────────────
1961–'69

Did it happen?

in a way

                but the real revolution
                was the beginning of the liberation
                                of women

Novum Sub Sole '69:
    the Union of Concerned Scientists
            formed by students and faculty at MIT
                an excellent, longevitous organization
                which issued reports & offered analyses
                of US policies
                        during the ensuing decades

            in order to help create a
            "cleaner, healthier environment and a safer world"

    the National Environmental Policy Act
        requiring an environmental-impact statement
                                for each government decision

    the Fermi National Accelerator Lab near Chicago
    the first effective artificial heart
            used *pro tempore* for patients awaiting transplants

    the ankle length maxi-dress
    "Sesame Street"
            with Jim Henson's puppets such as
                    Big Bird   Bert and Ernie   Cookie Monster

    Astronomers Thomas Gold and Franco Pacini
    proposed that pulsars are rapidly rotating neutron stars

    & the rise of
        multiculturalism (and its good friend friendshipism)
                                made r.w.n.'s groan and plot!

Libri '69:
    Philip Roth's *Portnoy's Complaint*
                inspired at least in part by watching Tuli Kupferberg
                sing "Jack Off Blues" in a Fugs show back in '66
                        at the Players Theater in Greenwich Village

    John Berryman's *The Dream Songs*
    Gary Snyder   *Earth House Hold*
    Theodore Roszak   *The Making of a Counterculture*

338

Vine Deloria, Jr.   *Custer Died for Your Sins*
Gunslinger, Book II   Edward Dorn
The Godfather   Mario Puzo
Kurt Vonnegut   *Slaughterhouse-Five*
Lillian Roxon's   *Rock Encyclopedia*
& *The Trial of Dr. Spock* by Jessica Mitford

Pinched Tapers '69:
          Jan 30 ex-CIA chief Allen "Nobody Reads" Dulles at 75
          Boris Karloff at 81 on February 3
          Vito Genovese, crime king, February 14 at 71
          Karl Jaspers on February 26 at 86
          Max Eastman, March 25 at 86
          Coleman Hawkins at 63 on May 19
          June 22 Judy Garland at 47
          July 5 Walter Gropius at 86
          August 6 the philosopher Theodor Adorno
          Ludwig Mies van der Rohe in Chicago at 83 on August 17
          Joseph Kennedy at 81 on November 18
          Joseph von Sternberg December 22 at 75

More Novum: the 747
          Yale allowed women undergrads
                    the ATM machine in NYC

          "Everyday People"   Sly & the Family Stone
          "Proud Mary"   Creedence Clearwater Revival &
          "Leaving on a Jet Plane" from Peter, Paul & Mary

The Who's *Tommy*
Frank Zappa   *Hot Rats*
MC5   *Kick Out the Jams*
The Fugs   *Belle of Avenue A*
Henryk Górecki   *Old Polish Music*
Olivier Messiaen   *The Transfiguration of Our Lord Jesus Christ*
Captain Beefheart and the Magic Band   *Trout Mask Replica*

Woody Allen   *Play It Again, Sam*
Joe Orton   *What the Butler Saw*
Neil Simon   *Last of the Red Hot Lovers*

& a David Smith and Roy Lichtenstein retrospective
                    at the NYC Guggenheim

Films '69:
Midnight Cowboy (the Oscar)
Butch Cassidy and the Sundance Kid
Jane Fonda in *They Shoot Horses, Don't They?*
John Wayne's *True Grit*
Satyricon
Z   directed by Constantin Costa-Gavras &
Max Ophüls' 4 and 1/2 hour *The Sorrow and the Pity*

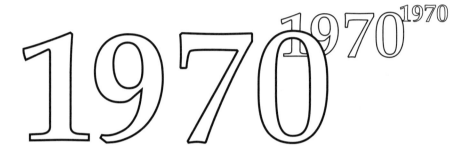

There were 204,765,770 in the USA
as the '60s passed away

"Who killed the '60s?" they ask.

Time did,
the Spirit of Napalm did
& his bone-pal

Scythe Man the Lurker

─────────────────── **Type A** ───────────────────

The decade ahead was the time that
2 American cardiologists
Meyer Friedman and Ray Rosenman
isolated the Type A person

—impatient, someone w/ too many lists & projects
jittery, prone to ire-flash,
w/ too many phone calls
& too many dready projects

a life-path that was shown to lead to
heart attacks, mental problems
& early encounters with
the Scythe Man

Grrr   Grrr   Grrr

January 4
in the Beatles' final recording session
they added some harmony to "Let It Be"
& also a brass section with
trumpets, trombones & tenor sax

plus a lead guitar part by Harrison
maracas by McCartney & some cellos
(though not used on the final mix)

for a Type A band just 3 months
away from official break–up

January 12
After 2 1/2 years of struggle
the starving Ibo people of Biafra gave in to Nigeria
and no longer demanded independence

January 21
the big Boeing 747
began flying passengers

January 24

There was a benefit that evening at composer Leonard Bernstein's place
for the NY Panther 21 Legal Defense Fund

—it was one of a series of events in the homes of
well-to-do New York City liberals during those months
to hear about & flash cash for causes
(such as César Chávez's United Farm Workers)

(The January soirée was to benefit
the 21 black New Yorkers charged with plotting to
blow up department stores, the NY Botanical Garden
& kill police officers—

The case was based on the testimony of 3
undercover police officers who infiltrated the BPP in NYC.
One of the police infiltrators had also been
Malcolm X's personal bodyguard

All 21 were found not guilty in a trial in '71

For more on the Panther 21 see *Agents of Repression*, p. 396
by Ward Churchill and Jim Vander Wall or
Murray Kempton's
*The Briar Patch: The People of the State of New York v.
Lumumba Shakur, et al.*, E. P. Dutton, 1973)

The fundraiser at Leonard & Felicia Bernstein's apartment
featured—shudder shudder—ACTUAL Black Panthers
which brought forth the fluffy, breathy
condemnation of a writer named Tom Wolfe
famous for his breathy, envious book on
Ken Kesey and the Merry Pranksters

who penned an enormous article for
the June 8 issue of *New York Magazine*
titled "Radical Chic: That Party at Lenny's"

a flow of ink which followed the long-standing
British/American Empire pattern of
ridiculing those with money helping the non-rich

You could see Mr. Wolfe in 1827
    snickering at the paint-stained clothing of William Blake
    (and his egalitarian politics)
    after a breathy-prosed snickery visit

The Bernsteins' Panther benefit also triggered the ire
                          of *The New York Times.*

It was just a few weeks after Fred Hampton's murder in Chicago
& the FBI-Red Squad assault to smash the Panthers
                    was in Full Swing across the nation

—as traced in this volume of *America, A History in Verse*

        The choke-off of
        money & good will
        from the wealthy
            & influential
        to good & even controversial
                left liberal causes
        is always the gritty-clawed goal of the right

        & the catch-sentence "Defund the Left"
        was surging by the 2nd year of Nixon
        in the temporary ebb of its sister sentence
                    "Defund the Right"

February 2
    the great Bertrand Russell
    who'd not long ago organized the Stockholm War Crimes Tribunal
                that judged against US policy in Vietnam
    & winner of the Nobel Prize for Literature in 1950
                passed away at his house in Wales

February 14
    Nixon expanded the biological weapons ban to include
                    all "toxic agents"

    The CIA ignored the ban
    and took two cans of extremely lethal shellfish toxin,
        called saxitoxin
        (for which it had developed pistols
        to shoot saxitoxin-tinged darts at victims)

into freezer storage
the US Navy Bureau of Medicine and Surgery
23rd Street in DC

February 21
Kissinger's first meeting, in secret, with Le Duc Tho in Paris

Le Duc Tho insisted on a coalition gov't in the South with
the Viet Cong as a member

(as JFK had proposed allowing the
Pathet Laos to help rule Laos)

but the Kiss-Nix complex would
use uberbombing
as an answer

February 24
racist ax-head Governor Lester Maddox of Georgia
handed out ax handles in a
Washington restaurant

in honor of the pukish time years before when he
waved ax handles to keep blacks from
coming into his restaurant in Atlanta

——————————— **Chicago 7 Convicted** ———————————
February 14

The trial at last came to a clamorous closing
after 5 1/2 months of mishugáss
and the jury went away to deliberate.

There was a kind of collective "Whew!" that the defendants
could have uttered just then
except that as soon as the jury had departed
the ghastly and arbitrary judge named Julius Hoffman
sentenced the 7 defendants and attorneys Wm Kunstler and
Leonard Weinglass as well
to jail terms of up to 4 years
for contempt of court

On February 18, all 7 were acquitted of "conspiracy" to incite riots
but the jury convicted 5 of the 7

Dave Dellinger, Rennie Davis, Tom Hayden,
                Abbie Hoffman, Jerry Rubin

      of violating the so-called Rap Brown amendment
      to the 1968 Civil Rights law
      i.e., crossing state lines to foment a riot
      (John Froines and Lee Weiner were acquitted)

& then on February 20 Judge Hoffman
      added five years to the five for Rap Brown

(Bobby Seale was tried and convicted separately
after being bound and gagged
      when he demanded his own attorney)

By February 27, all were out on bail
         & began to appeal their convictions

February 25
    the Abstract Expressionist Mark Rothko
        had suffered a heart attack, was despondent at 66
        and cut his wrists

      to join the dark vista of
         some of his somber-paneled paintings

─────────────── **Unfortunate Headline** ───────────────
February 1970

There was a 10-day trial for Timothy Leary
in Orange County, California
for the 2 roaches found in his station wagon
              in late '68

    His chances for favorability were diminished
    the morning the case went to the jury
        by the newspaper headline
    "DRUG-CRAZED HIPPIES SLAY MOTHER AND CHILDREN"

    as an army medical officer, Jeffrey McDonald
    claimed that hippies killed his family after chanting
        "Acid is Groovy, Kill the Pigs"
        (a couple years later McDonald himself was convicted
                of the murders)

They found Leary guilty
   and the judge immediately sent him to jail.

Then March 2 a US district court in Houston
gave him 10 years for the Laredo pot bust back in 1965

and the judge in Orange County
   appended another 10
   to run after the federal sentence

Leary was 49
   and was facing confinement for maybe the rest of his life
    for holding up the

 sign

And thus the right-wing pot hounds
   brought down another very public person
     of the 1960s
   (just as they did Ken Kesey & John Sinclair)

March 1
   Socialists surged to "unexpected" triumph in the
     Austrian elections

—————————— **War in Greenwich Village** ——————————
March 6

Three were killed
   when an SDS bomb went off by accident
   in a Greenwich Village townhouse on West 11th
   (owned by a dad who was away on vacation
      in the Caribbean)

    The building was totally levelled

Police were looking for the 2 known survivors
Kathy Boudin and Cathlyn Wilkerson
     who fled the area

─────────────── **Charges for My Lai** ───────────────
March 10

The army indicted five men
                    for murder at My Lai
Captain Ernest Medina, Captain Eugene Kotouac,
and 3 other soldiers
                    (for a variety of offenses
                              —murder to rape)

Lt. William Calley
had already been arrested for pre-meditated murder
                    and faced execution

─────────────── **A Coup in Cambodia** ───────────────
March 13–18

For 29 years Prince Norodom Sihanouk
                    had governed Cambodia
The prince had striven to fashion a neutralist time-flow
while the war planes cratered the nations around him

North Vietnamese & and Viet Cong troops
                    had used part of Cambodia
                    for what the West called "staging"

On March 18 the Prince was ousted by
                    the right-wing premier,
                    a human named Lon Nol

who opened the door to an American invasion.

─────────────── **Invasion** ───────────────

The biasmophilia that cracked ancient Cambodia
        can be traced in the
        even-handed book by William Shawcross
        Sideshow—Kissinger, Nixon and the Destruction of Cambodia.

The US had conducted secret bombing of Cambodia
        throughout Nixon's first year-and-1/3 of rule

during which there had been falsification of bombing records,

wiretaps to head off the leaking of truth &
    lies for the ink-man's eyes

all to deceive the American people
    in a time when the war was supposed to shrink

The US military was convinced
—or was convinced for the purpose of the cause—
that the nerve center for the Viet Cong war-course
   —called COSVN, for Central Office for South Vietnam—
   lay in a certain area of Cambodia.

  That was the main excuse for the attack which
      Nixon soon would order
       —to snuff out COSVN

  (though COSVN was never located
     & likely never existed)

    Not a good moment for America

──────────── **A Bomb at the Electric Circus** ────────────
March 23

First it had been the Polish National Home
then in 1964 the Dom
   a post-Beat dance place
then it was called the Balloon Farm
where Andy Warhol's Explosive Plastic Inevitable
    & the Velvet Underground performed
& then by 1970 it was the Electric Circus
   on St. Mark's between 2nd Ave and 3rd

Terror struck on a rainy night
not long before midnight
someone had shoved a short lead pipe bomb
with clock detonator packed with small-bore ammo
     beneath a mirror-paved stage

150 were in the club, and 17 were injured

  I don't think anyone was ever arrested for it.

348

April 8
    Just 4 1/2 months after rejecting Clement Haynsworth for
                                                    the Supreme Court
    the Senate, to its credit, again rejected
    a right winger, this one was Harrold Carswell
                                        51–45

April 10
    Paul McCartney announced he was leaving the Beatles

───────────────────── **Harry Blackmun** ─────────────────────
                        April 14

        The Fates were snicker-weaving that April
        when Nix appointed

        Harry Blackmun of Minnesota to the Supreme Court

        Blackmun was supposed to be a conservative
                    but then reversed course
                                    when on the court

                        heh heh heh

April 18
    An activist named Bob Channey spoke at a statewide anti-war rally
                                        in St. Petersburg, Fla.

    "Let's bring the goddamn war home," were among his remarks,
    "and begin dealing seriously with the problems
                            which confront us here"

    There were about 1000 people on hand
    He was arrested for profanity
                & also charged with resisting arrest

            after which he was given a 2-year sentence
            which he actually had to serve
                    beginning in 1975
                            after a long legal struggle

            (and of course lost his teaching job
                        at the U of Florida)

April 20

Nix announced another 150,000 troops to be withdrawn in a year
but 2 days later he was plotting how to take advantage of
Lon Nol's coup in Cambodia

(Prince Sihanouk had formed a gov't in exile
with the Khmer Rouge.)

General Creighton Abrams, now commander of forces in Nam
taking over from William Westmoreland
urged bombing of bases in Cambodia

Bomb, said Nix
Bomb, said Kiss
Bomb, said Creight'
Bomb, said Apopis

Earth Day
April 22

The first Earth Day was organized by
Senator Gaylord Nelson and Denis Hayes

& featured parades, seminars, metal-recycling
across the nation
w/ millions taking part

Congress recessed for the day
and 10,000 gathered at the Washington Monument

an event of such treasonous & seditious magnitude
the FBI felt compelled to surveill it
to protect America

Springing a Rain of Death on the People
April 27–30

The night of April 27
Nixon saw *Patton* for the second time

George Patton was the general, however brilliant, who said things like
"We're not going to shoot the sons-of-bitches,
we're going to rip out their living goddamned guts
& use them to grease the treads of our tanks...."

Refreshed by *Patton*, the next morning
        Nixon & his bombophilic advisor Henry Kissinger
                ordered the invasion of Cambodia

—a project dubbed "Operation Shoemaker"—

& then on the evening of the 30th the President told
    a war-weary & startled nation
    after the fact
        that several thousand American troops were moving
            into Cambodia 50 miles northeast of Saigon

    It was to be a "limited incursion" he said
    but his television manners fibbed the pledge—
    He seemed strained and nervous
    & his upper lip roiled with sweat

Thus continued the years of bombing & slashing
that would lead in the end to the

 's of Pol Pot

    Thanks Nix
    Thanks Kiss
    Thanks Mil

After the sweat-roiled performance
    students went on strike across the nation
        about a third of campuses were shut down
    and a few ROTC buildings were torched
        including the one at Kent State in Ohio

Nixon Affirms the Berkeley Radical Adage
"The Issue Is Not the Issue"
May 1

The next morning Nixon went to a briefing at the Pentagon
& out in a Pentagon corridor uttered some scornful remarks:

"You see these bums, you know, blowing up the campuses.
Listen, the boys that are on the college campuses today
are the luckiest people in the world... and here they are
burning up the books,
storming around about this issue. You name it. Get rid of the war and
there will be another one. Then out there (SE Asia) we have kids
who are just doing their duty.
They stand tall and they are proud...."

Then on May 2 *The New York Times* learned that
the US was about to bomb North Vietnam for the first time since
Johnson's halting halt in Nov '68

and refused Nixon's plea not to publish it

Four Dead in Ohio
May 4

In the days before the evil at Kent State
some entity or entities
perhaps military intelligence
fed a stream of fake reports into the eyes & ears
of the mayor of Kent, Ohio:

There were Weathermen seen on campus
Banks were going to be burned
LSD was going to be zapped into the water supply.

There was some mild unrest the night of Nixon's speech
a few youths tossing bottles
& windows broken downtown

so that the Mayor declared a State of Emergency
and an 11 pm curfew for the city
1 am at the college

and called the Ohio governor's office to say
        "SDS students have taken over a portion of Kent."

Ohio's Governor, one James Rhodes, was a guard-caller
He'd already summoned the National Guard into action
        40 times
          in '69 & '70

& so on April 29, the Governor ordered
the 107th Armored Cavalry & the 145th Infantry
into active duty
        to deal with a truckers' strike in Akron.

It was 4 hard days of duty
          for the guardsmen

who then on Saturday, May 2
were sent to Kent State & Kent
        after only 3 hours sleep

The troops arrived around 10 pm
& then the ROTC building on campus began to burn
          with explosions of live ammo.

Governor Rhodes was running that year for the US Senate
& faced a primary opponent
on the coming Tuesday, just two days away

& so he plunked down the law and order card
at a press conference on Sunday, May 3
where he called the Kent State demonstrators
        "worse than. . . brownshirts."

        Classes resumed
        on Monday
        Students & some faculty were upset
        over armed soldiers
          patrolling their campus

(plus being called bums by the president
& nazis by the governor)

        so a noon rally was called
        Teachers announced it in class

Maybe a thousand gathered
near the gentle rise called Blanket Hill
behind the Victory Bell
on the Commons

when the 99 guardsmen
strode to the kill

with bayonets affixed to M-1 rifles
so powerful they could kill
someone 2 miles away

A bullhorn told the students to disperse—
guardsmen fired tear gas
& anger grabbed
the hillside

Sung: *Tin soldiers & Nixon's comin'*
We're finally on our own
This summer
     I hear the drummin'
Four Dead in Ohio

They marched to the top
of Blanket Hill
The protesters parted to let them through
then filled in behind them
w/ boos and anguish

The 99 soldiers then walked
back down to an athletic field
where they waited 10 minutes
with rocks tossed at them
by a few
& a few tear-gas canisters & insults
tossed too

Not all of the guardsmen, of course,
were wasp-eyed murd-spores
as the photo below
taken at Kent State at the time
illuminates:

A Kent State student named Allison Krause
spotted the flowers in the barrel
        (perhaps the very guardsman above
        in a photo taken that day)

Krause went over & talked with the guardsman
till an officer approached
        & ordered him to pull out the blossoms

Then came evil
on a warm spring day
with gas masks fogging up

as the bayonets marched back again
                    to the summit
                          of Blanket Hill

Sung: *Gotta get down to it*
         Soldiers are cutting us down
         Should've been done long ago.
         What if you knew her and
         Found her dead-on-the-ground?
         How can you run when you know?

At the hillock's summit
the troops walked between
      the Pagoda & Taylor Hall.

All at once the trailing right of the wedge
      turned
         & readied their rifles

It was 12:25 when 28 guardsmen fired
There were 2 quick fusillades
      with 55 M-1 bullets
      5 pistol shots & a shotgun blast

      spraying down upon the
      students in the parking
      lot more than a football
      field away.

      Dead were Jeffrey Miller
      Allison Krause, William
      Schroeder & Sandra
      Lee Scheuer
         plus 9 wounded

Sung: *Tin soldiers & Nixon's comin'*
      We're finally on our own
      This summer
         I hear the drummin'
      Four Dead in Ohio

In the photo you can see the death-heads
      bent down and firing

After the killings the city was closed off
& helicopters circled above without cease
shining big spotlights down on houses & yards
                         in a totalitarian dazzle

Four Dead in Ohio

It has not, as far as I know, been shown
what person in the military
issued loaded rifles to the National Guard
                    to kill unarmed student protesters

nor is it known whether or not the military had placed
any Vietnam Special Forces veterans into
the Ohio National Guard
           (as it did, say, in the National Guard unit in
                              Birmingham, Alabama)

———— Counter-Insurgency Comes Home ————

"The killings at Kent State and Jackson State
show clearly enough that sooner or later
our counter–insurgency methods
                    would be applied at home."
              —Philip Agee, former CIA officer

———————— No Justice ————————

Nixon that June appointed a 9-person
           Commission on Campus Unrest, headed
           by the former governor of Pennsylvania, William Scranton
           The Scranton Commission issued a report on
           Kent State, dated October 4, 1970
           which stated

"The Kent State tragedy must surely mark the last time
that loaded rifles are issued as a matter of course to
           Guardsmen confronting student demonstrators."

———————— National Rage ————————

After the murders there was national rage
with something like 400 colleges closed
               for the remainder of the school year

and day upon day   night upon night
        there were vigils in DC

    There was a huge one the night of May 9–10
    which covered the mall from the Lincoln Memorial
                all the way to in front of the White House

    At 5 am Nixon sauntered forth
            to the Lincoln Memorial
                to talk to some protesters.

As for the bombing of Cambodia
so desired by Tricky & his would-be Metternich sidekick

it went on and on
scarring that nation with wounds of evil
that enabled the Khmer Rouge communists
                to take over in 1975

            Thanks Nixon
            Thanks Kissinger
            Thanks bombopaths in the military
                an ugh! in the abyss to 'ee &

        A time of disgrace for America

May 4
    the Pulitzer Prize for International Reporting to Seymour Hersh
        whose articles on My Lai were distributed by
                the Dispatch News Service in the fall of 1969

———————————— **"Four Dead in Ohio"** ————————————

            A few days
            after the shootings
            Dave Crosby was hanging out
            w/ Neil Young.
            On hand was the
            May 15 *Life* magazine
            with those shocking photos
            especially the one with the
            young woman kneeling &
            holding up her arms

& a yellow-hued headline
"TRAGEDY AT KENT"

Young wrote a song on the spot
& right away they recorded it.
Ahmet Ertegun of Atlantic Records
flew to NY w/ the tape
& it was released
in a week
surging #1 on the charts
following CSNY's
"Teach the Children"

———————————— **FBI Smears Jean Seberg** ————————————
spring & summer of '70

The actress famous for her roles in *Saint Joan*,
Godard's *Breathless* & the '69 *Paint Your Wagon*
was pregnant

The FBI, bugging the Black Panthers in LA
thought perhaps the father was
the Panther's Minister of Information
& began a smear campaign in the media

J. Edgar Hoover ruled that since she'd given $ to the Panthers
she "should be neutralized," to use Eddie's own language

The FBI prepared a fake, anonymous letter
which it sent to a gossip columnist named Joyce Haber
at *The Los Angeles Times*

who dutifully published the smear on May 19

The day the *LAT* smear appeared
J. Edgar Hoove-sleaze sent a report on Seberg
to the White House, depicting her as a "sex pervert. . . .
presently pregnant by Raymond Hewitt of the Black Panthers."

The Hollywood Reporter picked up the smear & then
on August 7, Jean Seberg attempted suicide.

Next, on August 19
　　　　after an article in *Newsweek*
　　　　saying her baby was by a "black activist"
she went into labor prematurely and the baby died.
She insisted on an open coffin at the funeral

Each year on the anniversary of the baby's death
she tried to kill herself
　　　　She succeeded in 1979

　　　　Not a great moment for America

─────────────────── **Walter Reuther** ───────────────────
　　　　　　May 9

He was a great labor leader
—president of the United Auto Workers
from 1946 until his chartered Lear jet crashed
　　　　　　　　　　　this day

His leadership evolved during the historic
sit-down strikes of the 1930's
　　　　　　that helped create the UAW

He demanded his union's workers get
cost-of-living raises
health and pension benefits

　　　　　& when he was president of the
　　　　　Congress of Industrial Organizations
　　　　　he worked to merge it in '55
　　　　　　　w/ the American Federation of Labor

A Democratic Socialist of great charisma
he'd recently chaired a convention of the UAW
　　　　　　　with 4,000 delegates

J. Edgar Hoover had hounded him
　　　　　　　　for decades
& Reuther had the day before his crash
come out strongly against
　　　　　　the invasion of Cambodia.

He had cooperated with his brother Victor Reuther's
successful exposure of CIA manipulation
                    of labor unions

The twin-engine Lear Jet
had brought the singer Glen Campbell
                    to Detroit earlier in the day
and then in the evening
carried Walter Reuther, his wife May & 4 others
                    toward a spot in northern Michigan
where it crashed about 9:30 into trees as it was coming in to land
killing all

There has always been a trickle of speculation
                    that it was sabotaged

The federal study of the crash
indicated that the altimeter had 7 defects
                    & possibly had malfunctioned

& it's possible someone had tampered with it

truncations shift nations

──────────── **Police Murders at Jackson State** ────────────
May 14

The murders continued
This time it was
two protesters at Jackson State College in Mississippi

where police shouldn't have responded
                    to a mere disturbance with violence

After all, many of the nation's schools
                    had already been shut down for the year

Apparently some students shouted pigs! & honkies!
          out of the windows
                    of dormitories

and then about 40 police officers
lined up facing the buildings
just 50 feet away and opened fire

killing students Philip Gibbs & Earl Green

The Scranton Commission on October 1, '70
issued a report that said, "even if there were sniper fire
at Jackson State—
a question on which we found conflicting evidence—
the 28-second barrage of lethal gunfire partly directed into
crowded windows of Alexander Hall was
                    completely unwarranted and unjustified"

June 22
    18 became the voting age, as Nixon signed a law
    attached to a bill extending the Voting Rights Act of 1965

———— **An Example of the Military-Industrial Shove** ————
                    June

        After its formidable lobby
                had bully-shoved its will

        North American Rockwell,
        later to warmorph into Rockwell International
        was given a contract of $1.4 billion in '70 tax dollars
                to build 3 B-1 bomber prototypes

June 18
    In the British general elections
    Conservatives won 330 seats,
                Labour 287, Liberals 6.

                —Conservatives w/ 46.4% o' votes
                    Labour 43   and Liberals 7.4

        Harold Wilson resigned & Edward Heath formed
                            a Conservative gov't

———————————— **The Huston Plan** ————————
                    June–July

        Sometimes out of the ooze of time
        someone can strut on the stage of power
                        almost by accident

and so it was that a young attorney named
                              Thomas Charles Huston
—a former Army intelligence officer—
went to work on the White House staff
where he had been assigned
                              since the summer of '69
to examine possible linking of rubles & Russkies
                              to campus protests

By the spring of '70 Mr. Huston
had successfully urged Richard Nixon to order a meeting
of uppermost intelligence heads
              for the purpose of a coordinated effort to
                     root out the commie disorder-moles.

The meeting, chaired by Nixon, was held on June 5
with the chiefs of the CIA, FBI, NSA & the DIA
plus H. R. Haldemann, John Ehrlichman
                     and Mr. Huston

Nixon approved the 43-page plan Huston had melanged
allowing intelligence agents to
burglarize anyone they deemed a "threat to internal security"
bug and tap anyone, read anyone's mail and communications
              & in general to clean their eyeglasses
              with the Bill of Rights

              (Of course it turned out that
              the NSA and the CIA were already doing
                     much of what Huston was urging)

The Huston Plan was "approved" on July 23
then apparently was killed
              and sank into the dry-as-dust
              stacks of police-state proposals
                     in the vast vaults of the War Caste

(The Plan was among the prizes squirreled away
              in his top secret safe
              by White House counsel John Dean
              who used it as a poker chip
              to help avoid a jail term
                     during Watergate)

June 29
　　US troops retreated out of Cambodia into southern Nam,
　　　　　　　　　　　　　　　　　　　after 2 months

　　This was a few days after the Senate voted 81-10 to repeal
　　　　　　　　　　Johnson's '64 Gulf of Tonkin resolution.

　　Way overdue.

────────── **The Cooper-Church Amendment** ──────────
June 30

　　There was a heroic generation of Democratic Senators
　　those years
　　such as Frank Church of Idaho
　　George McGovern of South Dakota

　　　　who stood up for the Constitution
　　　　in matters of going to war

　　& so this day the Cooper-Church Amendment passed in the Senate
　　to ban combat troops in Cambodia after June 30
　　　　as well as any bombing in support of
　　　　　　Cambodia's troops

────────── **The Environmental Protection Agency** ──────────
July 9

　　In a message to Congress Nixon proposed the creation of the EPA
　　thus pulling together
　　　　many of the US govt's environmental activities
　　　　　　　　within a single bureaucracy

　　By the end of the year
　　　　after the scrutiny of Congress the EPA
　　　　　　(on paper a great good
　　　　　　but only modestly successful the next 30 years
　　　　　　in reducing cancer-causing poisons
　　　　　　from the American economy)
　　　　　　　　was legally established

364

The Evil of the Phoenix Program
July 1970

A Marine Corps Criminal Investigation Division officer
named William Taylor

was working at Da Nang
     as a CID investigator

He'd been investigating
a US Army Intelligence officer
     the CIA had recruited for its Phoenix Program

He'd opened a case file
after complaints from Vietnamese sources
that an Army Mil-Int officer
     w/ the help of Korean officers

was murdering Vietnamese civilians for the CIA

The American had been seen
at the Da Nang Interrogation Center
     forcing sex from women

Investigator Taylor followed the officer
     who was traveling with a Korean accomplice
one Sunday morning
     —not to church for sure—
but to an open air café
filled with middle-class Vietnamese
     (including children and mothers)

The 2 killers opened a briefcase
     & pulled out 2 hand grenades

then lifted up the bamboo curtain
that bordered the café
     and rolled the grenades inside

(an act of terror
     they thought would be blamed on the Communists)

Taylor watched with horror
　　　　as body bits blasted the Sunday

He chased the murderers
　　　　rammed his jeep into theirs

and attempted to arrest them
　　　　but the Establishment
　　　　　　　—the CIA & their kill-mavens—
　　　　　　　　　did nothing

Out, demons, out!

(for more on the Phoenix, you can read Douglas Valentine's
interesting book, *The Phoenix Program*)

July 17
　　　　the US announced that Israel might have the a-bomb

─────────── **Fear by the Tropicana Pool** ───────────
mid-July

I attended the Manson family trial in Los Angeles that summer
researching my book *The Family*

Miriam and I and our 5-year-old daughter Deirdre
stayed those months at "Sandy Koufax's Tropicana Motel"
on Santa Monica Boulevard
　　　　always a place where rock bands stayed

The Fugs had roomed there several times
　　　　during the late '60s

And so it was during the summer of '70, at various times
that Lou Rawls, Kris Kristofferson, the 5th Dimension,
& Janis Joplin and her band
　　　　(she was completing her final album, *Pearl*)
　　　　stayed at the Trop

When the famous residents realized that I was spending
time with the M group at the Spahn Ranch
          & had even camped out with them near Death Valley

I was told that if I ever brought any of the M-group
to the motel, people would move out pronto

One afternoon, 2 rather scruffy young men with long hair
came to the Tropicana pool, asking for Ed Sanders

A surge of raw fear spread among the poolside musicians.
Had Sanders violated the M ban?   One very famous
songwriter later told Miriam he'd figured the best way to escape
                      in case of flashing steel
         was to hit the water and swim to the far edge

But no.   The 2 young men were Glenn Frey, the future leader
of the rock band the Eagles, and John David Souther,
         later a well-known composer of movie scores

        You can't judge a hippie by its cover.

August 4
    Charles Manson held a newspaper up to the jury
    at his murder trial in LA:

———————— **Violence in Another Courtroom** ————————
August 7

Back in January a guard at Soledad Prison in California
killed 3 black inmates during a disturbance

and then in March a white guard was killed
& 3 black activists

soon to be dubbed the Soledad Brothers
were charged with the murder

but claimed it was a frame
    because of their pro-Panther leftist politics

One of the Brothers was the writer George Jackson

& then, in a strange weave of history
        difficult to explicate in a few lines
        there was a very botched and violent
            attempt to free the Soledad Brothers.

26-year-old Angela Davis
formerly a student of Herbert Marcuse at UC San Diego
had lost her teaching job at UCLA
        after she joined the Communist Party in 1968

George Jackson's 17-year-old brother Jonathan
used guns registered in Davis's name
to take hostages in a courthouse in Marin County,
            where 4 were killed
including Jonathan Jackson, Judge Harold Haley
            & 2 men on trial in the room.

Young Jackson apparently shouted for the release of
            the Soledad Brothers
                before bullets
                    ended his voice.

Within days Angela Davis was accused of
            murder, kidnapping and conspiracy
& went on the lam
with the FBI chasing her
        till she was caught in October in Manhattan

(The charismatic Davis attracted the fascination of the media
            & radicals as well
with "Free Angela" decals on walls & phone booths
            around the world.

She was stuck in jail for more than a year
before being released on bond
during which time George Jackson himself was killed

in the late summer of '71
under peculiar circumstances at San Quentin

and then finally Angela went on trial in '72
and an all-white jury set her free

—a time-flow worthy of study)

———————————— **USPS Goes Independent** ————————————
August 12

Nixon signed the Postal Reorganization Act,
making the United States Postal Service an "independent agency"

August 13
Consumer activist Ralph Nader
settled his lawsuit against General Motors
for $425,000
after their secret campaign
to try to scrape up some dirt
after his influential book
Unsafe at Any Speed was published
and helped save countless lives
in the campaign for auto safety

August 18
an old Liberty ship loaded up with 66 tons of nerve gas
was deliberately sunk 300 miles off Florida
in a skullic glub-glub

———————————— **Murder Comes to Wisconsin** ————————————
August 24

Some students who hated the University of
Wisconsin's participation in war research
blew up the Army Mathematics Research Center
killing a graduate student and a computer
worth $1.5 million in 1970 money

———————————— **The Fiftieth Anniversary of Suffrage** ————————————
August 25

There were rallies & marches throughout the nation
including a big march down Fifth Avenue

by Women's Strike for Equality
a coalition including NOW and women's liberation groups
to celebrate the 50th anniversary of women's suffrage

Calling for the 3 preconditions of liberation:
- 24-hour childcare
- abortion on demand
- equal opportunity in education and employment

September
in Boston, two Brandeis students
out to snuff capitalism

took part in a bank heist, during which a cop was killed

& the two women went underground
eluding the police for over a decade

────────── **Socialist Elected President of Chile** ──────────
September 5

Salvador Allende Gossens won the presidential election in Chile

Right-wing democracy-bashers in the CIA
hated the election of a Marxist

Chile's citizens were for the most part poor
& Allende wanted to nationalize all the mines,
the finance biz, major industry
and to redistribute land and wealth
to all the citizens

Allende vowed to nationalize
without trampling on Chile's democratic traditions

Former CIA head John McCone
now a director of the International Telephone & Telegraph Co
told Kissinger and CIA head Richard Helms
that ITT was willing to death-spew up to
$1,000,000 to help overthrow Dr. Allende

whose election on October 24
was ratified by the Chilean Congress.

Meanwhile the authoritarian would-be Metternich Henry Kissinger
—then very much in control—
told a meeting of the National Security Council's 40 Committee
about 2 months before Allende's election

"I don't see why a
country should be
allowed to go Communist
through the irresponsibility
of its own people."

Roll, o Kiss-eyes, roll
roll & wreck

One question lurking in the time-track
is whether Kissinger urged the removal—
i.e., the murder—of General Rene Schneider
head of the Chilean armed forces
who refused to allow the military
to crush Allende's presidency

The CIA's own later report admitted
it tried to "instigate a coup to prevent Allende from taking office
after he won a plurality in the 4 September election
and before, as Constitutionally required because
he did not win an absolute majority,
the Chilean Congress
reaffirmed his victory."

The CIA fed weapons to the groups in Chile
who were lusting to kill General Schneider

September 15
Nixon and Kiss met with Helms and A.G. Mitchell
and, in the words of the CIA, "President Nixon and his
National Security Advisor, Henry Kissinger, directed the CIA
to prevent Allende from taking power."

Helms' notes indicate that either Nix or Kiss
ordered the CIA to "make the economy scream."

Nixon authorized $10 million for the overthrow.

October 22
    Right-wing military sleaze
        killed the democracy-respecting General Schneider
  & the CIA ("for humanitarian reasons" it later said)
        gave $35,000 to the kill-group
            to keep the CIA's contact with the
            group
            omerta'd.

He's still alive as I write this—
Indict Henry Kissinger

September 12
    Tim Leary was in a minimum-security prison in San Luis Obispo

The Brotherhood of Eternal Love
    a group of psychedelicists
        had put up $25,000 for his escape

& the underground Weatherpeople
        made it happen:

the former Harvard professor climbed a tree, scaled a wall
& walked barefoot across the roof,
donned a pair of baseball gloves
        then went hand over hand
        across a thin steel wire
        to a utility pole

    slid down and was met by a woman in a pickup truck
    who uttered the password "Nino"
    & he responded with "Kelly"
        and off fled they

    to a Weather safehouse in the Bay area.
    & then Tim and his wife Rosemary wended to Algiers
        to join *pro tempore*
        the "government-in-exile"
        set up by Eldridge Cleaver & the Black Panthers

September 18

the great Jimi Hendrix
     choked on his stomach flow
         & passed away in London

     after too much Too Much

September 30
   the Commission on Obscenity and Pornography
   set up by LBJ in early 1968
   released a 12-person majority report

     which angered the right
     calling as it did on
     massive sexual education

     & finding "no evidence that exposure to or use of explicit
     sexual materials play a significant role in the causation of
     social or individual harms such as crime, delinquency,
     sexual or nonsexual deviancy or severe emotional disturbances."

     The majority report urged the repeal of laws preventing adults
     from having free use of sex-text & sex-materials.

     VP Spiro Agnew responded that
     "as long as Richard Nixon is President,
          Main Street is not going to turn into Smut Alley."

Operation Tailwind—
—— **Did the US Military Use Sarin Death-Gas in Laos?** ——
September, 1970

The military secretly bombed Laos
almost every day from 1964 through most of '69

in a form of warfare I have called "Layered Robo-Kill"
         (see the entry for May 1964)

In an investigation conducted long after the end of the war
it was alleged that that US Special Forces used sarin
         a deadly nerve gas

on a Laotian village
in September '70

which, it was thought, harbored American soldiers
who had defected

The operation to gas the defectors was
part of a covert mission called Operation Tailwind.

According to the later sworn testimony of
Admiral Thomas Moorer
        the Chair of the Joint Chiefs of Staff in 1970
the military viewed such defectors as
                kill-worthy spores
                who were helping the enemy

(sarin, methyl-isopropoxy fluoro-phosphine oxide
                had been developed in the 1930s
                by the German company I. G. Farben

It's deadly in small amounts
                —convulsions, paralysis, thanatos

The US called sarin CBU-15 and GB
and it was stockpiled in 1970
                at a base in Thailand)

Admiral Moorer confirmed in his testimony that
sarin was carried in helicopters
                used in rescue operations
                        when planes were down
                                in hostile territory

When used to rescue a downed pilot, say,
the gas had to be plied with caution
                & downwind from the target
"Hopefully the pilot can tell you" (by radio)
said Moorer
                "'I'm just behind the oak tree up the hill.'"

The Admiral admitted the use of poison gas, while
not at the time illegal,
                was controversial because

there was pressure on the Senate to ratify
(at last)
the 1925 Geneva Protocol
                    against the use of chem/bio in war

(The Senate finally ratified the treaty in '74)

In his testimony Admiral Moorer was
very clear that the use of sarin
                    was justified:

"The US is the garden spot of the world. . . ." he said
"I would have used any weapon, any tactic and
any move to defend the security of the United States."

—who knows how long it will last in the electro-liquid haunts of
the Internet, but Admiral Moorer's deposition is contained at the
e-address: http://copvcia.com/PDF/MOORER.TXT
with the pertinent sections beginning around deposition p. 217

———————————— **Janis** ————————————
October 5

Janis Joplin had finished the beautiful vocals for
                    "Me and Bobby McGee"

and in the evening she and her band
                    recorded a Happy Birthday salute to John Lennon

The session ended around midnight
          & she returned to her room
                    at the Landmark Motel in Los Angeles

where she took a shot of dangerous, un-cut heroin
then went out to the lobby
          & purchased some cigarettes

chatted with the lobby man
how happy she was with her new record

                    returned to her room
                        & fell to the floor
                            not to rise

uncut dope
tied the rope

————————————— **Grrrs in Bolivia** —————————————
October 7

Bolivia already had a tendency to nationalize
such as when back in '52
to the megaroll of the cap-eyes
a revolution had nationalized the tin-mines
& restored vast agricultural land
    to Indian agrarians

& then in October of '70 a leftist general named Juan José Torres
    assumed power in Bolivia

    where the memory of Che Guevara & '67
    still stirred the people

His government nationalized the
   operations of a Dallas-based metal processing company

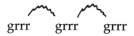

grrr grrr grrr

  & a zinc mine whose major owners
    were US Steel & Engelhard Minerals

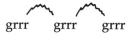

grrr grrr grrr

  & then Torres wanted to develop huge new
    iron deposits for the people of Bolivia

  so that the military government of nearby Brazil
    & the US-trained officer corps in Bolivia
  in cahoots with the right-wing Falange political party

  began to scheme
    to topple Juan Torres

  so that he would only survive
    till the summer of '71

Nixon Pledges Not to Invade Cuba
October/November

Messages were exchanged between Kissinger/Nixon and Sov Amb
Anatoly Dobrynin
> to affirm the '62 US pledge not to invade Cuba
> and the Soviets for their part made clear
> their continuing commitment
> not to place offensive missiles in Cuba

RICO
October 15

Congress passed the Racketeer-Influenced and Corrupt
Organizations Act

> which allows the government to grab assets illegally
> gained or used at "the time of the indictment"

> & allows for triple damages if private plaintiffs
> can prove that defendants engaged in a
>> "pattern of racketeering activity"

If a prosecutor could show a pattern, say one or more
related felonies, the prosecutor could
> indict the putative perp under RICO

Nixon said it would allow the government
"to launch a total war against organized crime."

It wasn't used till 1985.

(The RICO law had begun as a measure shoved
upon Congress by Arkansas' Senator John McClellan
> to gouge into the power of unions

There had been the 1959 Landrum-Griffin Act,
> which had placed restrictions on labor unions
but McC complained that "union lobbyists"
> had "knocked the teeth right out"
>> of Landrum-Griffin)

October 16
   25 were indicted after the Kent State shootings
                       none of them National Guardsmen

October 19
   Its topmost floors still under construction
          at the southern tip of Manhattan
              the World Trade Center
                       opened today for buying and selling

October
   Common Cause was founded by John Gardner
                       former secretary of HEW under LBJ

   The group was forged as a "third force"
   independent of the republicrats
                       & worked to end the Vietnam War

November 1
   the *Sunday Times* of London frothed forth that Jack the Ripper
   was in fact the Duke of Clarence, a human named Albert Victor

          to the multi-century murd-fascination of the populace
                          for
              panem et circenses et homicidium

November 3
   Nelson Rockefeller was reelected as governor of NY
                       still thirsting for the Rose Garden

   while down in Georgia
   a wealthy peanut farmer named Jimmy Carter
   was chosen Governor
   after 8 years in the state senate

   Carter had graduated from the US Naval Academy in '46
   & was an engineer in the atomic submarine program
                       & was always a nuclear-power-o-phile

   When his dad passed away in '53
   he resigned from the Navy and went home
              to run the family peanut farm

And so the two elected governors
one perennially
      & the other perhaps for the first time
no doubt spent election night '70
            pondering the presidency

November 12
    Charles de Gaulle was buried
          to the grief of a nation
             he helped keep whole
             in the era of Hitler

— The War Crimes Tribunal Marches upon Teller's House —
November 23

In Berkeley there was a War Crimes Tribunal that night
held in the Pauley Ballroom on the UC Berkeley campus

It was clearly inspired by Bertrand Russell's 1967 Tribunal

One of the Tribune's subjects was Edward Teller
and a flier was circulated around town
      "Edward Teller—War Criminal"

If not that, most certainly an Angel of Death

      Some built landmines
         the body-claimer
    Teller built h-bombs
         the Dream-maimer

I've long wondered if Teller held a secret patent
on at least part of the so-called Teller-Ulam Configuration
the h-bomb trigger
      (the credit for whose invention he
      hogged from his co-inventor Stanislaw Ulam)

   & if so, did Teller secretly pick up royalties
for all those 1,000's of h-bombs
      built in the era of
      Counterforce & Mutual Destruction?

If he did, it lights a big, greedy candle
                              on the century.

Anyway, the anger pulsed in Pauley Ballroom that night
till a crowd of about 50 decided to
          march across Berkeley to Teller's house
          which was protected by a line of police

          where the Bomb Man, so accustomed to
          the plotting of his schemes of mass slaughter
                    in national security privacy,

          received a scary taste
          of being yelled at in public

November 27
     Aleksandr Solzhenitsyn announced he would not go to Sweden
     to receive his Nobel Prize for literature.
     He said he was afraid he wouldn't be allowed to return
                                        to the Soviet Union

Hoover Flumph-Flumphing a Plot
———— That Turned Out Not to Be a Plot at All ————
November 27

J. E. Hoover was flumphifying in front of a Senate Committee
and announced that the Bureau had broken up a plot
"composed of Catholic priests and nuns,
teachers, students, and former students who have manifested
opposition to the war in Vietnam by acts of violence against
Government agencies and private corporations"

Hoover flumphed onward that Philip and Daniel Berrigan had
"plans to blow up underground electrical conduits and steam pipes
serving the Washington, D.C., area in order to disrupt Federal Gov't
operations. The plotters are also concocting a scheme to kidnap a highly
placed governmental official. The name of a White House staff member
(later id'd as Kissinger) has been mentioned as a possible victim."

The gov't had gathered letters, thanks to an FBI informant,
back & forth 'tween Father Philip Berrigan & Sister Elizabeth McAlister
with vague proposals to perform a "citizens' arrest" on
                    the would-be Metternich Mr. Kissinger

380

Hoover got what he craved: budget-boosting gluts of fake ink, but
in spite of a huge FBI campaign to get convictions
the "East Coast Conspiracy to Save Lives"—the name of the Berrigan
group, were acquitted, all of them, on April 2, 1971.

See *The FBI and the Berrigans: The Making of a Conspiracy*
by Jack Nelson and Ronald Ostrow
Coward, McCann & Geoghegan, NY, 1972

The Great William O. Douglas Survives
————————— Assault by Right-Wing Nuts —————————
December 3

There was a drive through much of 1970
by the right wing
to force the great great William O. Douglas
from the Supreme Court

(After all, they had snarl-fanged Abe Fortas
out of there just a few months previous)

but Douglas had what they prize in America: guts

He'd been a close advisor to Franklin Roosevelt
during the '30s
and there was a move to make him the VP candidate in '44
when Henry Wallace was ousted at the Democratic Convention
(which would have made Douglas President
in '45, and Douglas no doubt
would have been able to
stand up to
General Groves. . . .)

He was also a genuine environmentalist
a friend of Rachel Carson
and an actual friend of Actual Freedom

but back in April o' '70
Representative Gerald Ford of Michigan
arose in the House to accuse Justice Douglas
of promoting a "hippie-yippie style revolution"

and Ford shrilly complained that Douglas had allowed
the avant-garde literary magazine *Evergreen Review*
(famous for printing early on important texts by the Beats,
Samuel Beckett, Sartre, Che Guevara, et al)
to print a section from his book
                Points of Rebellion
(whose theme was the right-wing assault
going on—and still going on—
                against Actual Freedom of Speech)

After the accusations by the mean-dull Ford
a committee was formed in the House to
                look into impeachment

& then on December 3 it was announced that
                no such impeachment would occur

& the tough/gentle Justice Douglas
cheerily announced
                toward the end of the mean year known as
                '70

that he would remain on the Court

It was a moment for America

December 4
    César Chávez was sent to jail for 10 days for
    continuing the increasingly successful
                nationwide boycott of lettuce

Chávez, the head of the United Farm Workers Organizing Committee
    campaigned that sweetheart contracts set up 'tween Teamsters and
    many lettuce growers were robbing farm workers

December 10
    Dr. Norman Borlaug
    whose research on new strains of high-yield rice and wheat
    led to what they called the Green Revolution
                received the Nobel Peace Prize this day

Since '44 he'd worked at the
                International Maize and Wheat Improvement Center
                        in Mexico.

December 18
    a vom-forth of atomic cancer-gas
        forced hundreds to flee the test site in Nevada

────────────── **OSHA** ──────────────
December 29

The Occupational Safety and Health Administration (OSHA)
was set up by the Occupational Safety and Health Act
to give "every working man & woman in the nation
        safe & healthful working conditions"

Tox-lovers & right-wing slime have tried ever since
        to wreck OSHA & weaken it

────────── **The Dungeoning of America** ──────────

There were 400,000 in US prisons
        at the end of 1970
(according to the *Scientific American*)
a number which would 'shroom up
        to a ghastly 2,100,000
        by 2000
thanks to the dungeony dragnet on
        nonviolent drug users

& the slow seizure of the American mind
        by the right

Novum Sub Sole '70:
    floppy disks for computer-data storage
        from IBM

Robert Smithson finished his earthwork
        Spiral Jetty
    on the north shore of the Great Salt Lake

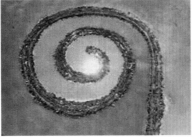

—a fine American Geo-Glyph   383

David Baltimore
    the microbiologist
discovered "reverse transcriptase"
a viral enzyme
    able to reverse the usual
        DNA-to-RNA
            transcription

    It was key to the development of genetic engineering

———————————— **The Gray Panthers** ————————————

It was the year the Gray Panthers were founded
        a senior citizen group led by Maggie Kuhn
            funded by the United Presbyterian Church
            & th' United Church of Christ

                which decided to shake the system
                rather than fade and acquiesce

                on issues such as better senior health care
                raising the mandatory retirement age
                getting rid of nursing home abuse
                & lifting the level of Social Security payments

More Novum 1970:
    An art song named "Bridge Over Troubled Water" by Paul Simon

    Michael Tippett's *The Knot Garden*
    Black Angels and
    Ancient Voices of Children by George Crumb

    32 études australes by John Cage

    the Beatles' final album, *Let It Be*
    Sondheim's *Company*

    Workingman's Dead and *American Beauty*
                from the Grateful Dead

    "Raindrops Keep Falling on My Head" the number 1 tune in sales
    Joni Mitchell *Ladies of the Canyon*

Drama:
Dario Fo's *Accidental Death of an Anarchist*

The Farm of Endlessness:
the bard Charles Olson
author of *The Maximus Poems*
and *Projective Verse*
on January 10 at 59

Alexander Kerensky, head of '17 provisional gov't in Russia,
June 11 at 89
Erich Maria Remarque on Sept 25 at 72
John Dos Passos on Sept 28 at 74
Gamal Adbel Nasser on Sept 28 at 52

Libri '70:
Germaine Greer's *The Female Eunuch*
Kate Millet's *Sexual Politics: A Surprising Examination of Society's
Most Arbitrary Folly*
Shulamith Firestone's *The Dialectic of Sex*
Philip Foner's *The Black Panthers Speak*
Gary Snyder's *Regarding Wave*
My Lai 4: A Report on the Massacre and Its Aftermath
by Seymour Hersh

The Diary of Samuel Pepys began to be published
—an engrossing read

& *A Heritage of Stone* by New Orleans DA Jim Garrison
another heroic American
someday due his due
whose book laid it out
for what it was
—a coup d'etat

Films o' '70:
Five Easy Pieces   The Passenger   Love Story
*M*A*S*H   Catch-22   *Wadleigh's *Woodstock*

On th' tube: "The Mary Tyler Moore Show"

And so ends Volume 3 of
America, A History in Verse
in a whirling hurry of years
whose slogans, song hooks, banners & fragments of verse
throng in the mind 34 years later

What a flash of time it was!

So much creativity & expectation
so much strife & rebellion
so much shaking the Puritan portals with naked bodies
so much daring & walking on the moon
so much kissing the sky & thirsting for Vision
yet so much hesitance, so much anger
so much violence & napalm
so much reaction & hunger for a safety
                    the universe will never allow

Coming up in *America, Volume 4*:
the slow biasmophilic closure of the war
the sabotage of the '72 election &
then the long fade of Nixon
the stingy but honest years of Ford
in the temporary triumph of reform & modern muckraking

386

& then the years of Human Rights and
the disco late '70s with its mantram of "Stayin' Alive"
the hesitant era of President Carter
Three Mile Island & the anti-nuke movement
a revolution in Nicaragua & the first bullets of the Contras
the ghastly karma of '53 burst outward
in '79 Iran
followed by the triumph of Reagan

all in the rhapsody of a great nation
where so many sing without cease
work without halt
shoulder without shudder
to bring the Feather of Justice to every
belltower, biome & blade of grass

in Graceful America

Long may it dwell in peace, freedom and equality
out on its spiraling arm

EDWARD SANDERS was born in Kansas City, Missouri, in 1939. He studied Greek and Latin at New York University, graduating in 1964. As owner and operator of the Peace Eye Bookstore (1964–1970), he was the spearhead of New York City's underground press movement. He was also the founder and leader of the Fugs, a satirical folk-rock band that has issued many albums and CDs during its forty-year history.

Sanders' book *The Family*, a nonfiction account of the Charles Manson group, was published in 1971. A perennial bestseller, it has been translated into several languages and was updated in 1990 and again in 2002.

It was while researching *The Family* that Sanders developed the ideas expressed in his manifesto *Investigative Poetry* (1976), an impassioned call for poets to take up the writing of history. In 1993, in the collection *Hymn to the Rebel Café* (Black Sparrow), Sanders published "Melville's Father," the first of his investigative poems. It was soon followed by the book-length verse biographies *Chekhov* (Black Sparrow, 1995) and *The Poetry and Life of Allen Ginsberg* (2000).

In *1968, A History in Verse* (Black Sparrow, 1997), Sanders mixed autobiography with national history. His current project, *America, A History in Verse*, is his most ambitious to date, an epic attempt to "trace with grace / what the Fates & Human Mammals have wrought / in the Time-Track of the USA." The first two volumes, chronicling the years 1900 to 1961, were published by Black Sparrow in 2000.

Sanders is the recipient of a number of grants and awards for his poetry, including fellowships from the Guggenheim Foundation, the National Endowment for the Arts, and the Foundation for Contemporary Performing Arts. His *Thirsting for Peace in a Raging Century: Selected Poems 1961–1985* was honored with an American Book Award. In recitals throughout the United States and Europe, Sanders performs a mix of chanted, spoken, and sung poetry, sometimes accompanying himself on musical instruments of his own invention, including the Talking Tie, the Light Lyre, the Microlyre, and the Mona Lisa Lyre. His musical cantatas and dramas include *Star Peace* (1987), *The Karen Silkwood Cantata* (1980), and *Cassandra* (1993), all of which have received theatrical productions.

Sanders' prose includes *Tales of Beatnik Glory*, a four-volume cycle of short stories set in the late 1950s and 1960s, two volumes of which were published in 1990. Sanders has also written journalism for many publications, including *The New York Times*, *The Village Voice*, and *The Kansas City Star*.

For almost thirty years, Sanders has lived in Woodstock, New York, with his wife, the artist and writer Miriam Sanders. Believing that investigative poetry begins at home, the couple founded and edited *The Woodstock Journal*, "a poetry-suffused, center-left biweekly newspaper working for an organic food supply, safe air, unpolluted water, national health care, human freedom, and fun" that recently ended its eight-year run.

Photo: Miriam Sanders